Ten Years After Helsinki

About the Book and Editor

Divided between two military alliances, Europe has maintained stability based on political status quo and military power balance. However, European states—including neutral and nonaligned countries—have felt a need for a common policy to guarantee their security, and the Conference on Security and Cooperation in Europe (CSCE) was convened to address this concern. Ten years later, the authors of this study find that the outlines of a European security regime are indeed discernible.

The conference in Helsinki initiated efforts for negotiated and controlled change in Europe. Contributors to this volume analyze the achievements of CSCE, consider more recent models of collective or common security systems, and deal with political and military processes at work in Europe as well as relationships with great powers and the Third World. The role of Western Europe, and particularly Finland's role as an initiator of the CSCE process, receives special attention. Documentation of the tenth anniversary meeting and the CSCE process in general are also included.

Kari Möttölä is director of the Finnish Institute of International Affairs, editor of *Nuclear Weapons and Northern Europe* and *Yearbook of Finnish Foreign Policy,* and co-editor of *Finnish-Soviet Economic Relations.*

Published in Cooperation with the
Finnish Institute of International Affairs

Ten Years After Helsinki

The Making of the
European Security Regime

edited by Kari Möttölä

Westview Press / Boulder and London

Westview Special Studies in International Security

This Westview softcover edition was manufactured on our own premises using equipment and methods that allow us to keep even specialized books in stock. It is printed on acid-free paper and bound in softcovers that carry the highest rating of the National Association of State Textbook Administrators, in consultation with the Association of American Publishers and the Book Manufacturers' Institute.

Published in 1986 in the United States of America by Westview Press, Inc.; Frederick A. Praeger, Publisher; 5500 Central Avenue, Boulder, Colorado 80301

Library of Congress Cataloging-in-Publication Data
Ten years after Helsinki.
  Includes index.
  1. Conference on Security and Cooperation in Europe—
Addresses, essays, lectures. 2. Europe—Defenses—
Addresses, essays, lectures. 3. European cooperation—
Addresses, essays, lectures. 4. Europe—Foreign
relations—1945—   —Addresses, essays, lectures.
I. Möttölä, Kari.
D1053.T46 1986   327.1'7'094   86-1646
ISBN 0-8133-7192-9

Composition for this book was provided by the editor.
This book was produced without formal editing by the publisher.

Printed and bound in the United States of America

 The paper used in this publication meets the minimum requirements of the American National Standard for Permanence of Paper for Printed Library Materials Z39.48-1984.

6   5   4   3   2   1

Contents

Preface

Kari Möttölä

The European political scene is a mix of stability and change. The existing security system has prevailed largely unchanged since the aftermath of the Second World War. It is a negotiated order, based on the recognition of political *status quo* and depending heavily on the balance of military power between East and West. In many ways, it is a traditional security order. Force is the accepted ultimate guarantee of security even though only as a threat, not as a usable instrument of policy.

At the same time, however, there are factors of change in the European system. These trends point to an idea of **Europe as a whole**, overcoming some of its divisions. There are common norms and joint institutions that are all-European. They give coherence and purpose to the relations between European states in a way that transcend the classic anarchic order. There is a security regime emerging in Europe — of converging expectations regarding the behaviour of European states *vis-à-vis* each other and regarding their common goals as European states.

The main embodiment of the common European idea is the Conference on Security and Cooperation in Europe (CSCE). Certainly, the CSCE is very much a forum for alliance politics but its working practices as well as its political life so far witness **a much more complicated European polity**. In many ways, the CSCE process activates those impulses for cooperation that grow out of material welfare and human needs, and those aspirations for security that are common for the Europe that has lived through two world wars and still carries memories and signs of those catastrophes.

At the same time, the CSCE is a forum where the participating states look after their vital national security interests with the utmost care. The CSCE has not changed security arrangements but it has touched upon issues where all the states have to demonstrate and crystallize their basic course. So, the CSCE is both an innovating and reinforcing exercise.

The CSCE process has proved to be durable but its concrete effects on the European scene are difficult to determine. Has Europe changed because of the the CSCE — and how? Does the CSCE process make Europe something more than its parts? Can the idea of a Europe as one change the existing security structures or security thinking among the European states?

Preface

These are some of the points of departure for this book which has grown out of the international round table seminar "Ten years after Helsinki: European security — a new beginning?" that was arranged by the Finnish Institute of International Affairs (FIIA) in Haikko Manor, outside Helsinki, in June 1985. The immediate cause for the seminar where participants from 20 CSCE countries were present was the tenth anniversary meeting of the Final Act held in Helsinki, 30 July — 1 August. But the focus was, from the beginning, on the European security system as a whole, albeit with special emphasis on the CSCE process.

The essay on theoretical aspects of the research on détente and the CSCE by Juha Holma was prepared as a background study for the seminar whereas Klaus Krokfors' account of Finland's activities in the CSCE was originally written for the special issue on the CSCE process of *Ulkopolitiikka* (2/1985), the quarterly journal of the FIIA.

The other articles are papers presented at the Haikko seminar. Pierangelo Isernia and Esko Antola look at some general features of the European security system, the former on the interaction between external and internal factors in security policy and the latter on various models for security orders, historically and theoretically. Adam Daniel Rotfeld, Leo Mates, Philippe Moreau Defarges and Rudolf Th. Jurrjens assess the CSCE experience itself. Hans-Henrik Holm and Lars B. Wallin take up some of the key military issues for the future construction of European security.

The European security regime is outlined in the book from several angles, concentrating on different issue-areas and using varying approaches. No synthesis is attempted but even these articles demonstrate that a lot more is happening in the European political scene than is normally recognized. The CSCE process may not yet have chosen its course and emphasis. The third follow-up meeting in Vienna, starting in autumn 1986, will be the next opportunity for choosing the line and pulling the strings together. This book tries to show that there are materials and elements in the European scene for an emerging security regime but a lot of heavy and demanding political decisions will have to be made before any deep-going changes take place.

Acknowledgements

Firstly, I wish to thank the contributors to this book as well as all the participants of the Haikko seminar for lending their interest, expertise and skills for this project of the Finnish Institute of International Affairs.

My best thanks go for Martti Korpijaakko, Katariina Koivumaa, Pirjo Hynninen and Asta Leppälä who all at various stages contributed to editing and processing the materials, and for Ulla Silvonen and Aija Virtanen who compiled the index.

Finally, the Finnish Institute of International Affairs is most grateful for Westview Press for publishing the book and offering its wide international contacts and channels for its marketing.

Kari Möttölä

Introduction
Europe - Détente -
CSCE 1975-1985

Juha Holma

Since the third phase of the Conference on Security and Cooperation in Europe in 1975, considerable changes have taken place in the relations between the participating states. The Final Act of the CSCE was signed in an atmosphere in which the high point of détente between the Great Powers had already been passed. A cooling of Great Power relations was already discernible at the follow-up meeting in Belgrade in 1977 and was clearly visible after the events in Afghanistan, when the United States refused to ratify the SALT II treaty.

The cooling of Great Power relations has placed the European states in a complicated position. Détente, which opened up new prospects for European security and cooperation, has been sorely tested by the events in Afghanistan and Poland and the deployment of new weapons systems in Europe. However, both economic interests and public opinion in many Western European countries call for a continuation of the policy of détente. For the European states, the CSCE process has also involved a psychological factor. On the one hand the meagreness of results and dependence on the Great Powers has caused frustration, but on the other hand the CSCE has kept alive hope in the possibility of finding European security solution.

During the past ten years, the CSCE has changed. In the initial phase of the conference, the most important issue for the European states concerned the approval of principles and rules concerning the recognition of the contemporary situation in Europe. The issue of human rights and "human contacts" played a central role at the Belgrade follow-up meeting. At the Madrid meeting the focus appeared to shift once again to Basket One matters, but with emphasis being placed on confidence-building measures and disarmament.

This paper attempts to find methodological points of reference for an examination of the entity formed by the states participating in the

CSCE, particularly in the field of security. Issues include methods for controlling conflicts and cooperation. Another issue concerns institutions linked to European security in the broad sense and their creation and development during the CSCE process. The paper is more a theoretical and methodological exercise on the basis of existing research than a study based on empirical data.

The International System, Europe and Détente
The Concept of System

The concept of **system** is part of the standard vocabulary of political research, although its meaning varies from one study to another. *Singer* distinguishes two predominant approaches to the system concept. One of these Singer calls the "system of action" school and the other the "system of entities" school.[1] In the former case, the "social system" is defined on the basis of interaction between the entities (beings) which comprise it, while in the latter case the "social system" is defined on the basis of these entities. In the system of action approach, the units of analysis are **action, behaviour, interaction, relation** or **role.** In the system of entities approach, the units are **the social beings comprising the system.**[2]

Singer's division can be made clearer by noting that the system of entities comes quite clear to equating the concepts of system and structure. In this case, the system equals its structure. The system of action, on the other hand, emphasizes the system's structural properties. Following *Giddens's* theory of structuration, it can be said that the system of action provides an opportunity to study the structuration of the international system. Attention is drawn to how the international system is created and reproduced in interaction between states by the application of developing rules and available means in circumstances shaped by unforeseen results. The structure of the international system is not only a barrier to action, but also its outcome and medium.[3]

In international political research the system of action focuses on interaction between states. Through its modes and means, phenomena linked to the international system and their background causes are studied. Tension reflects the state of affairs based on perceptions which exists between states in the international system. Tension grows out of threat perceptions involving other states' actions, intended actions or goals. Détente and the CSCE as part of this process are studied as a series of events as a result of which states' comprehension of one anothers' actions weakens as a tensioncreating factor. Détente includes a learning process which cannot be directly reduced to the state's capability to promote its interests.[4] Tension and détente are factors linked to states' actions.

The system of entities focuses research on states' foreign and security policy, studying states' goals and capability to carry out these goals. Research objects include national interest and military, political and economic power.[5] Tension is a result of different states' contradictory intentions and ends, whose achievement is influenced by available means. Tension arises between states to the extent that they expect conflict behaviour from one another.[6] Tension is directly proportional to the contradiction between states' goals and power resources. Détente signifies a process which reduces tension. It consists of an adjustment of states' ends and power resources in such a way that expectations concerning the opponent's conflict behaviour are reduced, mistrust involving actions is lessened and predictability is increased.

The division based on the different meaning of the term system concerns the emphasis of research. While the system of action focuses on communication and power relations, the system of entities focuses on goals and power relations. In the system of action, the basis for communication and power is the state's power resources. Similarly, the system of entities requires communication and interaction for the utilization of power resources to promote goals. Examination of détente from the system of action viewpoint appears fruitful. It points to a change in the international system which is deeper than the change in any single state's goals and power resources. **Changes in interaction indicate structural changes in the international system.**[7]

On the Concept of Power

The definition of power advanced by the realist school leads to an examination of the attributes of power. The basis for power is regarded as being the state's population, natural resources, geographical position, level of development etc. Power is expressed in military, political and economic forms. One of the characteristics of power is its manifestation in different power relations, e.g. in relationships of submission and dependence or in some type of hierarchy.[8]

When the point of departure is the system formed by states' actions, it is not fruitful to examine the basis of power or the power of some particular actor. Instead, the use of power can be viewed as a way in which certain actions direct other actions, which may arise in the present or the future. Power exists only when it is put in action. The relationship of power is not the difference between the power resources of the actors. A relationship of power is a form of action which is not directly aimed at others. Instead it is aimed at others' actions, either presently in progress or liable to occur immediately or in the future.[9]

A relationship of power can be articulated only when two necessary conditions exist: 1) the subject of power is and remains free to act, 2) the field of responses, reactions, results and possible inventions remains open.[10] The first condition refers to the experiencing of the use of power as legitimate, which means an acceptance of the relationship of power and submission to it, but not its justification. Military occupation and slavery, for example, do not include a relationship of power; the attitude of the subject of constraint has no significance. The second condition refers to both the legitimacy of the use of power and its generality. Legitimacy requires that the use of power allows the subject opportunities for action. In order for the use of power to direct other actors' actions, it must be generalized, i.e. it cannot be based on the threat of just one type of punishment.[11]

Power in the International System

Anarchy in the international system is generally defined as the absence of any dominating power holder among states.[12] Each state is on the basis of sovereignty free to protect its own interests. Sovereignty and anarchy constitute the opposite sides of the same political phenomenon, since each demand for sovereignty expressed by states automatically defines their relations as anarchistic.[13]

According to the realist school, power constitutes an organizing principle in the area of international relations. Power relations determine the state's position in the international system. Power relations are created as a result of states' actions toward one another. The international system involves a decentralized political order in which the actors belonging to the system have little authority. An anarchic system can vary in terms of characteristics from rough and conflicting to developed and stable.[14]

In the system of entities, the examination of power directs attention to the distribution of power within the system and the dynamics of the system. According to the realist school's definition, the structure of the international system is equal to the distribution of power within the system.[15] The dynamics of relations between states is determined from the point of view of the totality of international relations.[16] The dynamics of relations between states includes, for example, the maintenance of the balance of power.

In the system of action, power relations arising from interaction between states crystallize to form **a power structure.** All the states in the international system are the subjects of the system in that the system's power structure directs their actions. Within this power structure they, nevertheless, have different opportunities for action, which can lead to a change in the power structure and in the international system.

The examination of power can be linked to three different elements or the network of relations in interaction between states. Firstly, relationships of communication transfer information by means of language or some other symbolic medium. Relationships of communication refer to actors' perceptions concerning their environment, more precisely foreign policy leaders' perceptions concerning the state's operating environment. Secondly, objective capability is associated with real objects such as military and economic potential. Objects influencing the security of the international system include weapons systems, for example. Thirdly, relationships of power represent control through actions aimed at others, by means of inequality or constraint. In the international system, relationships of power are represented by alliance relations and the relationships between alliances, for example. The above-mentioned elements are in practice intermeshed and use each other as methods to achieve ends.[17]

The crystallized form of power relations arising from states' inter-action, the power structure, contains the international system's **means and techniques of control.** Military threat and armament to maintain it are the most important techniques for controlling the international system. Weapons ensure the maintenance of order. Different ways of using political and economical rewards and sanctions and even prestige can serve as techniques for controlling the international system.

Europe and the International System

The point of departure is the international system created after the Second World War with regard to the European states as well as the United States, the Soviet Union and Canada. After the war most of the world's states joined alliances led by the United States or the Soviet Union. Order in the international system was based on military threat and armament. This arrangement was called **the bipolar international system.** In the case of the European states, the dynamics of the inter-national system has been studied a great deal by examining the tight-ening of alliance contacts or polarization and the position of neutral states in this framework.[18] This definition in the international system has been regarded not only as a theory, but also as a world view or paradigm whose rise is linked to the Cold War period.[19]

After the Second World War the victors determined the rules for forming the international system. The grouping of European states into alliances and neutral and non-aligned countries represented the crystallized power structure of the post-war international system. An essential question for research is whether détente and particularly the CSCE process represent a type of interaction between states leading to a change in the international system. If this is the case, does this change mean only a replacement of a technique of control based on military threat with some other method or does it also affect the system's units, alliances and states?

The operationalizations required for research can be made with the help of the following questions: In what way are states differentiated in the field of détente and European security? What types of goals have states had with regard to détente and security? What means of producing power relations have states used in connection with détente? What forms of institutionalization have European security questions in the broad sense produced during détente? What is the degree of rationalization of the manifestations of power relations?

Operationalization Options
Modes of Differentiation between States

Modes of differentiation between states refer to states' hierarchy in the international system at a given moment. Modes of differentiation describe the power structure and relationships of power which deter-mine the order of importance of issues to be decided. In the case of European security questions, this brings up the interaction between states which determines forums and methods of solution. Issue-areas under study include political and military détente. Forums in the area of political détente include negotiations and measures aimed at increasing security. In the field of military détente, forums include arms limitation, arms control and disarmament negotiations and efforts to arrange negotiations.

Breslauer has noted that the success of détente was based on the following facts: 1) matters concerning European security were not located in the area of Great Power rivalry or cooperation; 2) Europe and arms control were matters which did not question the Great Powers' equal position; 3) European arms control had high priority; 4).European security and trade had a rather stable framework; 5) the Great Powers' control over the European states was much greater than monitoring aimed at the Third World; 6) agreements were not as "binding" as Third World conflicts and they focused on the easiest component of matters.[20] Breslauer divides states into two groups, with the Soviet Union and the United States in the first group and other states in the second. The power structure of the international system is formed on the basis of the relation between the Great Powers. The Great Powers decide methods and forums for solving issues and the order of importance of issues.

The Goals of States' Actions

The goals of states' actions can refer to their explicitly stated foreign policy objectives or states' "real" goals as revealed by research. Détente has been studied from both points of view. *Frei and Ruloff* begin with the assumption that the important thing is what the actors involved think is real. This leads to an examination of states' actions as their leadership sees them without prior theory concerning the goals of states' actions.[21] *Goldmann,* on the other hand, examines states' goals as revealed by research. The setting of goals is also influenced by domestic factors on which foreign policy is based.[22]

A change in states' "identity" may affect their goals and strategy for achieving them. A changing concept of states' role in international relations leads to changes in foreign affairs. According to Goldmann, domestic factors may act as stabilizers of détente in such cases as the FRG and the Soviet Union. In the United States, détente was seen as a stronger negator of fundamental beliefs and values, and détente did not achieve an established position.[23] In *George's* view as well, foreign policy leaders must obtain legitimacy for their actions in order to achieve goals. Policy must be in harmony with citizens' basic values. Leaders must show that they understand the world situation sufficiently well in order to be able to influence the course of events within the framework of available resources. Legitimacy has both a normative and a cognitive basis. George considers the break-down of détente to be due to a loss of legitimacy as a result of the Soviet Union's actions.[24]

Research can seek references to changes in states' "identity" from such texts insofar as their existence can be judged from changes in states' actions. In this case it is also possible to clarify the nature of the goals on which these actions are based, i.e. whether actions are based on fundamental goals or goals linked to a desired state of affairs.

Means of Producing Power Relations

The most typical means of producing power relations is **military threat.** Manifestations of the existence of military threat include the division of states into alliances, but also alliances' internal division into different types of states with regard to dependency relations. In East-West relations, military threat produces power relations in the form of participation in armament and military cooperation as well as arms control and disarmament. With regard to European security, one can ask what role the new weapons systems deployed in Europe play in the formation of power relations between states. One can also ask whether confidence-building measures influence power relations in a crystallizing manner by making military threat "safer".[25]

Another means of producing power relations is **economic** in nature. After the Second World War, the European states formed alliances economically as well as politically. The integration race led to institutional forms represented by the EEC and the CMEA.[26] With détente, states' contacts in the economic area have changed their form. Both Western European integration and the CMEA countries' desire to increase economic ties with the West are signs of new interaction between states in the economic field.[27] One example of actions crystallizing the power structure is the economic sanctions which the nations of the Western Alliance placed on the Soviet Union after the events in Afghanistan and the declaration of martial law in Poland.

Neutral and non-aligned countries have few means of changing power relations. One can nevertheless think that they strive by means of **international agreements** and **multilateral diplomacy** to influence power relations. This idea is supported by the observation that the neutral and non-aligned countries' point of view during the CSCE process has strongly emphasized the issues of disarmament, security, conflicts and peace.[28]

The Institutionalization of Power Relations

An historical example of the institutionalization of power relations is the United Nations Security Council, in which permament membership belongs to the former and current Great Powers with the exception of Germany and Japan. Both military alliances and economic associations represent institutionalization of power relations. In addition to various types of alliances and organizations, power relations can take the form of law or be manifested in established habits, be crystallized in agreements or organizations or form looser frameworks of action.

The CSCE as an institution constitutes one form of the institutionalization of power relations. Although the era of détente has given way to an era of international tension, the CSCE still goes on. An essential question is whether the CSCE constitutes a code of guiding and directing actions which can be considered an attempt to remodel power relations.[29]

The concept of a **regime** is close to a code of conduct. In American research, a regime is defined as "sets of implicit or explicit principles, norms, rules and decisionmaking procedures around which actors' expectations converge in a given area of international relations".[30]

Seen from the viewpoint of the system of action, a regime represents one form of the institutionalization of action which includes aspirations with regard to power. One can imagine that the regularity, discipline, authority and purpose signified by a regime are based on something else besides military threat. A regime would thus represent **a new method of control** in the international system. Furthermore, a regime includes the crystallized power relations resulting from the interaction aimed at forming it. In this respect a regime implies not only voluntary cooperation, but expediency in the maintenance of power relations.

With regard to détente and the CSCE it is of interest whether states' interaction implies the creation of a regime for handling matters related to European security. Are there any apparatuses, forms of cooperation, methods of observation, verification agreements etc. on the basis of which a control system or systems would appear to exist?

Degrees of Rationalization of Power Relations

Détente is often explained by saying that high-level tension and the Cold War system became irrational for one reason or another. The slipping of the Great Powers toward nuclear war, the maintenance and development of enormous military potential etc. are often regarded as reasons for the fact that the costs of maintaining the international system in a state of rigid confrontation became excessive for the Great Power blocs. Different explanation models strive to show that détente is advantageous either for the socialist countries or for the Western Alliance nations.[31]

The degree of rationalization of power relations refers to the action necessary to achieve relationships of power. The rationalization of power relations depends on the effectiveness of the means of power and the reliability of the results of action and their relation to possible costs. In brief, the rationalization of power relations depends on the relation between the costs of achieving and maintaining power relations and the benefits to be gained from them. From the point of view of research, it is of interest whether expectations involved in détente concerning a change in power relations in a more rational direction have proved to be correct.

European Security: Forums and Regimes

The following section examines, on the basis of the literature, how the European states differ from one another in certain forums of détente and how the institutional solutions included in détente can be analytically described from the point of view of changes in power relations.

Europe and Forums of Détente

As a result of interaction between states, the international power structure and power relations subject to constant change determine states' significance and weight in the international system at any moment. The totality comprising states' foreign and security policies determines each state's position in relation to other actors. The hierarchy of states in the international system thus describes different states' relation to the international system's communication events, its real objects and power relations at a given time.

Action between states includes not only bilateral interaction but also coordinated forms of interaction which are usually called multilateral diplomacy. Multilateral negotiation processes developing on the basis of different issues compose forums. Usually forums are seen merely as negotiation processes. On the other hand, forums are both signs of a change in the international system and elements in this change. Forums are more than mere negotiation processes. They include forms of social action between states which by regulating communication events, influencing real objects such as weapons systems and being reflected both within alliances and between them help determine change in the international system.

Forums included in détente, under the concept of security, include the Strategic Arms Limitation Talks (SALT I and II), the Strategic Arms Reduction Talks (START), the Mutual Force Reduction (MFR) talks in Vienna and the Conference on Security and Cooperation in Europe (CSCE) in its different stages. European security questions are also discussed regionally, like public debates concerning a Nordic nuclear-free zone and negotiations concerning a Balkan nuclear-free zone.

In individual forums differentiation between states takes place on the basis of 1) the right of participation; 2) the choice of issues to be settled; and 3) methods of resolution. These can also be examined from the point of view of the intermeshing of forums. Evaluation focuses on a) the order of forums with relation to each and b) the formation of forums in the areas of political, military and economic détente.

The right of participation not only describes states' legal position in relation to forums, but also determine more broadly states' possibility to participate in interaction shaping the power structure of the international system. In this sense participation rights manifest power relations between states. In the literature participation rights are often studied from this point of view. The basis for talks aimed at limiting and controlling strategic weapons is generally considered to be the establishment of strategic nuclear balance between the Soviet Union and the United States in the 1960s. The Great Powers' bilateral SALT talks differentiated the basic dimension of the power structure of this system from other interaction between states. At the same time, the Great Powers recognized each other's equality in the area of strategic nuclear weapons.[32]

The right to participate in the Mutual Force Reduction talks is based on military presence in Central Europe, i.e. in the area of the Benelux nations and the Federal Republic of Germany among NATO countries and the German Democratic Republic, Poland and Czechoslovakia among the countries of the Warsaw Pact. A total of nineteen states have participated in these talks. Participation rights are based on the military power of the NATO Alliance and the Warsaw Pact but are also connected to concepts of security interests within the alliances.[33]

The right to participate in the Conference on Security and Cooperation in Europe is based on **the principle of equality between states.** All thirty-five participants were, at least formally, willing to respect the idea of a conference of individual equal states. Within détente, the CSCE is an exceptional forum because it offers all European states an opportunity to bring up matters regarding security and cooperation from their own point of view. According to the literature, differentiation between states goes on within the CSCE and is influenced by different issue-areas and the way they are treated at different stages of the CSCE process. One might ask in what way the principle of states' equal participation has influenced the shaping of the different stages of the CSCE and the emphasizing of different issue areas at the conference.[34]

The right to participate in solutions involving nuclear-free zones is regarded as being determined either on the basis of joining the zone or on the basis of repercussions which the zone has on the security interests of other states. The latter approach links the formation of the zone and joining it with other disarmament, arms limitation and control solutions decided at other forums.[35]

The selection of issues to be settled and agreement on the way they will be handled includes three elements: a) a communication structure which provides a common language and, on this basis, an understanding as to the issues to be settled; b) real objects of discussion and associated issues and c) issues to be left out of discussions and associated real objects. These are intermeshed with one another in the political and diplomatic practice associated with the creation of forums.

The choice of issues settled in the CSCE Final Act was guided by the bilateral agreements reflecting the lessening of tension in Europe which preceded the conference. The choice of issues to be settled was guided by problems inherited from the final solution of the Second World War, the settling of which made it possible to draw up principles guiding relations between states in a final document.[36] As far as the CSCE is concerned, it remains to be seen how the participating states will implement the Final Act and what development will take place in the area of confidence-building measures.[37] Research findings concerning speeches made during the CSCE process support the idea that relations between states have retained their central role on the conference agenda.[38]

In contrast with the CSCE, the Strategic Arms Limitation Talks emphasize the significance of creating a closed communication structure. The tight isolation of the talks has made flexibility and compromises possible.[39] In connection with SALT I the Great Powers' communication contacts where institutionalized by establishing a permanent consultative committee to decide disagreements and seek new means of limiting strategic weapons. The problem of forward based systems (FBS) illustrate the selection of issues to be settled when it comes to objects to be included in and left out of talks.[40] The question of forward based systems in connection with SALT appears to demonstrate not only the United States' desire to coordinate its negotiation policy with its allies but also its wish to keep power relations within NATO intact.

The deadlocking of the MFR talks over the quantity of forces in Central Europe is seen in the literature as a sign of the difficulty in harmonizing differing concepts of military balance. This is due to the alliances' different deterrence warfare strategy, which is manifested in different military systems.[41]

Methods of settling issues link forums to means of producing power relations and the institutionalization of power relations. The view has been presented, for example, that the United States has attempted to tie strategic nuclear armament talks to the Soviet Union's policy in the Third World.[42] On the other hand the United States is regarded as having striven to abandon institutionalized solutions agreed during the era of détente and revert to control of the international system based on military superiority.[43] Both views emphasize the possession of nuclear weapons as a means of producing a power structure in the international system.

In the case of the CSCE, methods of resolution were initially concentrated on determining principles of action between states.[44] After the Madrid follow-up meeting the CSCE has entered a new phase in which the emphasis has shifted from principles of action to the achievement of gradual change through confidence-building measures and in this way progress toward disarmament in Europe. Both aligned and non-aligned states are participating in the solution of security issues at the Conference on Disarmament in Europe (CDE), so a larger number of special security policy interests are brought out. The CDE also serves as a forum for discussing national issues within military alliances which could not be brought up in bilateral contacts.[45]

The right of participation, the choice of issues to be settled and the way in which decisions are made can also be examined from the point of view of links between forums. The point of departure for evaluation is détente as a coherent phenomenon which creates a series of negotiation processes, a kind of network of forums, in which individual forums are related not only to events in international politics but also to one another. The order of forums and its formation illustrate change in power relations between states.

The formation of forums dealing with European security has been affected by the development of weapons systems, e.g. intermediate-range nuclear missiles and the increase in the destructive power of conventional weapons, which for their part are reflected in pressures for change in military doctrines. Discussion has brought out the need to link different forums, such as those involving strategic nuclear weapons, intermediate-range nuclear weapons and conventional weapons. In addition, proposals for individual political solutions such as refraining from the first use of nuclear and conventional weapons and collective security solutions involving Europe as a whole have been presented.[46]

The examination of the network of forums also draws attention to links between different areas of détente, i.e. political, military and economic détente. One can for example ask whether political détente is a precondition for military détente and whether increased cooperation in the economic area is tied to political and military tension in Europe.

Regimes as a Mode of Institutionalizing Power Relations

The view has been presented that détente reflects both conflict and cooperation between East and West. During the era of détente a body of rules and principles took shape to guide practical politics. Expectations and disappointments concerning détente are based on the interpretation of these rules and principles in evaluating the actions of other states. The drawing up of norms formulated in different forums and bilateral interaction makes them a measure of states' goals. States' foreign policy leaders evaluated political goals in relation to rules of conduct approved in the international system.[47]

The totality formed by the above-mentioned principles and rules is called **a code of conduct.** The rules it contains are political or law-like in nature. The formulation of a code of conduct calls for a consensus between actors. Mutual understanding is based on states' foreign policy leaders' observations concerning the environment. According to this approach, the totality of principles and rules only tells what lines of action the actors have agreed on through negotiations or implicitly. Different action strategies affect the formation of the code more than the structural characteristics of the international system.[48]

The concept of a regime has also been used as an analytical concept for explaining states' actions. A regime is defined as a set of principles and norms from which rules and decisionmaking procedures can be deduced in certain areas of international relations.[49] The creation of a regime is linked to actors' observations concerning their environment. The creation of security regimes first of all requires the Great Powers' willingness to form a regime and secondly confidence in common values in the areas of security and cooperation.[50] The dynamics of regimes is tied to actors' observations concerning the environment, on which mutual understanding concerning goals and means of achieving them are based.[51]

According to *Keohane,* cooperation between states maintains regimes although their creation may depend on the hegemony of one state in the international system. A change in the structure of the system does not lead to the end of cooperation efforts; instead, states strive to adjust their conflicting interests by means of joint institutions. Regimes are created to overcome the difficulties which otherwise would prevent useful solutions between states. At the same times regimes decrease insecurity and limit asymmetry associated with the availability of information. For this reason regimes are also persistent. States find it worthwhile to reshape existing regimes instead of rejecting unsatisfactory ones.[52]

From the viewpoint of the power structure of the international system, a regime forms an intermediate concept between decision makers' observations and the systems' structural properties.[53] Regimes are man-made arrangements, social institutions, whose purpose is to regulate conflicts in a framework of interdependence. The purpose of regimes is to create orders of rank among actors. The order refers to the benefits which the regime produces. The system is the totality in which action toward order takes place.[54] One can thus think of regimes as being linked to the power structure of the international system, as being methods and techniques for its control.

The formation of regimes connected with European security can be examined on the basis of two different questions. First of all one can ask whether the era of détente produced a set of principles and norms, as well as rules and decision-making forms based on them, which create one or more regimes. Another question is connected to the relation between efforts to form regimes and the power structure. Do the solutions included in détente demonstrate an effort toward new types of methods and techniques of control to ensure the security of the states of Europe?

One can find signs of the development of principles and norms and also rules and decision-making forms in détente between the Great Powers. Among the former is the Basic Principles Agreement between the Soviet Union and the United States which was signed in 1972. This agreement does not, however, include rules for its practical implementation.[55] In practice, the SALT I treaty recorded the principle of equality between the Great Powers, since it confirmed the existence of nuclear balance. SALT also included rules concerning verification of nuclear weapons systems covered by the treaty and the interpretation of agreements. On the other hand, SALT left open the question of the continuation of armament qualitatively through the development of weapons systems.[56]

In the Mutual Force Reduction talks the original starting point of both alliances was the reduction of forces in Central Europe by maintaining the *status quo* at the minimum level of military force. The main problem in the negotiations has been disagreement concerning the definition of military balance.[57] The dispute concerning the principle of maintaining balance has taken concrete form in the question of the strength of forces in Central Europe. The principle of balance is also connected to disagreement concerning the procedure for monitoring force reductions and movements in the area covered by the negotiations. The development of weapons systems is undermining efforts to define balance in the MFR talks. The introduction of new nuclear weapons systems and the increase in the range and destructive power of conventional weapons change the content of the concept of balance and the military doctrines on the basis of which balance is defined.

The Final Act of the Conference on Security and Cooperation in Europe is regarded as including a plan concerning how the principle of refraining from the use of force can in practice be turned in international dealings into positive actions and rules to determine mutually approved constraints.[58] The three baskets of the Final Act and the principles and recommendations they include are seen as modes of applying the principle of refraining from the use of force. There is little research concerning how the principles of the CSCE and the rules based on them act in relations between states. According to Goldmann, in crisis situations, such as in connection with the events in Poland, it is of consequence whether or not détente has become established in the parties' policies in the similar way.[59] The formation of a regime would thus be linked to the shift from emphasis on military force to political or economic sanctions, for example.

From the point of view of a regime, the evolution of the CSCE includes the question of the European power structure which the signing of the Final Act *de facto* confirmed and the processes of change which influence European security. The principles of the CSCE Final Act are by nature political and lawlike, and monitoring of their implementation takes place at follow-up meetings. On the other hand, the confidence-building measures discussed at the Stockholm Conference (CDE) are to be directly implemented and are binding on the parties. In the case of confidence-building measures the Final Act also includes a kind of evolution clause according to which measures will — voluntarily — be developed and expanded later on. From the point of view of institutionalization of the solution of European security problems, it is a matter of importance what kind of position the CDE acquires in the CSCE process and how it is linked to the arms reduction talks in Vienna, for example.[60]

Notes

1. David J. Singer 1971, pp. 8—9; quoted in Kjell Goldmann, *Tension and Détente in Bipolar Europe*, Stockholm 1973, p. 14.
2. Ibid. p. 14.
3. Anthony Giddens, *Yhteiskuntateorian keskeisiä ongelmia. Toiminnan, rakenteen ja ristiriidan käsitteet yhteiskunta-analyysissä* (Central Problems in Social Theory. Action, Structure and Contradiction in Social Analysis), Keuruu 1984, pp. 112—119.
4. Renate Fitsch-Bournazel, "Gefahren für die Entspannung in Europa", in Josef Füllenback & Eberhard Schulz (eds.), *Entspannung em Ende?*, München 1979, p. 37.
5. Concerning the difficulty involved in defining national interest, see James N. Rosenau, *The Scientific Study of Foreign Policy*, New York 1980, pp. 282—293.
6. Goldmann, *op.cit.* 1973, p. 19.
7. Rosenau, *op.cit.* 1980, pp. 267—270.
8. Kjell Goldmann, "The International Power Structure: Traditional Theory and New Reality", in Kjell Goldmann & Gunnar Sjöstedt, *Power, Capabilities, Interdepence. Problems in the Study of International Influence*, London 1979, pp. 9—35.
9. Michel Foucault, *Power/Knowledge. Selected Interviews and Other Writings 1972—77*, Suffolk 1980, pp. 788—789 and Talcott Parsons, "On the Concept of Political Power", in R. Bendix & S.M. Lipset, *Class, Status and Power: Social Science in Comparative Perspective*, 1966, pp. 240—243.
10. Foucault, *op.cit.* 1982, p. 789.
11. Parsons, *op.cit.* 1966, pp. 243—245.

12. Robert Gilpin, *War and Change in World Politics*, London 1981, pp. 27—28.
13. Barry Buzan, "Peace, Power and Security: Contending Concepts in the Study of International Relations", *Journal of Peace Research*, Vol. 21, No. 2, p. 113.
14. Ibid., s. 114.
15. Goldmann, *op.cit.* 1979, p. 14; Gilpin, *op.cit.* 1981, p. 85—88.
16. Osmo Apunen, "Johdatus kansainväliseen politiikkaan tieteenalana", *University of Tampere. Department of Political Science.* Mimeo 1982.
17. Foucault, *op.cit.* 1982, pp. 786—787.
18. Harto Hakovirta, "Kansainvälinen järjestelmä ja puolueettomuus Euroopassa 1946—1980—2000", *Politiikka* No. 3, 1980, p. 15.
19. Björn Hettne, "Conceptics of the Present World Order in the Social Sciences", *University of Gothenburg. Department of Peace and Conflict Research.* Mimeo 1982., pp. 9—11.
20. George W. Breslauer, "Why Détente Failed: An Interpretation", in Alexander L. George (ed.), *Managing U.S.-Societ Rivalry, Problems of Crisis Prevention*, Boulder, Colorado 1983, p. 331.
21. Daniel Frei & Dieter Ruloff, "Détente on Record: Applying Social Science Measurement Techniques to East-West Relations in Europe, 1975—79", in Daniel Frei (ed.), *Definitions and Measurement of Détente*, Cambridge, Mass. 1981, pp. 3—5.
22. Kjell Goldmann, "Domestic Politics as a Stabilizer of Foreign Policy, *Group for Research on Peace and Security Policy, Report no. 1.*, Department of Political Science, University of Stockholm 1984.
23. Ibid., s. 86.
24. Alexander L. George, "Détente: The Search for a 'Constructive' Relationship", in Alexander L. George (ed.), *Managing U.S.-Soviet Rivalry. Problems in Crisis Prevention*, Boulder, Colorado 1983, (b), pp. 26—28.
25. Adam Daniel Rotfeld, "CBM's between Helsinki and Madrid. Theory and Experience", in F. Stephen Larrabee & Dietrich Stobbe (eds.), *Confidence-building Measures in Europe*, East-West Monograph Number One, New York 1983, pp. 192—193.
26. Raimo Väyrynen, "Dynamics and Non-Peace in Europe", in Rudiger Jutte (ed.), *Détente and Peace in Europe*, Frankfurt 1977, pp. 44—45.
27. Anne-Marie Grosse-Jutte, "Peace and the Structure of the East-West Conflict", in Rudiger Jutte (ed.), *Détente and Peace in Europe*, Frankfurt and New York 1977, pp. 60—61.
28. Daniel Frei & Dieter Ruloff, East-West Relations, Volume I: A Systematic Survey, Cambridge, Mass 1983, pp. 211—212.
29. Osmo Apunen, "Understanding Détente", in: Osmo Apunen (ed.), Détente — a Framework for Action and Analysis. University of Tampere, Department of Political Science. Research Reports No 61, pp. 45—52.
30. Stephen Krasner, "Regimes and the Limits of Realism: Regimes as Autonomous Variables", *International Organization*, Vol. 36, No. 2, 1982 (a), p. 186; Robert Keohane & Joseph S. Nye, *Power and Interdependence. World Politics in Transition*, Boston 1977, p. 19.
31. Frei & Ruloff, *op.cit.* 1983, pp. 220—223.
32. Oleg Bykov, "Any Alternative to Military Equilibrium", in *Peace and Disarmament. Academic Studies.* Moscow 1982, pp. 77—78; Coit D. Blacker, "The Kremlin and Détente: Soviet Conceptions, Hopes, and Expectations, in: George (ed), *op.cit*, p. 122; Uwe Nerlich, "Nuclear Weapons and East-West Negotiations", in Cristoph Bertram (ed.), *Arms Control and Military Force*, London 1980, pp. 32—33.
33. The Stanford Arms Control Group, *International Arms Control. Issues and Agreements*, (Eds.) Coit D. Blacker & Gloria Duffy, Stanford, California, 1984, pp. 269—299; Lothar Ruehl, "MBFR: Lessons and Problems", *Adelphi Papers* 176, The International Institute for Strategic Studies, London 1982, pp. 6—10.
34. Karl E. Birnbaum, "East-West Diplomacy in the Era of Multilateral Negotiations: The Case of the Conference on Security and Cooperation (CSCE)", in *Beyond Détente: Prospects for East-West Cooperation and Security in Europe*, Netherlands 1976, pp. 139—141; Frei & Ruloff, *op.cit.* 1983, pp. 10—68.
35. Tapani Vaahtoranta, "Nuclear - Weapons and the Nordic Countries:

16   *Juha Holma*

Nuclear Status and Politics", in Kari Möttölä (ed.), *Nuclear Weapons and Northern Europe*, Problems and Prospects of Arms Control, Finnish Institute of International Affairs, Helsinki 1983, pp. 57—63.

36. Osmo Apunen, "The principles of relations between the States of Europe", *Yearbook of Finnish Foreign Policy 1975*, Helsinki 1976, pp 36—47.

37. Kari Möttölä, "Euroopan aseidenriisuntakonferenssi: tausta, sisältö ja rooli", *Arnek* 1984, A 2, pp. 5—6

38. Frei & Ruloff, *op.cit.* 1983.

39. The Stanford Arms Control Group, *op.cit.*, 1984, p. 228.

40. Nerlich, *op.cit.* 1983, pp. 31—48.

41. Ruehl, *op.cit.* 1982, pp. 28—36.

42. The Stanford Arms Control Group, *op.cit.*, 1984, 267—276.

43. Bykov, *op.cit.* 1982, p. 87.

44. Apunen, *op.cit.* 1978, pp. 5—21.

45. Möttölä, *op.cit.* 1984, p. 59.

46. Alan F. Neidle, "Introduction — The Political Process of Arms Control", in Alan F. Neidle (ed.), *Nuclear Negotiations. Reassessing Arms Control Goals in U.S.-Soviet Relations*, Austin, Texas 1982, xiii—xxxiv; McGeorge Bundy, George F. Kennan, Robert S. MacNamara & Gerard Smith, "Nuclear Weapons and the Atlantic Alliance", *Foreign Affairs*, Vol. 60, No. 4, 1982, pp. 753—768; The Report of the Independent Commission on Disarmament and Security Issues under the Chairmanship of Olof Palme, *Common Security. A Programme for Disarmament*, London and Sydney 1982, pp. 138—176.

47. Apunen, *op.cit.* 1981, pp. 45—46; Gerhard Wettig, *Konflikt und Kooperation zwischen Ost und West*, Bonn 1981, p. 13; Breslauer, *op.cit.* 1983, pp. 320—321.

48. Apunen, *op.cit.* 1981, pp. 45—46; Wetting, *op.cit.* 1981, p. 13; Breslauer, *op.cit.* 1983, pp. 320—321.

49. Stephen Krasner, "Structural Causes and Regime Consequences: Regimes as Intervening Variables", *International Organization*, Vol. 36, No. 2, 1982 (b), pp. 187—188.

50. Robert Jervis, "Security Regimes", *International Organization*, Vol. 36, No. 2, 1982, pp. 360—362.

51. Kari Möttölä, "Consensus and Conflict: the Dynamics of the Nonproliferation Regime", In Osmo Apunen (ed), *Détente - A Framework for Action and Analysis*, University of Tampere, Department of Political Science, Research Reports No. 61, 1981, p. 175.

52. Robert O. Keohane, *After Hegemony. Cooperation and Discord in the World Political Economy*, Princeton, New Jersey 1984, pp. 85—109.

53. Krasner, *op.cit.* 1982 (a), pp. 498—499.

54. Ernst B. Haas, "Words Can Hurt You; or Who Said What to Whom about Regimes", *International Organization*, Vol. 36, No. 2, 1982, pp. 210—211.

55. Alexander L. George, "The Basic Principles Agreement of 1972: Origins and Expectations", in Alexander L. George (ed.), *Managing U.S.-Soviet Rivalry. Problems of Crisis Prevention*, Boulder, Colorado, 1983 (a), pp. 107—117.

56. The Stanford Arms Control Group, *op.cit.* 1984, pp. 234—242.

57. Jonathan Dean, "MBFR: from Apathy to Accord", *International Security*, Vol 7, No. 4, pp. 116—121; Y.A. Kostko, "Military Détente in Europe", in *European Security and Cooperation. Premises, Problems, Prospects*, Moscow 1976, pp. 188—190.

58. Apunen, *op.cit.* 1981, p. 52.

59. Kjell Goldmann, "Détente and Crisis", *Cooperation and Conflict*, Vol. 18, No. 4, 1983, pp. 215—232.

60. Möttölä, *op.cit.* 1984, pp. 5—6.

2

The CSCE Process and European Security

Adam Daniel Rotfeld

Introduction

Europe is growing more and more aware of the necessity to work out mechanisms of consultation and cooperation to eliminate in practice the possibility of contradictory interests and tensions turning into open hostility and prevent the outbreak of nuclear war in Europe.

Meanwhile, East-West relations have for several years been deteriorating and recently entered into the phase of an acute crisis embracing practically all areas of international cooperation and contacts: politics and economics, military and social relations, scientific and cultural cooperation, and even spheres remote from politics, such as sports and tourism.

The causes of this state of affairs are seen differently in the East and in the West. It would, however, be a gross simplification to believe that appraisals and opinions are determined solely by membership in politico-military groupings or by other ties of alliance of various states. Apart from considerable differentiation of views on the causes of problems and difficulties in East-West relations, there are some common elements in the presented evaluations. No one questions the general thesis that the European reality is determined by both the relations between states as well as relations within individual states and groupings. Nor is the thesis disputed that militarization and ideologization of international relations are the main source of tension and aggravation of the present situation. However, fundamental differences exist in the interpretation of these general theses, in identification of the sources of phenomena, and especially in determining the responsibility for the dangerous development of the situation in Europe.

The state of the relations between the Eastern and Western states which ten years ago participated in the Conference on Security and Cooperation in Europe distinctly departs from the standards expressed in the form of principles and recommendations in the CSCE Final Act, and in many instances is **an outright denial** of them. The debates held in Madrid on the question of implementation of the Helsinki decisions as well as the negotiations aimed at agreeing on new recommendations focused on discerning the causes of the alarming deterioration of the situation, that is, on making a correct diagnosis and finding ways of increasing the effectiveness of the CSCE resolutions, so that they exert a tangible positive influence upon the state of East-West relations.

Ten years ago, during the preparations in Helsinki and Geneva for the CSCE Final Act, the work of the Conference was treated as the crowning stone of a whole series of bilateral agreements and relaxation of tension in East-West relations. It was the period of withdrawal of the United States from Vietnam. In Europe it was the time of democratic changes in Spain, Portugal and Greece. Europe seemed to be entering on a path of construction of a system of security and cooperation, on a path from which there was no point of return.

The development of events questioned, however, the concept of détente developing continuously and along a steadily rising curve. This reasoning posited a kind of automaticism of détente. There appeared a theory of the cyclical nature of development of international relations. After a phase of détente, an outbreak of tensions in East-West relations occurred within a few weeks of the historic meeting of the leaders of 35 states in the Finlandia Hall. As the month and years passed negotiations and cooperation gave way to increasingly vehement political confrontation, polemics and mutual accusations. The reasons of this state of affairs are complicated. In short: assessment of the CSCE process runs all the way from an unqualified approval to extreme criticism. It has been accompanied both by great hopes and expectations and by disappointment and disillusion.

In this context the following questions deserve consideration:

1. What is the essence of the CSCE process? Is this concept confined to the implementation of the principles and provisions of the Helsinki Final Act, or does it embrace the whole of the policy of détente between the East and the West?
2. What is the nature of the CSCE provisions and what function do they perform in relations between the CSCE participating states?
3. Do the difficulties that have occured in East-West relations possess a structural and lasting nature, or do they result from phenomena of a transitional and subjective nature and thus possess a temporary character?
4. What are the prospects for the CSCE process?

The Essence of the CSCE Process

The multilateral process initiated ten years ago in Helsinki was the most comprehensive and ambitious attempt to harmonize the conflicting interests of states from the East and West and to replace the confrontational and hostile posture by a cooperative.

Among the elements constituting the new quality of the process, one should mention:

— **first,** the setting in motion of the multilateral pocess; in the process

initated in Helsinki, all states of Europe and North America have participated since the beginning;

— **secondly,** the democratic character of this process; in the Final
Recommendations of the Helsinki Consultations, the participants
agreed that all states would take part in the CSCE as sovereign and
independent and in conditions of full equality; respect for equal rights is
guaranteed by the provision that resolutions will be adopted by
consensus, construed as the lack on the part of any representative of
objections which would be treated by him as an obstacle to making a
decision in the question under discussion;

— **thirdly,** the comprehensive character of the principles and decisions
of the CSCE, which encompass practically all areas of international
life: politics and economy, military affairs, cooperation in the humanitarian field, protection of the environment, exchange in the domain of
culture, science, and technology, human contacts, information, and
education. This made it possible to harmonize the interests of states in
various domains. On this basis, the CSCE Final Act is described as an
expression of the *equilibrium* achieved, which integrally embraces all
Baskets (concessions in some areas were compensated for in other
domains). Hence, a selective approach to the implementation of the
CSCE resolutions, an exaggeration of the significance of some aspects
at the expense of other aspects (e.g., evaluating the CSCE process
exclusively from the viewpoint of human rights), leads, in fact, to
upsetting the equilibrium and to a deformation of the whole process.
The meaning of the compromise accomplished consists not only of
adopting definite agreements, but also of respecting in practice the
interests of all participants in the CSCE process, interests expressed in
concrete provisions of the Helsinki Final Act;

— **fourthly,** ensuring the continuity of the initiated process without
creating a new organization. Initially, the idea of calling new institutions
into being gained wide popularity[1]. It manifested itself in both official
proposals of states and models solutions suggested by theorists in
both the East[2] and the West[3]. In time, however, the search was concentrated on pragmatic solutions.

It is worth noting that in the period of preparations for the CSCE, the
NATO states were firmly opposed not only to any institutionalization,
but also to a continuation of the multilateral process. As the debate on
the contents of the principles and provisions of the CSCE Final Act
lengthened, one could observe an evolution of standpoints in this
question. The Socialist states, which were the authors of the idea of
setting up a permanent organ, insisted on political rather than technical
solutions. The point was that the initiated process should not lead to
'multiplying new organizational entities', but should rather serve the
strengthening of security and the development of cooperation in Europe.

On the other hand, the Western states, during the second stage of the
CSCE in Geneva, would not assume "any obligation for the future"[4].
Their stance resulted from the conviction that an institutionalization
of the CSCE process was subordinated to the interests of the Warsaw
Treaty countries and would lead to undermining the unity of the Atlantic

Alliance[5]. Under the circumstances, neutral and non-aligned countries were the main advocates of ensuring the continuation of the Helsinki process, supported by a group of small and medium-size states of the East and the West, belonging to existing politico-military groupings.

In effect, the continuity of the CSCE process (and this is the essence of the compromise in this matter) consists not only of the decisions to hold multilateral meetings, such as Belgrade 1977 or Madrid 1980, and meetings of CSCE experts (as in Montreux in 1978, in La Valetta in 1979, in Hamburg in 1980, in Athens 1984, in Ottawa 1985 or in Budapest 1985), but, above all, of implementing the principles and provisions of the Helsinki Final Act on a uni-, bi-, and multilateral basis. In other words, **content and substance rather than form are more important for the continuation of the process.**

What is important in the CSCE process is that the participating states have given priority to their common interests over the differences which divide them. The CSCE provisions do not eliminate the sources of differences and controversies but create instruments to resolve conflicts through peaceful means, through negotiations, political consultation and cooperation.

In practice, all areas of international activities and mutual relations among CSCE participating states should be adjusted to the set of rules adopted in Helsinki. The entire Final Act and the CSCE principles in particular set up **an integral whole**[6]. These and other provisions were intentionally included in the Final Act in order to prevent a selective approach of the adopted decisions and to rule out any attempt at overemphasizing some principles at the expense of others. Officially, all the countries in East and West reaffirmed in various ways the fact that — in accordance with the Final Act — each area is of equal importance to security and cooperation in Europe.

In practice some NATO states, and in particular the United States, consider only the human rights provisions as the centerpiece and the core of the whole CSCE process[7]. Such a reduction of the practical significance of Helsinki Final Act to certain aspects of human rights (individual vs. collective; political vs. economic) was persistently pursued at all stages of the CSCE to the detriment of other provisions, and especially of those regulating the areas of security and economic cooperation. In general, although the aim of the Helsinki Conference was to elaborate the framework of **inter-state relations,** the main concern of the NATO representatives was: how to replace the role and responsibility of states by the individuals and non-governmental organizations in the process initiated by the CSCE. This approach reflected the political philosophy and ideological values of the Western countries.

The documents adopted in Helsinki, Belgrade and Madrid express a compromise. But it would be a gross oversimplification to say — as it is often presented in some publications[8] — that Basket One (Questions Relating to Security in Europe) reflected principally the interests of the Socialist countries, whereas Basket Three (Co-operation in Humanitarian and Other Fields) suited the needs and the expectations of the NATO states. One should not imagine the compromise as a simple trade-off; as a "price" which had to be paid by WTO or NATO countries for adopting certain provisions unacceptable to them. The compromise is expressed in an agreement reflecting a balance of interests not only in the entire document, but also in its parts and even in specific, carefully and thoroughly negotiated phrases and wordings of some provisions.

The process of the CSCE was "motivated by the political will in the interest of peoples, to improve and intensify their relations and to contribute in Europe to peace, security, justice and co-operation as well as to rapprochement among themselves and with the other states of the world."[9] In other words, it was intended to establish a confidence building system encompassing all the areas of international activities. In order to achieve this aim, the central problem was to find a balance between goals and means. This implies respect for socio-political diversity. On this basis a systematization and codification of principles and norms proved possible, which were to constitute, to the agreed extent, **a joint regime** for all European and North American states. Specific solutions were to be subordinated to these goals.

The Nature of the CSCE Decisions

Exploring the causes of the limited effectiveness of the Helsinki Final Act, some observers express the view that the source of the weakness of the CSCE lies in the moral-political — as opposed to legal — character of its provisions and in the limitation of the scope of their application to the territories of the signatory states. The character of the CSCE resolutions is the outcome of a definite compromise. **Three ways of thinking** on this question have emerged which could be characterized briefly as follows:

1. The Final Act is not an agreement in the understanding of the law of treaties and does not give rise to obligations under international law. This way of reasoning is widespread among Western authors.[10]

2. The Final Act contains provisions of a varying legal nature; nonetheless, the CSCE Declaration on Principles is the most significant, its provisions being unreservedly binding in the sphere of international law. This view prevails in the professional literature of the Socialist countries.[11]

3. The Final Act systematizes and concretizes norms of a political nature[12] which possess a varying but essential legal significance, since they reinforce the binding rules of international law or further the development of this law; nonetheless, the sources of the binding force of the CSCE resolutions are of a non-legal nature[13].

Misunderstandings arising with regard to the politico-legal qualification of the CSCE provisions are connected with a textbookish approach to new phenomena and solutions which — satisfying as they do the definite needs of international life — transcend the bounds of the traditional science of law. The opinion is quite widespread among specialists in international law that **only legal rules possess a binding force in international relations.** Any non-legal, political, moral norms are regarded as not being binding. This is doubtless a correct reasoning as far as international law is concerned.

However, the CSCE resolutions are designed **as an instrument of action in the sphere of politics,** and not in the domain of international law. This distinction is clearly drawn in the text of the Helsinki Final Act. Principle X (Fulfillment in good faith of obligations under international law) states, *inter alia:* "In exercising their sovereign rights, including the right to determine their (the participating states — A. D. R.) laws and regulations, they will conform with their legal obligations under international law; they will furthermore pay due regard to and implement the provisions in the Final Act of the Conference on Security and Cooperation in Europe". In addition, the parties to this document stated that "the text of this Final Act (...) is not eligible for registration under Article 102 of the Charter of the United Nations", which, as a note of the Finnish government to the UN Secretary General explains, would be the case if an international treaty or agreement was involved[14].

Under the circumstances any attempts at imparting a legal character to the Final Act are futile, since it was a clear intention of the parties not to give a legal form to the principles and provisions adopted. Moreover, those authors are right who emphasize that this does not detract from the significance and effectiveness of the Final Act[15]. One can, of course, ponder over the motives which guided the signatories of the document in giving it a form which "goes beyond the known categories of documents containing the results of international conferences"[16]. At this point, it seems relevant to remark that **the non-legal nature of the CSCE provisions** is the outcome, not of an oversight, but of the political will of the states participating in the Conference. Consequently, a legal interpretation can only help to understand the function of this document. For example, the statement that this is not an international agreement or that the document does not create laws and obligations in the sense of hard law, but only in the sense of soft law, does not explain anything, since the intention of the participants in the CSCE was not to make law, but **to search for effective political mechanisms** to strengthen security and develop cooperation in Europe.

In other words, criteria of political rather than legal evaluation are suitable in an analysis of the accords reached in Helsinki, Belgrade and Madrid[17] since the problem lies not in a qualification of the CSCE provisions from the point of view of the theory of international law, but in defining the role and function which these provisions ought to fulfill in the practice of international relations.

Considering the problem in practical categories, one can set forth a thesis that the CSCE provisions had, and have, **a dual function** to perform. On the one hand, they definitely closed the postwar period in Europe; on the other, they rendered concrete the principles of peaceful coexistence in Europe and defined the rules of conduct of states in their mutual relations in the future.

The political nature of the obligations undertaken in the Final Act presupposes political responsibility for the fulfillment of these obligations. What determines the efficacy of international political norms in general, and of the CSCE provisions in particular, are **the principles of reciprocity and interdependence.** Interestingly enough, the effectiveness of a number of international-legal obligations which states had assumed long before the signature of the CSCE Final Act (e.g., in the International Covenants on Human Rights) increased only after their inclusion in the provisions of the Final Act. This concerns not only human rights, but also some other generally binding principles of international law which, after their inclusion in the CSCE Declaration on Principles, exert a much stronger influence on the practice of international relations than they did prior to the Helsinki Conference. One could mention here, in particular, references to territorial principles, to the principle of self-determination, and to the principle of non-intervention in internal affairs. Also worth noting is the fact that during the meetings of representatives of the participating states in Belgrade and Madrid, delegations presented in detail and of their own accord, not only the achievements in the realization of the Final Act provisions regarding operative matters (economic cooperation, cooperation in science and technology, the protection of the environment, human contacts, information, culture, and education), but also in the observance and implementation of the CSCE Decalogue of Principles. In other words, the fact that the CSCE process has so far had a rather limited effect on the improvement of relations between the states of Europe does not result from the limited binding force of the decisions of the Helsinki Conference, but from a whole chain of causes beyond the sphere of influence of this process.

The Problems and Difficulties

How did the provisions and the whole mechanism of the CSCE function **in practice?** The evaluation of this process is not unequivocal even from the point of view of individual states, so a convergence of views is much more difficult to achieve in multilateral documents to be agreed upon by representatives of the 35 states participating in the CSCE (the attempts at formulating, in Madrid, joint opinions on the subject of the implementation of the CSCE provisions encountered insurmountable difficulties). This is comprehensible if one considers that the Helsinki document was, and still is, treated in practice by all countries as an instrument for the realization of group and national interests. This approach raises no objections if the interests of the individual states or groups of states are not incompatible with common goals and the foundations of the whole process.

Attempts at summing up the implementation of the CSCE provisions were made at various stages, both in Socialist countries and in a majority of Western states. Unlike the materials of the US Congress, however, the attention (e.g., in reports worked out in Spain, Denmark, Finland, or Canada) was as a rule focused on the foreign policy of the given state in the context of the implementation of the CSCE principles and recommendations. Although a collection of reports of this kind would not provide a sufficient basis for an objective summing-up of the implementation of the Final Act, nonetheless, these reports testify to the need of presenting by the signatory states of their accomplishments in this domain. Interestingly enough, the European surveys on

this subject identify the CSCE process with détente in East-West relations. Disturbances in this process are treated as departures from the
normal state of international relations, although there exist fundamental
divergencies in the evaluation of the sources and causes of difficulties
and problems now arising along the East-West line.

During the past years that have elapsed since the signature of the
Final Act, a significant evolution has occurred in the Western appraisals
of this document: initially criticized as an expression of the West's
unilateral concessions toward the Socialist countries, this document
today is treated as the basis for relations with the Socialist countries
over a historically long period of time.

Practice is the touchstone of the durability and effectiveness of international mechanisms. The positive achievements of the CSCE process
should not be limited to maintaining channels of communication and
understanding between the East and the West in conditions of a deteriorating international situation. The measure of the effects of this process
are not single agreements, facts, and developments, but the sum total
of phenomena that have brought about lasting changes in the international system — changes in the sphere of politics (the state of inter-
bloc relations and the equally important changes within the blocs), of
social psychology (overcoming the barriers of hostility and animosity),
of economy (awareness of interdependencies), of the military aspects
of security (awareness of threats and of the need to create new structures
for confidence and security).

A positive aspect of the CSCE process is that **Europe has been brought
closer to the vision of common security:**
— territorial-political stability has been achieved; the problem of
frontiers has been removed from the agenda of the international
debate;
— tendencies toward emancipation in Western Europe have been
strengthened and the foreign policies of the states of that region have
been diversified (the European NATO states do not want to subordinate
their interests to the US global policy);
— the CSCE process is clearly shifting to the sphere of military
aspects of security (Stage I of the Conference on Confidence- and
Security-Building Measures and Disarmament in Europe has been
convened in Stockholm);
— old economic, cultural, and other ties between the East and the
West have been restored and new ones established;
— continuation of the détente process in the long run may create
for all CSCE participating states optimum external conditions for resolving difficult economic and social problems.

There are **negative phenomena** as well:
— an "ideologization" of the CSCE process;
— the utilization by some countries of détente and CSCE process
as an instrument, in a more distant perspective, for a revitalization of
the German problem, which would upset the European equilibrium;
— attempts by some NATO states in making Socialist countries
economically dependent on the West (inadequate instruments of inter-

dependence).

Altogether, the process initiated in Helsinki has released immense energy and activated the policies of all participants in the CSCE. Various unilateral actions have been undertaken: in many countries changes have been introduced in legal regulations; steps have been taken to provide material premises for the realization of the adopted decisions. On a bilateral basis, along the East-West line: reviews of bilateral relations are carried out regularly with a view to a more effective implementation of the CSCE resolutions; new agreements are being concluded, which concretize the general principles and recommendations contained in multilateral documents. Finally, on a multilateral basis: a dialogue is continuing, the successive stages of which were marked by the CSCE follow-up meetings in Belgrade and Madrid and by the meetings of CSCE experts (in Montreux, La Valetta, in Bonn, Hamburg, and in Athens, Venice, Ottawa and Budapest).

The question arises in this context: is the process initiated in Helsinki nearing conclusion? Do the possibilities for an improvement of relations and for a further positive influence on shaping the situation in Europe require setting up new mechanisms in motion?

Prospects for the CSCE Process

The increase of tension in the world necessitates searching for more effective means of surmounting this tension. Should we expect a new conference of the leaders of 35 states of Europe and North America? Such a solution cannot be ruled out. However, the problem must not be limited to holding successive conferences and adopting new declarations and documents, although in critical situations the negotiating process alone contributes to the relaxation of tension and plays a stabilizing role in East-West relations. Détente and the CSCE process, which is an institutional continuation of détente, do not function in a vacuum and are not linear phenomena.

In the 1970s, the framework and rules were defined for rivalry and clashes of conflicting interests in various areas of international life. These contradictions are not evanescent. What is more, in effect of accelerated armaments, the relations in the military field have gravely deteriorated. New threats have been added to the old ones. The question has arisen of **extending the CSCE process to the sphere of military relations.** This is a new and important dimension which will determine the essence of European security in the 1980s. The possibility is emerging of progress in the questions of the so-called second generation of military confidence- and security-building measures and of including them in the structures shaped in the multilateral CSCE process.

One should not expect that in the future the process of security and cooperation will proceed in conditions of harmonious interests and a lack of factors which adversely influence its development. Politics is an art of feasible things. Although it is obvious that diplomatic transactions are carried out to affect compromise and mutual concessions, one can at times have the impression that positive results of détente are expected without the readiness to bear the expenses of this policy. Such expectations are illusive and unrealistic. In practice, this means that two parallel political lines will continue to exist in the CSCE process: on the one hand, the striving to strengthen security and develop cooperation, on the other hand, attempts to employ CSCE mechanisms for the purpose of legalization of a policy of interference in the internal affairs of other states. This process will oscillate between security and cooperation, on the one hand, and confrontation and interventionism, on the other[18]. External developments and factors independent of the CSCE (political, economic, and military situation, conflicts, etc.) have so far had a stronger effect on the evolution of the process initiated in Helsinki than this process has had on the development of the situation.

In other words, security has its limits. They are determined by the vital interests of external and internal security of individual states and of the two alliances. A subjective approach to these interests and attempts by one side to pursue its own goals without regard to the goals of the partners may, and actually do, create threats to the functioning of the entire international system. An effective and realistic security system in present-day Europe, and, more broadly, in East-West relations, cannot be founded on a concept of domination and submission, that is to say, it cannot be a system of subordination in the sense that one grouping would recognize the superiority of the other and submit to its will.

Adopting as the initial premise the approximate balance of power that exists in East-West relations and the fact that the dividing line runs between the groups of states with different socio-political systems, the security system should perform the functions of **coordination** and of **maintaining the balance of power.** Leaving theoretical considerations aside, it is only worth noting that the development of this system in the 1980s will be determined by clashes of different conceptions in conjunction with the concrete military-political situation, and not in accordance with model constructions elaborated by theorists. Instructive in this respect is the experience of the past decade, when there appeared scores of different theoretical propositions which had no visible effect on the adopted solutions. There are chances to restore the practical significance of the CSCE process only if the following requirements are met.

(1) **Respect for the principle of "equal security" and the preservation of military equilibrium.** This demands, above all, acceptance of nuclear parity and renunciation by all sides of strivings to secure superiority. It also means refraining from the absolutization of one's own security at the expense of the other side and the treatment of the question of control and verification in a manner adequate to the agreed measures aimed at strengthening security, reducing armaments, and diminishing military activity.

(2) **The effective application of a policy of non-intervention and non-interference in internal affairs.** This involves the renunciation of expansionism and arbitrary recognition of various regions of the world as one's own "security zones"; full respect for the inviolability of existing and recognized frontiers (this concerns, above all, the situation in Central

Europe), the questioning of which is a destabilizing factor in the politico-military equilibrium, which constitutes the foundation of regional security.

(3) **The non-use of force in international relations.** This concerns both relations between states and between systems. This can be achieved in different forms: a treaty, or solemn declaration, or any other political act which would ensure the practical effectiveness of the principle of non-use of force.

(4) **Separating the ideological competition from interstate relations.** This means refraining from transferring ideological disputes into the sphere of relations between states and from tendencies to impose one's own value system as the only valid model and criterion in evaluating the policies of other states and social movements.

(5) **Joint action aimed at resolving global problems which condition the maintenance of world peace.** This concerns, in particular, steps designed to prevent nuclear war and bring about disarmament.

No one should cherish the illusion that a system of common security in Europe will be the result of a definite meeting or conference. This is a process with a historical dimension, a process taking place on many planes, complex, and not devoid of internal contradictions, a process of searching for the common denominator for different, at times antagonistic conceptions of security and confidence. The results of the Helsinki Conference were the first step along this road. The next step was done in Madrid. Some hopes are connected with the Stockholm Conference.

The initiated dialogue may be disturbed or even suspended, but should not be discontinued for good. Security and mutual trust are not, and will not be, a condition achieved once and for all. This is a process of searching for equilibrium and equal security in a world of conflicting interests, tensions and crises.

What Europe needs is a comprehensive agreement. Such an agreement cannot be worked out by experts or achieved as a result of detailed debates of a technical-military nature. The gravity of the situation demands serious decisions which would diminish distrust and suspicion and increase confidence and the will of cooperation, and which would eliminate more effectively the possibility of nuclear war in Europe.

Notes

1. The memorandum of ministers of foreign affairs of states parties to the Warsaw Treaty (Budapest, June 22, 1970) stated that it would be useful to hold a series of European conferences and to establish an appropriate organ, with the participation of interested states, to deal with the question of security and cooperation in Europe. The head of the Polish delegation to phase I of the CSCE in Helsinki, Minister of Foreign Affairs, *Stefan Olszowski,* said on July 7, 1973: "We think it necessary to set up suitable machinery for multilateral consultations involving all States participating in the Conference. Poland attaches particular importance to the establishment of such a mechanism, perhaps in the shape of a consultative committee". Conference on Security and Cooperation in Europe. Stage I — Helsinki, *Verbatim Records,* July 3—7, 1973, CSCE/I/PV. 2, p. 37. An expression of the official standpoint of the Warsaw Treaty states in this matter

was the Czechoslovak proposal submitted on July 4, 1973 (Doc. CSCE/I/5) and the communique of the Consultative Political Committee of States-parties to the Warsaw Treaty (Warsaw, April 18, 1974).

2. One could mention here the proposal to set up a Council for European Security, contained in the book of the Soviet author M. N. Minasyan: *Sotsializm i miezhdunarodnoye pravo*, Saratov 1975, p. 236. As regards Polish authors, cf.: A. Towpik, "Ogólnoeuropejski system bezpieczeństwa i współpracy" (The European System of Security and Cooperation), *Sprawy Miedzynarodowe*, 1972, no. 1, p. 13 and A.D. Rotfeld, "Ogólnoeuropejski system bezpieczeństwa i współpracy: Prawdopodobieństwo powstania, zarys struktury i funkcji" (The European System of Security and Cooperation: The Probability of Its Establishment: An Outline of Its Structure and Functions), *Studia Nauk Politycznych*, 1973, no. 2, pp. 165 ff.

3. A detailed proposal for an East-West Standing Commission — cf.: M. Palmer, *The Prospects for a European Security Conference*, London 1971, p. 50. For more on the subject of Western models of institutional solutions, see: A. D. Rotfeld, *Europejski system bezpieczeństwa i współpracy. Zachodnie modele a rzeczywistość* (The European System of Security and Cooperation. The Western Models and Reality), Warszawa 1973, mimeographed.

4. Ph. Devillers, "Conférence sur la Sécurité et la Coopération en Europe", *Revue de Défense Nationale*, 1975, no. 31.

5. The American authors T. W. Stanley and D. M. Whitt, *Détente Diplomacy: United States and European Security in the 1970's*, New York 1970, pp. 81 ff. defined nine Sovien policy objectives which the multilateral CSCE process will serve. For a critical analysis of this stance, see: A. D. Rotfeld, "The CSCE: Its Conception, Realization and Significance", *Polish Western Affairs*, 1973, vol. XIII, no. 1, p. 23.

6. The final clause of the Declaration on Principles Guiding Relations between CSCE States provides: "All the principles set forth above are of primary significance and, accordingly, they will be equally and unreservedly applied, each of them being interpreted taking into account the others."

7. In some American writings, one can find the following interpretation of the CSCE Final Act: "For the first time in history, human rights were formally recognized in an international agreement as a fundamental principle regulating relations between States." William Korey, "Human Rights and the Helsinki Accord. Focus on U.S. Policy", *Headline Series* No. 264, Foreign Policy Association, New York 1983, p. 15—17. These types of comments ignore the UN Charter (Art. 1, p. 3) and other documents, such as the Declaration of Human Rights or the Covenants on Human Rights.

8. Among the American publications — see: S. J. Flanagan, "The CSCE and the Development of Detente", in D. Leebaert (ed.), *European Security: Prospects for the 1980s*, Lexington, 1979, p. 190; Korey, *op.cit.*

9. "The Preamble of the CSCE Final Act"; in A. D. Rotfeld (ed), *From Helsinki to Madrid. CSCE Documents*, Warsaw 1983, p. 111.

10. Cf. H.S. Russel, "The Helsinki Declaration: Brobdingnag or Lilliput?", *American Journal of International Law*, 1976, vol. 70; G. von Groll, "Die Sohlussakte der KSZE", *Aussenpolitik*, 1975, vol. 26; K. Blech, "Die KSZE als Schritt im Entspannungsprozess", *Europa Archiv*, 1975, vol. 30.

11. Cf. e.g.: *Vo imia mira. Miezhdunarodnopravniye problemy yevropeiskoi bezopastnosti*, Moskva 1977; S. Bock, "Festigung der Sicherheit in Europa — Kernstück der Schlussakte von Helsinki", *Deutsche Aussenpolitik*, 1975, vol. 20; W. Poeggel, "Kwestia obowiazujacego charakteru Aktu Końcowego z Helsinek przy szczególnym uwzglednieniu 10 zasad" (The Question of the Binding Force of the Helsinki Final Act with Special Emphasis on the 10 Principles), *Przeglad Stosunków Miedzynarodowych*. 1976, no. 1.

12. This standpoint is widely represented in Polish writings. Cf. J. Symonides, "Deklaracja zasad stosunków miedzypaństwowych KBWE" (The CSCE Declaration on Principles of International Relations), *Sprawy Miedzynarodowe*, 1975, no. 10; A. Klafkowski, "Akt Końcowy KBWE — podstawy interpretacji prawnej" (The CSCE Final Act: The Basis for Legal Interpretation), *Sprawy Miedzynarodowe*, 1976, no. 7—8; A. D. Rotfeld, "KBWE. Zagadnienia prawne" (The CSCE: Legal Questions), *Państwo i Prawo*, 1976, no. 1—2; K. Skubiszewski, "Akt Końcowy KBWE w świetle prawa miedzynarodowego" (The CSCE Final Act in the Light of International Law) in *Państwo i prawo*, 1976, no. 12; R. Bierzanek,

Bezpieczeństwo regionalne w systemie ONZ (Regional Security within the UN System). Warszawa 1977, ch. VIII.

13. Cf. Th. Schweisfurth, "Zu der Rechtsnatur, Verbindlichkeit und völkerrechtlichen Relevanz der KSZE-Schlussakte. Ein Diskussionsbeitrag zum Phänomen der ausserrechtlichen zwischenstaatlichen Abmachung", *Zeitschrift für ausländisches öffentliches Recht und Völkerrecht*, 1976, no. 4.

14. Cf. *UN Office of Public Information*, NO/464/ — note of September 19, 1975.

15. "The fact that the CSCE Final Act is not a treaty, is by no means disadvantageous. And even on the contrary, a treaty could be renounced and then various doubts would arise as to the attitude of the withdrawing state toward European cooperation. The CSCE Final Act is not subject to renunciation because the law of treaties is not applicable to it". K. Skubiszewski: *op.cit.*, p. 7.

16. Ibidem, p. 15.

17. Cf. J. Gilas, "Miedzynarodowe normy polityczne" (International Political Norms), *Przeglad Stosunków Miedzynarodowych* 1978, no. 3.

18. Cf. the collective work: *Zwischen Intervention und Zusammenarbeit. Interdisziplinäre Arbeitsergebnisse zu Grundfragen der KSZE*, Berlin 1979.

3
Structure and Regime in European Security

Pierangelo Isernia

Introduction

This essay tries to point to a set of factors explaining the growing "politicization" of the security issue-area in Western Europe. By politicization it is meant here that an issue-area — in our case, military defence of Western Europe against the Soviet threat — gains a primary role on the political agenda of a country or a set of countries so that its content, limits and rules are put into question. Two manifestations of such a politicization were, on the one hand, the vast mass mobilization across Western Europe against the NATO decision to deploy cruise and Pershing II missiles, and, on the other hand, the intense debate on defence and security postures in Western Europe.[1]

The study of the evolution of an issue-area is affected, much more than in any other case, by the theoretical perspective the analysis stems from. This is so because both domestic and international factors, material and perceptual variables must be taken into account, in an attempt to link together different levels of analysis.

In my attempt to single out and assess the relative weight domestic and international variables have in the politicization of the security issue-area, I will use a two-dimensional framework. Accordingly, the essay is articulated as follows: first, a brief presentation of such a framework is offered; secondly, this framework is used to describe and explain the nature, characteristics and evolution of the security issue-area in Western Europe; thirdly, some conclusions are drawn upon the theoretical and methodological problems this effort has raised.

I would like to stress three main limitations of this analysis. First of all, it takes into account only Western European NATO industrialized countries, with particular reference to Great Britain, France, FR Germany, Italy and the Netherlands, together with the United States. No attempt whatsoever will be made to address the motivations and sources of the Soviet Union's behaviour and policy. (CALZINI, 1985) Secondly my interest, at this point in time, is devoted mainly to stressing international and national similarities, rather than differences. Due to the obvious importance national differences have in explaining foreign policies, this is seen as an avoidable simplification. Thirdly, this is intended to be a first attempt toward a much more scrupulous empirical analysis.

The Security Issue-Area in Western Europe

An issue-area, in the words of Keohane and Nye (1977), is a set of issues, mutually interrelated, about which policymakers are concerned and which they believe are relevant to public policy. The issue-area sets the boundaries of relevant issue-policies, that is, the policy processes and policy outcomes deemed and perceived as legitimate and feasible in a given context. In this sense, still in accordance with Keohane and Nye, an issue-area is both an empirical field and a perceptual area, in which policy makers and the public opinion play a major role.

An issue-area is stable when no relevant and far-reaching conflict among relevant actors arises. An issue-area becomes unstable when a process sets in through which values, rules of the game, norms and principles are increasingly questioned and their legitimacy eroded. One of the main manifestations of an issue-area instability is its "politicization". Politicization is defined by Keohane and Nye (1977:157—158) as increasing controversiality and agitation that raises an issue's priority on the policy agenda and the level of government on which it receives attention.

Two forces concretely shape the issue-area stability: the structure of the international system and the regime of the issue-area. Their role can be depicted as shown in **Figure 1**.

FIGURE 1

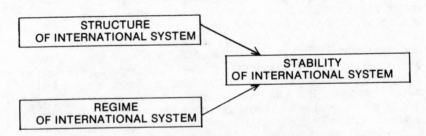

The Structure of the International System

The stability of the international system, and therefore of each issue-area, rests on the hierarchical structure of the international system.[2] Hegemonic power sets the political and economic framework in which international interactions take place. A hegemonic power is able to maintain a given structure of power until its economic and military predominance is overwhelmed. Military and economic power are mutually interrelated. (MODELSKI, 1978; BERGSTEN, KEOHANE and NYE, 1979) Military superiority is made possible by a wide economic base, and in turn, political order — one of the main offsprings of political hegemony — is a *conditio sine qua non* for a successful international economy. Several authors have underlined that an "open" international economy is associated with hegemonic powers (Great Britain in the nineteenth century and United States in the second half of this century), whereas protectionism, trade wars and instability are associated with a lack of leadership, and power fluidity. (KRASNER, 1976; KINDLEBERGER, 1981; KEOHANE, 1980)

Four main variables are traditionally indicated as characterizing the structure of the international system:[3] (a) the stratification of the international system; (b) the concentration of power; (c) the polarization of the international system; and (d) the nature of interdependence (symmetrical or asymmetrical) among countries.

Stratification is the degree of rank-concordance of each state of the system on several different rank-dimensions. Rank-concordance is a measure of the hierarchic order in the system. High concordance means that all nations have the same rank-position on several different dimensions. A high rank-concordance tends to produce a stable rank-role, that is, a coherent pattern of attitudes and behaviours according to the different positions occupied. Rank-discordance, on the contrary, means that each state occupies different positions on several dimensions of rank. (GALTUNG, 1964; WALLACE, 1972; 1973)

Concentration of power is a measure of dispersion of power resources among the actors of the system. Concentration of power is a distributional variable. A high power concentration in the hands of one actor makes it a pole. *Rapkin et al.* (1979) tends in fact to equate system concentration with system polarity. According to *Modelski* (1983; see also THOMPSON, 1983), a ten per cent power concentration in the hands of one actor makes it a great power. When 50 per cent or more of power resources (military expenditure, GNP, GDP, etc.) belongs to an actor, the system is unipolar. A bipolar system is characterized by the concentration of at least 50 per cent of power resources in the hands of two powers, each of them accounting for at least 25 per cent. (RAPKIN, THOMPSON, CHRISTOPHERSON, 1979:261—264; BUENO de MESQUITA, 1975; 1979)

Polarization is a relational variable. It depicts the degree of tightness of a cluster of states around a pole. (RAPKIN et al. 1979; BUENO de MESQUITA, 1975) Polarization is a measure of both internal cohesion of the alliance and distance among blocs. When all positive and cooperative interactions occur within a bloc and all negative and conflictual interactions occur between blocs, the system is highly polarized. I will focus exclusively on the degree of tightness or cohesion among the members of an alliance, without taking into account the volume and nature of interactions among blocs.

Eventually, the nature of **interdependence** is a measure of hegemonic power as control over actors and their behaviors in a non-coercive way. (HART, 1976) In looking at a structure of exchange one has to ascertain the symmetrical or asymmetrical nature of the relationships. A structure can be balanced or symmetrical and unbalanced or asymmetrical. It is unbalanced when an actor is much more dependent in terms of size of dependency, importance of the goods exchanged and availability of substitutes than the other (CAPORASO and WARD, 1979). Applying these criteria to a hegemonic power one can establish its capacity to control the international structure through non-coercive tools.

These four variables affect positively an issue-area. When stratification is highly concordant, polarity and polarization are high and power relationships are asymmetrical in favour of the hegemonic power, the structure of the system is hierarchic and one can predict a stable issue-area. When hierarchy starts to crumble, then the issue-area stability decreases and politicization is much more probable. Nevertheless, it may also occur that the hegemonic power declines, and nothing happens in the power structure. *Krasner,* for example, found an interesting temporal lag between changes in power positions and a change in the structure of trade. People need time in order to become acquainted with the new situation, and often no change occurs until a traumatic event makes all things to fall apart. (KRASNER, 1976:341) In order to explain these anomalies, a second set of variables has to be introduced: the regime.

The Regime of the Issue-Area

According to the classic, realist tradition, state-power determines political outcomes. Therefore, a change in the structural variables brings forth an equivalent change in norms and principles. Moreover, the weaker actor will always give way to the stronger, until the differential rates of growth will turn the chances in favour of the former, against the latter. In this arena, normative and cognitive aspects have no role.

This perspective has been progressively challenged in the last few years. Several authors have stressed the role of decreasing legitimacy in explaining system instability (MODELSKI, 1978; BONANATE, 1976; the power of smaller countries in constraining the stronger ones (KEOHANE and NYE, 1977); and the role of perceptions and beliefs systems on behaviours and policies. (ALLISON, 1971) The realist model seems particularly unable to explain change in the context of a patterned set of relationships in which role variables and expectations play a great role, together with cognitive aspects. (KRASNER, 1982)

In other words, it seems reasonable to assume that the international system, as every hierarchical structure, needs an institutional framework in which norms and rules shape objectives and procedures, define problems and guide the search for solutions. This framework sets the "regime" of the international system.

Krasner (1982:186) defines **regime** as "sets of implicit or explicit principles, norms, rules and decision-making procedures around which actors' expectations converge in a given area of international relations". At this level, political elites are the crucial variable. When the structural perspective, that sees foreign policy and international politics shaped by material resources and interests, is replaced by "cognitive behavioralism", the ways in which people see their milieu acquires importance. (TROUT, 1975; GEORGE, 1979; 1980; SPROUT and SPROUT, 1979)

Two dimensions of a regime are particularly relevant: its organizational nature and its legitimacy.

The **organizational nature** of a regime has to do with the procedures through which collective choices are conceived, taken and implemented. Two fundamental kinds of procedures are discernible: institutional and non-institutional. Institutional procedures are such as an international organization, a regular system of international consultation (for example, summitry between the most advanced industrialized countries) (PUTNAM, 1984; 1985). Non-institutional procedures are such as agreements and treaties determining specific matters. In the first case, there is a strong expectation of reciprocating behaviour in the future, within set patterns of behaviours, based on long-term interests. In the second case, no long-term interest is involved, and cooperation is limited in space and time. Institutional procedures imply a greater constraint of national decision-making autonomy and therefore greater effects on domestic dimensions.

Regime legitimacy is grounded on the national elites' perceptions of the "oughtness" of the structure of power. Legitimacy is an essential requirement of any political system, (EASTON, 1979) and therefore of the international system as well. (BONANATE, 1976) Regime legitimacy plays two essential roles in the international arena. First, it shows the fundamental coherence between a given structure of power and a commonly accepted definition of major national goals and values. Secondly, it gives specific and contingent political acts a broader normative and cognitive meaning, so as to grant decision-makers leeway for an effective and autonomous policy (expecially under democratic conditions). These two tasks correspond approximately to the distinction between regime and policy legitimacy introduced by *George and Trout* (1980; 1975).[4]

Regime legitimacy means that the national image of international politics is rooted within a broader normative framework whose sources are in domestic arena. **Policy legitimacy** is the connection between concrete acts and more general ideological and interpretative frameworks which give them "meaning". Both of them have two fundamental components: a normative and a cognitive one. The normative component shows the desirability of a given regime or of a given policy in the name of a set of domestically values based. The cognitive component shows the utility of a given regime in order to better implement a set of domestic values and the feasibility of a given policy to carry out a present or future regime. (See also KELMAN, 1969) The regime legitimacy, as *Trout* (1975) intends it, rests on the coherence between an image of international politics and the broader normative order on which the society is established. Therefore an international regime is deemed desirable and effective to the extent that it helps to realize profoundly imbedded social goals. The policy legitimacy, on the other hand, stresses the coherence between a "design-objective", the strategies and, lastly tactics deemed useful to achieve it.

Although both aspects contribute to regime stability, they have a different nature. Regime legitimacy pertains to a deeper level and therefore is much more stable and internalized than any specific policy legitimacy. Policy legitimacy can be undermined by domestic sources without affecting negatively — at least on the short term — the regime legitimacy.

Moreover, these two components have different degrees of complexity, both for elite and public opinion belief systems. Political elites have a much more complex and articulated conception of the regime and its policies and are much less rapidly disposed to a change between them. Public opinion, on the contrary, has a much simpler level of articulation on these matters, but its orientations are volatile.

Winding up the definitional task so far accomplished, we can assume that the factors as shown in **Figure 2** contribute to explaining the stability of an issue-area.

FIGURE 2

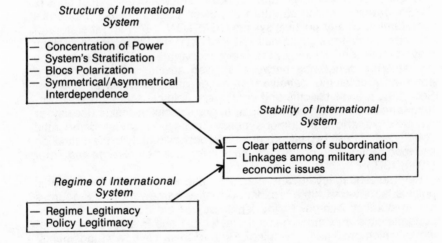

An Historical Overview

The Hierarchical Structure and the United States' Hegemonic Role

The Second World War ended with two big Powers, a bundle of weak and worn-out European countries and a colonial world in disarray. The United States and the Soviet Union, though the latter one was severely strained by the war, came out as the two major world Powers, in terms of economic and military capacity and political leadership. (KOLKO, 1970;

GADDIS, 1982; ALPEROVITZ, 1966) International relations were shaped, since the very beginning, by the bipolar nature of the structure of the international system. In Europe, military conquest, the Tehran, Yalta and Potsdam conferences produced a special reflection of this bipolarity. Each superpower, in stages partially brought about by their mutual competition, organized their relationships with their area of influence according to their forms of social, economic and political organization.

In Western Europe, the distribution of power resources, in the years immediately after the Second World War, was characterized by a highly asymmetrical pattern among the US and the European countries. The US had the economic size, the productive capacity and the financial infrastructure capable of exerting an effective leadership in world affairs. Moreover, "the lessons from the past" had a profound impact on orientation of American elites. (HOLSTI and ROSENAU, 1980) The poor economic conditions of European countries shaped the nature of the bipolar relationships with the USSR much more than the outward-looking attitudes and the "Cold War" orientations of the American inter-nationalist groups, based around the financial, banking and commercial sectors of the East coast, the President and the State Department.

On the other hand, this same bad situation made Europeans particu-larly sensitive to American economic and political help. Some countries had an economic infrastructure completely destroyed by the war, others had debts, problems of underproduction and a shortage of foreign currencies liquidity. All of them perceived, with the passing of time, a growing apprehension for the intentions of the Soviet Union. Finally, in some countries (namely Italy and Germany) the democratic regimes were "insured" by the Allies with the help of political and economic groups close to Western ideals. (GAMBINO, 1972; KOGAN, 1974)

The US, therefore, played since the very beginning a crucial role in providing leadership in this area. The "lessons of the past" influenced the construction of such an hegemonic leadership around two points: first, a strict adherence to the rules of free trade, multilateralism and open markets; secondly, a strong determination of the Western democracies to act jointly against totalitarianism. These tenets characterized the way Western Europe was integrated within the American hegemony both in economic and military terms. Moreover, open world economy and nuclear deterrence were perceived as mutually linked together.[5]

The recovery of Western economies occurred with the US aid to the reconstruction of Western Europe's industrial and commercial infra-structure, the linkage of the European monetary system to the dollar and the gold, trade liberalization and free access of American investments to Europe. The threat of the Soviet Union was coped with through the extension of nuclear deterrence to Europe, the progressive politico-military integration of West Germany with the Western world and a stable presence of American troops in Europe. These two pillars were mutually reinforcing. Nuclear umbrella, trade liberalization, stable exchange rates were different facets of the same coin: a stable control of the Unites States over Western countries for the sake of dealing in a unitary way with the Soviet Union and of making possible the economic expansion of American firms and corporations.

The hegemonic US position made it possible for the American public to accept the costs the United States was ready to pay in order to maintain it. The United States in fact accepted trade discrimination against its products by European countries, an open domestic market and a budget deficit in order to guarantee the stability and growth of world trade and investments; and higher military burdens — in comparison to other Western countries — for the common defence, in exchange for an economic, political and military leadership. European countries from their side, accepted American investments and a "dollar-standard" together with support for the American foreign policy in exchange for the stable outflows of public goods such as security and welfare.

In such a situation, the linkages among economic and military issues were quite strong, but rarely came to the surface. The stable pattern of asymmetrical relationships had deep influences on the expectations and interests of the US and its allies. At the same time, it was inevitable that over time each issue-area — monetary, trade, security, etc. — would develop its own rules, principles and decision-making procedures, and that, in the long run, those would have an autonomous impact on foreign policies and international politics.

Security Regime in Western Europe

In principle, **military force** can have at least two roles. First, the overt and direct use or threat of use of force, in order to compel somebody to do something. Secondly, this same outcome can be achieved by withdrawing or threatening with the withdrawal of the protection that force assures to somebody. An example of the first case is a military intervention in a foreign country, and of the second case, the withdrawal of nuclear guarantee to defend an allied country. While force in the first sense played a negligible role in Western Europe-US relationships, the second, "latent" sense was relevant not only in inducing European elites to give in some occassions (GILPIN, 1981), but also in shaping, as a "second face of power", the context of the political debate in security matters.

The security issue-area in Western Europe, as it has been developing for the last forty years, rests on the doctrine of nuclear deterrence and its norms, principles and procedures can be aptly called a regime.[6] On a very general level, the nuclear deterrence regime in Western Europe rests on the determination of the United States to discourage the use or threat of use of military force by confronting it with a nuclear blow of incalculable costs. Therefore, NATO policy is based on an explicit linkage between European defence and the US strategic deterrence, in order to make it more credible.

The deterrent effect of this doctrine, as it has evolved since the '50s, is based on two main pillars:

(a) the political determination of NATO to resist jointly any form of aggression or blackmail that should occur, and in particular the political determination of the US to repel a conventional and nuclear attack by the Warsaw Pact with a nuclear strike;

(b) the capability of the Atlantic Alliance to react to an aggression flexibly, adapting the response to the level of the aggression.

This theory is intended to prevent any war, making it an irrational act of unbearable costs.

In its form this regime rests not only on organizational factors but also on some common-shared expectations of European and American elites about their mutual behaviour. This is particularly true for the US and West Germany, the latter supposedly being the first territory to be assaulted. More specifically, this doctrine rests on the conviction of European leaders and mass publics of the trustfulness of the American commitment to defend Europe even at the risk of a generalized nuclear war, and of the capacity of NATO to convey this unitary commitment to the opposite side. Assuming that this capacity to convey determination to the Warsaw Pact is a mere reflection of the first condition, it is important then to spell out the requirements of a credible determination of the US to intervene. This determination has historically depended on three elements:

(1) The seriousness and credibility of the Soviet threat. Such a danger, in fact, makes any alternative to nuclear deterrence under the American guarantee either too costly or politically unfeasible. Moreover, the fear of smaller countries of the withdrawal of the nuclear umbrella constrains the willingness of these same countries to pursue alternative ways within or outside the Alliance, therefore limiting their decision-making latitude and strengthening the Alliance cohesion.

(2) The technical credibility of the use of nuclear force. This has been the problem of nuclear strategy during the "massive retaliation" period. In order to be effective, nuclear deterrence must be credible. But when the destructiveness of nuclear weapons made them practically unusable in a concrete, limited, political crisis, then the political role of nuclear weapons became negligible. This condemned nuclear strategy to political rigidity among inconciliable alternatives: surrender or nuclear annihilation. Limited nuclear weapons and the "flexible response" doctrine were seen as the right answer to this dilemma. This solution, so to say, nevertheless raised paradoxically the dilemma that, in order to make nuclear strategy and deterrence more credible, one has to make weapons systems more usable. In the last resort, the credibility of nuclear deterrence would rest on an increased probability of nuclear war. The means conceived to make war less probable was condemned to be grounded on a logic which sees nuclear war as more likely.

(3) But these principles — together with the European commitment to support an increased conventional posture — were made acceptable by being inserted in a wider set of norms and principles, which determined the functional hierarchy of issues and goals among Western countries, and the inextricable linkage among security and welfare.

These are the terms of the "consensus":

— The world is a conflictual arena in which two fundamentally different ideological groups of states strive for victory or death: capitalism and communism. They spring from different traditions — liberal and democratic capitalism, authoritarian and egalitarian Marxism — and the very nature of Marxism makes this struggle an unending game, unless one of the two sides is defeated. (TROUT, 1975)

— Therefore, the economic recovery of Western Europe and the stability of Western economic process in advanced industrialized countries have to be the highest priorities on the agenda of European and American governments.

— Essential and paramount conditions to achieving this goal are Western European defence under the nuclear umbrella and an open, competitive world economy.

— The United States is the only actor able to offer economic leadership and nuclear protection in order to fulfill such conditions.

— This implies, necessarily, a politico-military and economic subordination of Western European countries to American leadership, and any threat to such a leadership is a direct threat to European welfare and security.

This linkage, stable and fundamental, between security and domestic welfare was made concrete and legitimate through many institutional fora — NATO, OECD, IMF, etc. This transgovernmental bureaucratic structure — under American hegemony —[7] allowed for the "technical" management of international issues, avoiding any politicization of the crucial economic or political issues from "below", through parliaments and party systems. Moreover, the connection between security and welfare assured automatically bipartisan support for the security regime. *Wildenmann* (1983) has interestingly pointed out that defence has never been a policy goal for the mass public. Only recently "peace" — as distinct from "defence" — has gained wide public attention.

From this point of view, domestic structures, political traditions and the relative role of state and society played only a minimal role in shaping the content and scope of regime legitimacy. The regime was mainly shaped by the bipolar nature of the international system and by the objectives of the hegemonic power. But over time, developments both at the structural and the regime level, have increased the role domestic factors play in shaping foreign policy issues.

The Evolution of the Security Issue-Area: Structural and Domestic Factors

An overall and exhaustive analysis of the evolution in the security issue-area in Europe is beyond this article. I will limit myself to outlining the change in the four structural variables depicted above in these forty years, and then pointing out to the possible impacts of these changes on the regime.

We are witnessing a growing "politicization" of defence issues in Western Europe, in the context of greater controversiality of many political and economic issues between European countries and the United States. The dollar crisis at the beginning of the 1970s and the American decision to change the monetary regime, the oil crisis, the Eurodollar market problems and the decision to modernize the theatre nuclear forces in Europe are some of the problems on the agenda the euro-atlantic relationships of this decade. According to the theory of hegemonic stability (KEOHANE, 1980), the relative decline of the US hegemonic position vis-á-vis stronger economic partners (EEC and Japan) and enemies (USSR) can explain much of this phenomena. On the one hand, the US is less and less able a n d disposed to manipulate linkages among the issues in order to achieve unilaterally its goals. On the other hand, Western European countries — economically — and the USSR — militarily — are less vulnerable to American pressures and are amplifying and diversifying their goals and policies in ways not immediately coherent with the previous regime and structure.

In connection with these changes, the order of priorities among Western countries is shifting. The above mentioned congruence between European elites and their constituencies on the US-centered definition of the security issue-area is declining. Public opinion is growingly concerned with security matters, although this does not seem to affect the legitimacy or support of the Western Alliance nor to lessen the distrust of Soviet Union. Elites and experts are split on the problems of Western conventional defence, relationships with the USSR, assessment of détente, etc. The linkage between security and welfare is increasingly challenged. People are less able or disposed to make sacrifice in order to strengthen militarily the NATO, and the connection between these sacrifices and domestic welfare is becoming loose. Even the major source of consensus in the 1960s — the Soviet threat — is declining. This does not mean in any way a more trustful attitude toward the Soviet Union, but rather reflects the idea that it is irrational to plan to wage a war with the Soviet Union.

In sum, security is no more seen, as during the "cold war" period, as a necessary condition for welfare in Western societies, rather it is perceived as a separate, autonomous goal, though still legitimate in itself. Only among the younger generations is security becoming to be perceived as an obstacle to the continuous growth of welfare or as a threat to the quality of life.

This growing interest by public opinion corresponds with a decreasing consensus among political elites, both in the United States and Western Europe, on the best way of managing the euro-atlantic relationships.[6] This lack of consensus is reflected in the widening spectrum of proposals on Western defence that have appeared in those last years.

To describe how this "politicization" has occured, our two main dimensions have to be taken into account: the structure and the regime.

The International Structure Evolution

The hegemonic stability theory would predict that any change in the overall distribution of power will affect political outcomes and regime stability. According to this perspective, regime is a d e p e n d e n t variable, not an intervening one. (STEIN, 1982) To assess the validity of such an argument, I will first take into account the structural variables, as depicted above.[8] If these variables do not seem to offer convincing explanations, I will then consider the regime variable as an autonomous factor.

To examine the structural evolution of power in the European context, I will examine trends in the following four variables:

a) system's stratification, examining the rank positions of five actors (France, West Germany, Italy, Great Britain and the United States) on two main dimensions: military expenditures and GDP, **(Tables I and II)**

(b) system's concentration, examining two aspects: first, the military bipolarity between the USSR and the US, as expressed by the percentage of military expenditure accounted for by these two countries on the world total **(Figure 3)** (see RAPKIN et al., 1979:272—285); secondly, the percentage of the US, GDP of the world total GDP, in comparison to the national share of the main European economies (Japan, West Germany, France, UK and Italy). The first is a measure of political concentration and the second of economic concentration. **(Table II)**

(c) system's polarization, as reported by Rapkin et al. (1979:272), using the bloc flow approach (Szalai-Brams index) **(Figure 4).**

(d) The United States' and the European countries' sensitivity and vulnerability, using data on trade proportion, namely, the ratios of trade to domestic product (GDP) and the national quota of export on the world total. **(Tables III and IV)**

FIGURE 3

POWER'S CONCENTRATION
(US/USSR Military Expend, as Percentage of World Total)

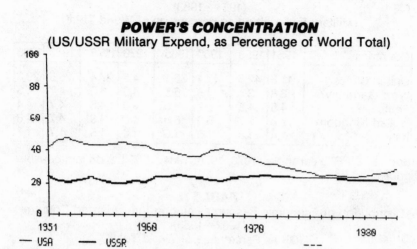

Source: SIPRI Yearbooks, 1973; 1978; 1984.

FIGURE 4

FLUCTUATIONS IN BIPOLARIZATION
1948—1973

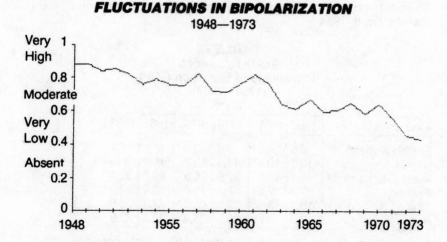

Source: *Rapkin et al., 1979:272—276.*

TABLE I
Distribution of Military Power among Industrialized Countries
(1951—1983)
(Military Expenditure as Percentage of World Total)

Countries	1951	1955	1960	1965	1970	1975	1980	1983
United States	41,3	42,8	42,4	36,1	34,5	27,4	25,5	29,3
West Germany	3,8	3,4	4,8	5,5	4,2	5,0	4,7	4,3
France	4,5	4,5	5,7	4,9	4,0	4,3	4,7	4,4
United Kingdom	7,8	7,7	6,9	5,9	4,3	4,6	4,7	4,6
Italy	1,4	1,3	1,5	1,6	1,4	1,5	1,7	1,7

Source: SIPRI Yearbooks, 1973, 1978, 1984. 1980 US dollars cousbut prices.

TABLE II
Distribution of Economic Resources among Industrialized Countries
(1962—1983)
GDP as Percentage of World Total

Countries	1962	1965	1970	1975	1980	1983
United States	41,5	39,3	37,7	29,2	25,4	32,1
Japan	4,4	5,2	7,8	9,8	10,2	—
West Germany	6,7	6,5	7,0	7,9	8,0	6,4
France	5,4	5,6	5,4	6,4	6,4	5,1
United Kingdom	5,9	5,7	4,7	4,5	3,9	3,5
Italy	3,4	3,6	3,8	3,7	5,2	4,5

Source: International Financial Statistics, IMF, Supplement on Output Statistic No 8, 1984.

TABLE III
Trade Resources
(Percentage of Export on GDP)
(1962—1983)

Countries	1962	1965	1970	1975	1980	1983
United States	4,6	4,9	5,4	8,4	10,2	7,7
Japan	10,1	10,9	11,3	13,7	15,1	—
West Germany	18,4	19,0	22,6	26,6	29,0	32,4
France	12,3	12,6	15,3	18,5	20,9	22,2
United Kingdom	19,2	18,6	22,6	25,6	27,5	26,5
Italy	12,3	13,9	15,9	21,0	22,8	23,6

Source: International Financial Statistics, IMF, Supplement on Output Statistics, No 4, 1984.

TABLE IV
Trade Resources
1951—1983
(Export as a Percentage of World Trade)

Countries	1951	1955	1960	1965	1970	1975	1980	1983
United States	17,5	17,9	17,4	16,1	15,1	13,4	11,8	12,1
Japan	1,4	2,3	3,4	5,0	6,7	6,9	6,9	8,8
West Germany	3,4	7,0	9,6	10,5	12,0	11,1	10,3	10,2
France	5,3	5,7	5,8	6,0	6,3	6,6	6,2	5,7
United Kingdom	10,8	9,7	9,0	8,1	6,8	5,4	5,9	5,5
Italy	2,0	2,1	3,1	4,2	4,6	4,3	4,1	4,4

Source: International Financial Statistics Yearbook, IMF, 1984.

This analysis is admittedly based on very simple indicators. Nevertheless, it is interesting to note how even this rough and initial attempt shows some remarkable face-validity results about the evolution of the system's structure.

The main evidence immediately arising from the data is a decline in the military and economic position of the United States. The American share of world military expenditure has declined from almost fifty per cent of the world total to a third of this total. In terms of military expenditure, the system has shifted from a unipolar to a bipolar structure. **(Figure 3)** The proportion of military expenditure accounted for by European countries has increased, although not affecting the rank position of the US vis-á-vis its allies, whereas the military position of the US in front of USSR has declined up to a substantial parity among them. The economic position of the US has declined as well. The economic size of the US economy in the world has decreased in absolute terms. Its share of the world GDP total has moved from 41,5 per cent in 1962 to 32,1 per cent in 1983. But US continues to score higher than any other industrialized country. In 1983 its GDP is still fivefold the GDP of its closer European competitor, West Germany, (6,4 per cent). Even Japan has an economy less than half the US economy. Moreover, in terms of sensitivity and vulnerability the US preserves a good position. Its share of world export has decreased from 17,5 per cent in the 1950 to 12,1 per cent in 1983; and the export/GDP ratio for the US in 1983 was 7,7 per cent. West Germany, undoubtedly the strongest European economy, has a ratio of 32,4 per cent on export/GDP. The gap between the more advanced European countries has therefore decreased, but the US maintains a substantially predominant position.

Two main conclusions can be drawn upon this data:

(1) The American position in the world has declined but not so much to justify a prognosis of proximate collapsing of its world hegemonic position. Its decline is more perceivable in relative than absolute terms. The network of mutual interdependencies is becoming more com-

plicated and a stiff competition is established both in economic and military terms. The confidence and credibility of American hegemony is eroded. The exercise of leaderships is more costly and other countries are less disposed to obeying the given regime. The American capability and willingness to establish linkages among different issues has decreased as well.

(2) The role of force has decreased both within the European context and vis-á-vis the Soviet Union. First, the nuclear parity among the two superpowers is starting to make its effects felt. Force, in particular nuclear force, seems to have higher costs in political, economic and moral terms and smaller utility in terms of objectives achieved. The implications of this parity, both domestically and internationally, are starting to be perceived by the political elites. Secondly, the degree of polarization among the two blocs is decreasing. **(Figure 4)** The Soviet Union is less and less perceived as a threat, although no sign of increased trust in its intentions is appearing. This declining appeal of the Soviet threat is reflected in the lesser cohesion of the Western Alliance, as expressed in the reluctance of the Europeans to sustain a greater burden of military expenditure for the common defense, in the suspicion with which any reference to "limited nuclear war" is received, and finally in the resistance to accept the modernization of nuclear forces in Europe.

All these trends notwithstanding, they do not seem to acquaint adequately the present decline in the regime stability, and especially the resistance against the implementation of objectives formulated within the common framework. In comparison to other areas, American hegemony is still firm in the security matters and therefore the theory of hegemonic stability would expect a low degree of conflictuality in this area. Moreover, many of the inferences made immediately above involve perceptual orientations and cognitive expectations which have nothing to do with the structural variables so far described. I am referring in particular to the role the perception of the Soviet threat could have on the growing controversiality within NATO. It seems thereby proficuous to move on to an examination of the regime as an a u t o n o m o u s variable in explaining the "politicization" of the security matters in Europe.

Regime Legitimacy and Delegitimatization

In assessing the autonomous role of the regime variable on foreign policy, I will distinguish three different aspects: first, the effects of the above-mentioned structural change on the regime stability; second, the autonomous effects regime is producing on the foreign policy orientations of Western countries; third, the strains and stresses domestic factors are exerting on regime legitimacy.

The main effect a progressive de-concentration of power produces on the regime level is probably an increasing u n c e r t a i n t y among political elites on the future stability of the regime. This uncertainty manifests itself on many levels. In the relationships with the USSR, in the sense of suspicion on the American intentions in dealing with the Soviet parity or alleged superiority, and, last but not least, in the linkage between security and welfare in the European context. This last effect seems to be one of the most relevant ones. The incongruence between the economic growth of European countries and their negligible military commitment implies, in fact, a delinking between the economic commitment and military defence, devolving the latter completely to the hegemonic power.

According to the **hegemonic stability theory,** such an uncertainty would imply an attempt to change the regime in order to bring it in tune with the actual structure of power. In particular, in the European context this would mean a deep reconsideration of the role of nuclear force and the autonomy of the European political posture. The reasons why this has not yet happened have to be looked for at the regime level itself.

When a regime is established it tends to acquire over time an "objective" reality which, to a certain extent, does not reflect the structure of power which created it. Thereby, a change in the structure of power may be not immediately followed by a change in the regime content. Many factors could explain this lag between structure and regime, and therefore even explain why the change in the structure of power has not produced a change in the regime but instead led to its growing politicization. Krasner (1982) has put forward some possible causes for this lag, and two of them seem particularly relevant to our case:

(1) Uncertainty about the crisis of the present regime and a future one. Two sources of uncertainty which can explain the slowliness of change are the following. First, uncertainty about the duration and result of the crisis of the present regime, which induces the political elites to let everything unperturbated. This uncertainty is particularly relevant in this area because although the sources of the present crisis are more acute now than before nevertheless they are not new. Doubts about the credibility of the extended deterrence, the scope of the Soviet intentions and the best way to cope with them have been with NATO since its beginning, and the adoption of the doctrine of nuclear retaliation has always been half-heartedly endorsed in both sides of the Atlantic, As *Bundy et al.* stresses: "in both decades the Alliance kept itself together more by mutual political confidence than by plausible nuclear war-fighting plans" (BUNDY et al., 1984:31). Therefore, there is always the hope that the present pressures will be overcome again by an act of political confidence. Secondly, uncertainty about the nature and content of a future regime. In the security area, where the security dilemma plays an important role (JERVIS, 1984) regime building and change are very slow, and elites are always reluctant to act in a coordinated way. In fact, not only regime change will presuppose joint coordination at least among the European countries, but also definite steps in the direction of either unilateral disarmament or of greater military burdens and responsibility for the European countries — all of them expected to raise resistance, suspicions and fears in public opinion and among elites. This uncertainty is moreover compounded with cognitive dimensions which are the second source of resistance to a change in the present regime and of the lag between structure and regime.

(2) Cognitive limits to an alternative framework for defence. Europeans and Americans have always had conflictual interests in the security context: the United States wants to keep a war started in Europe limited to such an area; whereas Europe wants to connect the European context with the US strategic forces. In this sense, both parts share a sense of uncomfortableness within the present regime. Nevertheless, neither of them is able to offer an alternative cognitive framework in which to solve their competing interests. The different proposals put forward in these last year can be tentatively summoned under three clusters:

(a) Proposals which aim at strengthening military and political cohesion of the Western Alliance and its credibility toward the USSR, lessening at the same time the rigid nuclear posture. In this perspective someone argues for abandoning the first-use policy (BUNDY et al., 1984), while others underline the need for the greater flexibility of responses to the Soviet threat, and therefore advocate a greater conventional force and its better utilization. (ROGERS, 1982) The latter position sees military strength and political cohesiveness as instrumental to a stronger bargaining position with the Soviet Union; whereas the former sees a no-first-use policy as a clear manifestation of goodwill aiming at establishing conditions for concrete and verifiable arms control agreements.

(b) Proposals which aim at reducing the risks of nuclear exchange in Europe through arms control negotiations aiming at reducing conventional and nuclear forces, enhancing confidence-building measures and creating nuclear-free zones.[9]

(c) Proposals which postulate a radical reversal of Western defence conceptions. According to this line of thought, alliance configurations and politico-military subordination to the US are powerful sources of instability. Reliance on nuclear weapons has to be abandoned, the Atlantic Alliance dissolved and defence based exclusively on defensive weapons, or even better, on non-violent means. Unitaleral steps — as the withdrawal from the Atlantic Alliance — are more effective than bilateral steps.[10]

Each of these positions can be assessed in terms both of structural implications and of capacity to gain wide popular consensus. It is obvious that the first group of proposals has the least structural implications in terms of regime change, but at the same time it raises the at least domestic resistance. On the other hand, the third group of proposals implies a structural change of regime, but at the same time will meet formidable international and domestic problems. The second group finds itself more or less in the middle in terms of feasibility and consensus.

As they are conceived, therefore, these proposals do not lend themselves to be easily espoused by European elites, who therefore prefer to stick to the present regime. Nevertheless, this very uncertainty makes political elites very sensitive to pressures coming from below.

In other words, a shaken regime, in which political elites are highly uncertain about the proper directions and unable to convey a coherent defence strategy is particularly sensitive to pressures and erosion from below, that is from public opinion attitudes and moves. In sum, one of the main effects of the lag between structure and regime changes could be the greater role domestic factors can play in shaping the security regime.

Public opinion polls reveal[11] that people are growingly concerned about nuclear war, and, at the same time, the support for NATO is high and the US-Western European alliance is deemed to be the best way to defend the common goals. The fear of the Soviet threat is diminished, but a substantial distrust for Soviet intentions remains. Peace is becoming an issue for Western publics, expecially younger generations. Without a precedent in the past forty years, defence and security mark high scores on the public opinion agenda. This is happening at a time when European (and American) elites seem to have an undermined image of international relations and a less coherent stance on many defence issues. (WILDENMANN, 1983; HOLSTI and ROSENAU, 1980) Cleavages among Western elites reflect political cleavages (SPD vs. CDU in West Germany; DC and PSI vs. PCI in Italy; Conservative vs. Labourite in England, etc.). At the same time, the erosion of bipartisan consensus produces consequences even at the transgovermental bureaucratic level within NATO, limiting the capacity of this organization to manage conflicts in a depoliticized way.

These multifaceted phenomena have been scrutinized from several points of view. Without any pretension of novelty, **Tables V—VII** give an illustration of the European public opinion mood on this subject using Eurobarometer surveys.[12]

Table V. Probability of War in the Next Ten Years (More than 50 %)

Countries	1980	1981	1982
France	41,9	25,1	20,3
West Germany	25,2	29,7	20,3
United Kingdom	37,5	21,2	16,9
Italy	32,0	18,2	14,3
Netherlands	23,6	19,6	19,1

Sources: Eurobarometer Surveys Nos 13, 16, 18.

Table VI. General Publics' Preferences for Foreign Policy (Percentages)

Countries	NATO Foreign Policy	Independent Europe allied with USA	Independent Europe not allied with USA	Independent Foreign Policy	Forces reduction better relations with USSR
West Germany	56,3	33,2	10,5	5,4	4,6
France	15,5	36,3	19,7	20,8	7,7
United Kingdom	52,6	23,8	8,5	11,7	3,4
Italy	29,6	36,9	21,0	9,3	3,2
Netherlands	40,5	35,4	8,3	4,6	11,2

Sources: Eurobarometer Surveys Nos 13, 16, 18.

Table VII. Agreement/Disagreement on NATO's defence effort (Percentages)

Countries	Agreement (1)	Disagreement (1)
West Germany	64,4	35,6
France	66,8	33,2
United Kingdom	74,2	25,8
Italy	52,7	47,3
Netherlands	53,6	46,4

Sources: Eurobarometer Surveys Nos 13, 16, 18.

(1) Agreement includes also strong agreements and Disagreement includes also strong disagreement.

A first observation is the remarkable share of people which is frightened by the possibility of a nuclear war in Europe, even after the sharp decrease in the number of people who esteem probable (more than 50 per cent of probability) a nuclear war in the next 10 years from 1980 to 1982. This decline is more striking for France (from 41,9 per cent to 20,3 per cent), Italy (32 per cent to 14,3 per cent) and the UK; less for West Germany and the Netherlands, the two countries in which the debate has a longer and more intense tradition. (VON BREDOW, 1982) This trend is completely different whether we look at the attitudes toward foreign policy or the defence effort. At the height of the mobilization against nuclear threat, only less than 10 per cent of the European population (except for the Netherlands) argue for an arms reduction policy and a better relationship with the USSR.[13] West Germany and the Netherlands are also the two countries were NATO policy has the highest support (together with England). Finally, in 1981, after almost two years of mobilization on such issues, the majority of population supported the Western military effort.

More difficult to assess are the attitudes of European and American elites on this subject. Wildenmann, quoting the only studies conducted in Europe (West Germany) on such a topic among positional elites, found great variations among experts and politicians on the assessment of détente and on many defence issues. A survey of experts in West Germany found: "very differentiated opinions... on the usefulness of détente policies, on MBFR, on the implications of deterrence, on the production and location of new nuclear weapons, on the evaluation of political and military developments in the USSR and on the global versus European approaches to security. ...These variations are similar to variation found among elites with respect to defence or détente", and Wildenmann concludes that "there is n o general consensus as to what should be the underlying rationale for defence policies — as was once the case in the 1960s — except that there is a consensus in preventing war." (WILDENMANN, 1983: 32 and 26) In a quite different context, Holsti and Rosenau (1980) found that the "consensus" about the nature of the international system, the Soviet threat and the appropriate policies to deal with external challenges and opportunities is declining among the American elites. The results of a nation-wide elites' survey show the appearance of a dominant cleavage in the US leadership opinions along the fault line defined by the Cold War versus post-Cold War belief systems.[14]

These strands of evidence make plausible to argue that both in Europe and the US the coherent consensus on security issue existing in the 1960s has disappeared. Therefore, the failure of political leaderships to shape a new coherent framework in which public anxieties and puzzles could find their answer account for the different ways these anxieties find expression and produce mass mobilization of wide scope. On the other hand, people are starting to become suspicious about the pretension of political leaders and experts to "know better". People more concerned with nuclear war are the younger generations, who have received higher education and have been exposed to "democratic socialization".

Summing up the three points so far outlined, I have argued that the change at the structural level produced a growing uncertainty about the regime legitimacy and stability, and the very nature of the security regime increased even more this uncertainty. This weakening of the regime made it more sensitive to challenges coming from below, and when a particular event like the decision to deploy the theatre missiles occurred a process of politicization from below started and reached the regime level.

Conclusion

In this paper, I have attempted to describe, in a very tentative fashion, the structural evolution in the European context and its effects on the security regime. This effort has revealed at least four interesting points:

(1) In terms of structural variables, the nature of asymmetrical relationships between Western Europe and the US has not significantly

changed since the Second World War. The US still remains the hegemonic power in the area, both in military and economic dimensions, although in more costly terms.

(2) The major significant effect at the structural level has been a progressive, though slow, delinking of the security and economic issues from one another. The main consequence of such a delinking has been the weakening of the security (and economic) regime in Western Europe and a growing uncertainty about its future directions and mutual expectations in Europe and the US.

(3) This uncertainty, compounded with the reluctance of European elites to change the cognitive framework of defence doctrines has made the security regime more sensitive to politicization from below.

(4) The lack of coherence and unity among the European elites on defence issue, together with a decreased threat from the Soviet Union, has coincided with a growing preoccupation of the European public — especially younger generations — on "peace" issues. Following the decision to deploy the euromissiles and in general the whole debate on "limited nuclear war", this interest has expressed itself through a growing fear of nuclear war. These fears appeared on the political agenda in the same moment when European elites were less able to cope with them. The elites' incapacity to convey toward the mass public a coherent and stable image of foreign policy has made politicization even more salient. Quite remarkably, however, this mobilization has not affected the public opinion's support for NATO or its defence policy.

This analysis has, however, some limitations as well. First, the analysis has been necessarily too cursory, jumping over some relevant logical connections, in particular the relationship between a structural change and growing regime uncertainty. Secondly, a much deeper and wider empirical analysis is needed in order to make really empirically founded statements around structural and regime levels. On the other hand, this analysis has shown interesting cues for further scrutinizing of the relationships between international structure, regime change and domestic constraint on regime legitimacy. It seems, however, incontrovertible that to build defence and foreign policy consensus in the future will need a much wider and substantial debate than in the past.

Notes

1. This analysis is limited to the consideration of the Western European context. In order to compare Western realities with Eastern ones, a completely different — and more complex — framework of analysis will be needed. However, rumors of growing concern for nuclear war in Eastern countries have been reported in the Western press.

2. Two main lines of thought in international relations theory are, on the one hand, **the equilibrium-parity school** and, on the other, the **hegemonic-disparity school.** The first school stresses the anarchical nature of the international system, made up of sovereign actors, not constrained by anything but force, and where the ruling mechanism is the balance of power. This line of thought assumes that all actors are fundamentally equal and war occurs when one state

attempts to establish a hegemonic position on the system. (MORGENTHAU, 1978; BULL, 1977; CARR, 1983) On the other hand, the second school underlines the orderly nature of the international system, ruled by hegemonic powers who guarantee peace and stability and an ordered set of relationships among minor actors. Peace rests on predominance or leadership by one actor and war is the consequence of hegemonic decline for deconcentration of power and leadership's delegitimation. Actors therefore are not equal in power and resources. (WALLERSTEIN, 1978; GILPIN, 1981; 1983; MODELSKI, 1978; 1983; BONANATE, 1976; 1981; LEVY, 1983)

3. The literature on the "structure" of international system is wide in scope although confused in content. Generally, two different aspects of the structure are underlined. Some equate structure with a given distribution of power; (WALTZ, 1975) others equate structure with interdependence, namely asymmetrical interdependence. (BONANATE, 1976) The first definition stresses the distributional or composite aspects of power, as the second the relational and configurational ones. (ZINNES, 1980)

4. The following pages draw upon the brilliant discussion of regime and policy legitimacy by *George* (1980) and *Trout* (1975).

5. On the role of linkages in the theory of hegemonic stability see *Bergsten, Keohane and Nye* (1977) and *Gilpin* (1981).

6. The security regime among Western countries seems to fulfill all the conditions put forward by *Jervis* (1982).

7. These organizations — especially NATO and IMF — legitimized normatively the crucial role of US leadership. The quota system in IMF assured the US a "last say" position in monetary matters. As to NATO, the decision to employ nuclear weapons is in the hands of American leaders. As the Athens Guidelines of 1963 state: "the United States will c o n s u l t with Allies on the use of tactical nuclear weapons time and circumstances permitting, therefore the US President retains the right to use American nuclear weapons without prior consultation" (quoted in the Second Interim Report on Nuclear Weapons in Europe, A Report to the SFRC, US GPO 1983). (SIPRI, 1984:25)

8. See the chapter 'The Structure of the International System'.

9. Different positions have been summoned in this group; see LODGAARD and THEE (1983) and SIPRI (1985) for a broad overview of positions.

10. See *Alternative Defence Commission*.

11. Many opinion polls have been conducted in these last few years on the subject. Analysis has been conducted by *Thies* (1983), *Capitanchik and Eichenberg* (1983); SIPRI (1983; 1984; 1985).

12. The following Eurobarometers have been utilized: nos 13, 16 and 18, respectively for 1980, 1981 and 1982. These data have been kindly made available through the Belgian Archives for the Social Sciences. BASS bears no responsibility for the analyses and interpretations presented here.

13. Attention must be given also to the form of the question. The last question in fact combines together references to a cooperative policy toward the USSR with support for an arms reduction policy. This combination could have biased the answers.

14. The Cold War axiom "depicts a conflictual world in which all issues and conflicts are related to each other...; the United States faces an implacable and united coalition of adversaries led by Peking and Moscow; the Third World plays a crucial role as both the battleground and the prize in the conflict between contending blocs; the United States have global responsibilities to meet any challenges from communism; and military instruments of policy are at least the necessary, if not the sufficient, means of securing vital interests."
The post-Cold-War axioms"... portray contemporary international relations quite differently. With a loosely structured international system there exist complex interests that do not always find the western democracies arrayed against the monolithic Soviet-dominated Communist bloc; the linkages between conflict issuea are at best modest...; third world conflicts are more likely to reflect nationalist than communist motivations but,..., they rarely pose a serious threat to vital U.S. interests; these interests are sufficiently varied and complex that they cannot adequately be met by employing such simple decision rules as 'oppose communism'; and the means by which foreign policy goal can most effectively be pursued are not limited to, or even primarily, military ones". (HOLSTI and ROSENAU, 1980:265—268)

References

Allison Graham T. (1971), *Essence of Decision. Explaining the Cuban Missile Crisis,*
    Boston, Little, Brown & Co., pp. 338.
Alperovitz Gar (1966), *Un Asso nella Manica. La Diplomazia Atomica Americana:*
    Potsdam e Hiroshima, Torino, Einaudi, pp. 309.
Bergsten Fred C., Keohane Robert O., Nye Joseph S. (1979), "International Econ-
    omics and International Politics: A Framework for Analysis", *International*
    Organization, Vol. 29, No 1, Winter, pp. 3—36.
Bonanate Luigi (1976), *Teoria Politica e Relazioni Internationali,* Milano, Comunità,
    pp. 238.
——— (1981), "Sistema Politico Internationale", *Il Mondo Contemporaneo,*
    Vol. X, Firenze, La Nuova Italia, pp. 332—347.
Bueno de Mesquita Bruce (1975), "Measuring Systemic Polarity", *Journal of Conflict*
    Resolution, Vol. 19, No 2, June, pp. 187—216.
——— (1979), "Systemic Polarization and the Occurence and Duration of War",
    in J.D. Singer et Associates, *Explaining War, Selected Papers from the*
    Correlates of War Project, London, Sage, pp. 113—138.
Bull Hedley (1977), *The Anarchical Society,* London, Macmillan Press, pp. 335.
Bundy McGeorge, Kennan George F., McNamara Robert S., Smith Gerard (1984),
    "Nuclear Weapons and the Atlantic Alliance", in Frank Blackaby, Jozef
    Goldblat and Sverre Lodgaard (eds.), *No-First-Use,* London, Taylor &
    Francis, pp. 29—41.
Calzini Paolo (1985), "Modelli di Interpretazione della Politica Estera Sovietica", *Il*
    Mulino, XXXIV, No 2, Marzo-Aprile, pp. 298—316.
Capitanchik David and Eichenberg Richard C. (1983), *Defence and Public Opinion,*
    Chatham House Papers — 20, London, Routledge & Kegan Paul, pp. 98.
Caporaso James A. and Ward Michael D. (1979), "The United States in an Inter-
    dependent World: The Emergence of Economic Power", in Charles
    W. Kegley jr. and Patrick J. McGowan (eds.), *Challenges to America,*
    London, Sage, pp. 139—170.
Carr E.H. (1983), *The Twenty Years' Crisis,* London, Macmillan, (1939), pp. 244.
Easton David (1979), *A Systems Analysis of Political Life,* Chicago, University of
    Chicago Press, (1965), pp. 507.
Gaddis John Lewis (1982), *Strategies of Containment,* Oxford, Oxford University
    Press, pp. 432.
Galtung Johan (1980), "International Relations and International Conflicts: A Socio-
    logical Approach", in Johan Galtung, *Essays in Peace Research,* Vol. IV,
    Copenhagen, C. Ejilers, pp. 316—351.
Gambino Antonio (1972), *Le Conseguenze della Seconda Guerra Mondiale,* Bari,
    Laterza, pp. 324.
George Alexander L. (1979), "The Causal Nexus Between Cognitive Beliefs and
    Decision-Making Behavior: The 'Operational Code' Belief System", in
    Lawrence S. Falkowski (ed.), *Psychological Models in International*
    Relations, Boulder, Westview Press, pp. 95—124.
——— (1980), "Domestic Constraints on Regime Change in U.S. Foreign Policy:
    The Need for Policy Legitimacy", in Ole R. Holsti, Randolph M. Siverson,
    Alexander L. George (eds.), *Change in the International System,* Boulder,
    Westview Press, pp. 233—262.
Gilpin Robert (1975), "Three Models of the Future", *International Organization,* Vol.
    29, No 1, Winter, pp. 37—60.
——— (1981), "The Politics of Transnational Economic Relations", in Robert
    O. Keohane and Joseph S. Nye (eds.), *Transnational Relations and World*
    Politics, Cambridge, Harvard University Press, pp. 48—69.
——— (1983), *War and Change in World Politics,* Cambridge, Cambridge Uni-
    versity Press, (1981), pp. 272.
Hart Jeffrey (1976), "Three Approaches to the Measurement of Power in Inter-
    national Relations", *International Organization,* Vol. 30, No 2, Spring,
    pp. 289—305.

Holsti Ole R. and Rosenau James N. (1980), "Cold War Axioms in the Post-Vietnam Era", in Ole R. Holsti, Randolph M. Siverson, Alexander L. George (eds.), *Change in the International System*, Boulder, Westview Press, pp. 263—301.

Jervis Robert (1982), "Security Regimes", *International Organization*, Vol. 36, No 2, Spring, pp. 357—378.

Kelman Herbert C. (1969), "Patterns of Personal Involvement in the National System: A Social-Psychological Analysis of Political Legitimacy", in James N. Rosenau (ed.), *International Politics and Foreign Policy*, New York, The Free Press, pp. 276—288.

Keohane Robert O. and Nye Joseph S. (1977), *Power and Interdependence*, Boston, Little, Brown & Co, pp. 273.

——— (1981), *Transnational Relations and World Politics*, Cambridge, Harvard University Press, (1970), pp. 428.

Keohane Robert O. (1980), "The Theory of Hegemonic Stability and Changes in International Economic Regimes, 1967—1977", in Ole R. Holsti, Randolph M. Siverson, Alexander L. George (eds.), *Change in the International System*, Boulder, Westview Press, pp. 131—162.

Kindleberger Charles P. (1981), "Dominance and Leadership in the International Economy", *International Studies Quarterly*, Vol. 25, No 2, June, pp. 242—254.

Krasner Stephen D. (1976), "State Power and the Structure of International Trade", *World Politics*, Vol. XXVIII, No 3, April. pp. 317—347.

——— (1982), "Structural Causes and Regime Consequences: Regimes as Intervening Variables", *International Organization*, Vol. 36, No 2, Spring, pp. 185—205.

——— (1982), "Regimes and the Limits of Realism: Regimes as Autonomous Variables", *International Organization*, Vol. 36, No 2, Spring, pp. 497—510.

Kogan Norman (1974), *L'Italia del Dopoguerra*, Bari, Laterza, pp. 283.

Kolko Gabriel (1970), *Le Radici Economiche della Politica Americana*, Torino, Einaudi, pp. 177.

Levy Jack S. (1983), "World System Analysis. A Great Power Framework", in William R. Thompson (ed.), *Contending Approaches to World System Analysis*, London, Sage, pp. 183—201.

Lodgaard Sverre and Thee Marek (eds). (1983), *Nuclear disengagement in Europe*, London, Taylor & Francis-SIPRI, pp. 271.

Modelski George (1978), "The Long Cycle of Global Politics and the Nation-State", *Comparative Studies in Society and History*, Vol. 20, No 2, April, pp. 214—235.

——— (1983), "Long Cycles of World Leadership", in William R. Thompson (ed.), *Contending Approaches to World System Analysis*, London, Sage, pp. 115—139.

Morgenthau Hans J. (1978), *Politics among Nations*, New York, A. Knopf (1948), pp. 650.

Putnam Robert D. and Bayne Nicholas (1984), *Hanging Together*, Cambridge, Harvard University Press, pp. 255.

Putnam Robert D. (1985), "I Vertici Occidentali: Interpretazione Politica", in Cesare Merlini (a cura di), *I Vertici*, Roma ADNKronos pp. 65-122.

Rapkin David P., Thompson William R., Christopherson Jan A. (1979), 'Bipolarity and Bipolarization in the Cold War Era", *Journal of Conflict Resolution*, Vol. 23, No 2, June, pp. 261—295.

Rogers Bernard W. (1982), "The Atlantic Alliance: Prescriptions for a Difficult Decade", *Foreign Affairs*, Summer, pp. 1145—1156.

Rosenau James N. (1967), "Foreign Policy as an Issue-Area", in James N. Rosenau (ed.), *Domestic Sources of Foreign Policy*, New York, The Free Press, pp. 11—50.

——— (1967), "Verso lo Studio dei Collegamenti Nazionali-Internazionali", in Luigi Bonanate (a cura di), *Il sistema delle Relazioni Internazionali*, Torino, Einaudi, pp. 266—290.

Sipri (1983, 1984, 1985), *World Armaments and Disarmaments*, London, Francis & Taylor-SIPRI.
—— (1985), *Policies for Common Security*, London, Francis & Taylor-SIPRI, pp. 250.
Sprout Harold and Sprout Margaret (1979), *The Ecological Perspective on Human Affairs*, Westport, Greenwood Press (1965), pp. 234.
Stein Arthur A. (1982), "Coodination and Collaboration: Regimes in an Anarchic World", *International Organization*, Vol. 36, No 2, Spring, pp. 299—324.
Thies Wallace J. (1983), *The Atlantic Alliance, Nuclear Weapons & European Attitudes*, Policy Papers in International Affairs, University of California-Berkeley, pp. 59.
Thompson William and Modelski George (1977), "Global Conflict Intensity and Great Power Summitry Behavior", *Journal of Conflict Resolution*, Vol. 21, No 2, June, pp. 339—376.
Thompson William R. (1983), "Cycles, Capabilities and War. An Ecumenical View", in William T. Thompson (ed.), *Contending Approaches to World System Analysis*, London, Sage, pp. 141—163.
Trout Thomas B. (1975), "Rethoric Revisited. Political Legitimation and the Cold War", *International Studies Quarterly*, Vol. 19, No 3, September, pp. 251—283.
Von Bredow Wilfried (1982), "The Peace Movements in the Federal Republic of Germany: Composition and Objectives", *Armed Forces and Society*, Vol. 9, No 1, Fall, pp. 33—48.
Wallace Michael D. (1972), "Status, Formal Organization and Arms Levels as Factors Leading to the Onset of War, 1820—1964", in Bruce M. Russett (ed.), *Peace, War and Numbers*, London, Sage, pp. 49—69.
—— (1973), *War and Rank Among Nations*, Lexington, Lexington Books, pp. 142.
—— (1979), "Alliance Polarization, Cross-Cutting and International War, 1915—1964", in J. David Singer et Associates, *Explaining War*, London, Sage, pp. 83—111.
Wallerstein Immanuel (1974a), "The Rise and Future Demise of the World Capitalist System: Consepts for Comparative Analysis", *Comparative Studies in Society and History*, Vol. 16, No 4, September, pp. 387—415.
—— (1978), *Il Sistema Mondiale dell'Economia Moderna*, Bologna, Il Mulino, (1974), pp. 514.
Waltz Kenneth N. (1975), "Theory of International Relations", Fred Greenstein and Nelson Polsby (eds.), *Handbook of Political Science*, Vol. 8, Addison-Wesley, pp. 1—85.
Wildenmann Rudolf (1983), "Public Opinion and the Defence Effort: Trends and Lessons Europe", in *Defence and Consensus: The Domestic Aspects of Western Security*, Adelphi Papers, No 182, London, International Institute for Strategic Studies, pp. 24—28.
Zinnes Dina A. (1980), "Prerequisites for the Study of System Transformation", in Ole R. Holsti, Randolph M. Siverson, Alexander L. George (eds.), *Change, in the International System*, Boulder, Westview Press, pp. 1—21.

4

Models of Peaceful Change and the Future of the European Security System

Esko Antola

From the Quantity of Order to the the Quality of Order

Bringing about changes peacefully in the European order is undoubtedly one of the most challenging tasks of the present work for security in Europe. Scholarly arguments stress repeatedly that, in the history of international relations, wars are the major agents of change. The dynamics of change is accordingly seen as a cyclical development from one international order to another.[1]

Breaking down this "vicious circle"[2] poses a major challenge to the current European system, founded on the outcome of a major war, which established the rules and norms of that order. The power relations therein are based largely on the resuts of that given war, the Second World War. The decisive difference between the current order and its predecessors is the fact that it relies heavily on nuclear weapons.

Scholarly models on how peaceful change could be promoted date back to the 1930s. The international order then existing was rapidly heading towards a collapse and the academic community wished to develop ideas and concrete models in the interest of preserving peace. The League of Nations' collective security system was, as a result of the First World War, designed to transform the traditional European Balance of Power -system into a collective security system. The competing option was, in Martin *Wight's* terms, to "relapse into the more primitive stage of rivalry between two dominant powers out of which it (i.e. the pre-war balance of power system: E.A.) had originally grown".[3]

The latter option, a relapse into a primitive rivalry, became evident in the Abyssinian War where collective security under the League was tested. Its system of sanctions did not work and an aggression was not prevented. Instead, international relations took a collision course which resulted in the outbreak of the Second World War.

In his later evaluation of the League collective security system Wight argues:[4]

> "The failure of the League of Nations was the most decisive occurrence in international history since the Peace of Westphalia. It ended the long period in which a degree of international order had been maintained by the rational, intricate and precarious system of the multiple balance of power; and by not carrying the system to a higher level, by failing to transform the quantity of order into confederal quality, it introduced a new chapter in which the ordering of international relations has been less under human direction and control".

It would not be historically sound to argue that the European order in the mid-1980s is in a similar situation. The greatest problem of the 1930s was, in E.H. *Carr's* terms[5] the conflict between the "haves" and the "have-nots": the then existing international order was challenged by dissatisfied Powers asking for compensation and rehabilitation as Great Powers. This is not the major problem of the current order.

In one respect, however, a similarity exists. We may express in Wight's terms: how to "transform the quantity of order into a confederal quality". Instead of a "confederal" we would write for instance "common security" or "peace structure" or even "détente". But the basic problem is the same: **how the stability and jointly established norms in the Helsinki Final Act could be transformed into a European order which is qualitatively more stable, more egalitarian and less dependent on the quantity of order, defined by arms.**

In this paper, an attempt is made to study the emergence of the post-Second World War European order from the point of view of peaceful change. It is assumed that the European order, in which the Conference on Security and Cooperation (CSCE) plays such an important role, is under stresses which call for changes in the basic structure of the order. To meet today's challenges, a mechanism of change is needed which would make a qualitative transformation possible.

An Order Based on Force

The problem of peaceful change has an intimate relationship with the configuration of the international order which serves as a starting point when evaluating the possibilities of peaceful change. It is also important to assess whether we face the problem of change **within** a given international order or whether we expect a change **from** one particular type of international orders **to** new models.

"By international order I mean a pattern of activity that sustains the elementary or primary goals of the society of states, or international society", argues Hedley *Bull* in his study of international orders.[6] The primary goals of a society of states are in Bull's definition the preservation of the system of states, the maintaining of independence and external sovereignty of states, the goal of peace and the limitation of violence.[7] The combination of these elementary goals, supported by a number of secondary and temporary goals, sets the rules and limits of a given international order. Changes, whether peaceful or not, are, accordingly, either strived for or fought against in the interest of the same primary goals.

For the purpose of this study the goal of peace and the limitation of violence are of special interest. If the procedures of peaceful change are to be realized in the interest of avoiding war, those goals would accordingly be realized or, at least, approached. The apprehension of force is in the core of our concept of an international order. The classification of international orders by Ian *Clark* serves as our frame in approaching the role of force.

Clark develops three ways of creating international orders on his premises:[8]

1. Order through the recognition of the central role of force creating and maintaining a given international order;
2. Order through placing constraints to the use of force, and;
3. Order through the eventual rejection of the special role of force in international relations.

Clark's first type of order is an example of a **classical concept of power politics** where sovereign states act in the conditions of international anarchy or an international state of anarchy. In such a situation, in Charles *Beitz*'s terms, four conditions prevail: actors of the international relations are states and only states; they are relatively equal in power; they are internally independent of each other; and there are no reliable expectations of reciprocity.[9] Beitz himself is dubious whether such an international order really exists, at least in the post-Second World War era when interdependences limit the policies of states and when international treaties and institutions add compliance to the state behaviour.

But in spite of compliance whit such an order, the use of force is ultimately the basis of an international order. Clark himself refers to deterrence as an expression of an international order concerned:[10]

"There is no consciously constructed mechanism that would constrain the use of force. To this extent, nuclear deterrence represents a *laissez-faire* situation in which order in the last resort depends on the free interplay of competing forces... There is no constraint of legal, institutional or physical nature."

In the history of European international orders, models of a balance of power have been the usual method of maintaining the order of the first type in Clark's typology.

Since:

"In international politics there is no authority effectively able to prohibit the use of force. The balance of power among states becomes a balance of all the capacities, including physical force, that states choose to use in pursuing their goals".[11]

The strive for a balance of power becomes both the very method of survival and peace as well in Bull's terms. The balance of power through alliances is seen as the basis of international relations where force is an essential element of state relations and where no effective constraints can be established. The rule to be followed in such an international order is that of the minimum common interest, survival, which becomes the primary goal of nations and which controls the use of force through a minimum of cooperation needed.

But the history also shows that such configurations of "balances of all the capacities" fail. The reasons are often sought from "power vacuum" theories which blame for the collapse of the order dovish states who do not pay enough attention to the realities of the basically game type of international relations. On the other hand, the highly competitive nature of balance of power systems with mutually reinforcing alliances make the balance highly unstable and inevitably increases the quantity of force, i.e. the quantity of arms.

Clark's second version of an international order is roughly the system of collective security. This means that **institutional, physical, legal or normative constraints should be placed on the use of force.** The idea of constraining force reflects a rationalist view of international relations confronted by the realist world view which is associated with Clark's first type of an international order.

As Geoffrey *Goodwin* points out, the rationalist view of collective security implies that three conditions must prevail:[12] peace is indivisible; aggression is a crime; and the "peace-loving majority" has the power to restrain those who threaten peace. Kenneth *Thompson* again argues that a system of collective security must include a mechanism of collective enforcement; that nations subscribing to collective security must be willing and capable of mastering overwhelming strength for collective defence and, finally, that at least a minimum of political solidarity and moral community must prevail.[13]

Inis *Claude* in his classical account of collective security furnishes us with the following definition:[14]

> "Collective security is a specialized instrument of international policy in the sense that it is intended only to forestall the arbitrary and aggressive use of force, not to provide enforcement mechanisms for the whole body of international law; it assumes that, so far as the problem of world order is concerned, the heart of the matter is the restraint of military action rather than the guarantee of respect for all legal obligations. Moreover, it assumes that this ideal may be realized, or at least approximated, by a reformation of international policy without the institution of a revolution in the structure of the international system".

The three different accounts of collective security reflect the division of opinions concerning the nature of this form of international relations. Both Goodwin and Thompson see collective security very much in the moralistic and legalistic way. Their views are inspired by institutionalized collective security arrangements reflecting very much the ideals of the

League. They both are also highly critical towards the performance of the UN as an institution of collective security.

On the other hand, Claude's definition seems to describe quite correctly the type of an international system where force is not denied as such but where constraints are sought in order to prevent its use. In a sense collective security is a tool which nations have at their disposal when aiming to limit the use of force in their mutual relations. Obviously goals of such arrangements are far more modest than the aims of institutionalized collective security measures with for instance mechanisms and rules of collective enforcement.

Claude admits himself that the working of the type of collective security he defines must meet its basic problems as well. He speaks about "the satisfaction of an extraordinarily complex network of requirements". For our purposes in particular his distinction into **subjective** and **objective** requirements is a suitable and valuable notion.[15]

Subjective requirements point to the need of positive commitments that nations have to the value of peace and the limitation of the use of force. The idea of the indivisibility of peace, as earlier mentioned by Goodwin is outspokenly also an element in the subjective side of commitments.

Objective requirements on the other hand refer to the satisfaction which a collective arrangement gives to those Powers adhered to it. Collective security must in real terms positively contribute to nations' security. Claude himself stresses the even distribution of powers as the most important objective requirement. It must be followed, however, by the general reduction of power which will imply disarmament of some sort. Finally, Claude points to the need to create a legal and structural apparatus, which could give an institutional expression to the basic principles of collective security.[16]

Thus the creation of a system of constraining the use of force has basically two elements: it must fulfill the task of producing a sense of security thus increasing the adherence of participating nations to the system; and, at the same time, nations must engange themselves into an institutionalized system where the use of force is not only prevented through collective commitments to restrictions but where also a reduction of force adds to their security.

Clark's third category consists of attempts to make the international order less dependent on the use of force. The utmost solution would be the establishment of a world government. In general the third category includes procedures which could **make force disappear.** Peaceful solution of conflicts, the extension of social contract theories to the international system as well as the establishment of common authorities are perhaps the most often debated items in this connection. We shall later discuss functionalism as an example of these methods.

Models of Peaceful Change

The issue of peaceful change is intimately linked to the content of order. Its intellectual roots are in the debate of the 1920s and 1930s, when its purpose was to study possibilities of change within the collective security system of the League, already in its collision course towards a war. The purpose was also to develop methods to make these necessary changes peaceful so that the *status quo* would not be destroyed.

The debate of peaceful change in the 1930s formulated two conceptions describing the content of the term. The first saw peaceful change as a method of avoiding war while the other stressed it as a procedure of restructuring the international order. The same distinction was expressed by Carr in his *The Twenty Years' Crisis* as a distinction between **utopian** and **realist** interpretations. The realist version sees peaceful change as a process of "adjustment to the changed relations of power" while the utopian school aims at eliminating power from international relations and instead hopes to base change "on a common feeling what is just and reasonable".[17]

When the realist interpretation of peaceful change is applied, the maintenance of order and the avoidance of war are stressed as its principal aims. As a method of international change, it appears as a substitute for war. A good example of such an argument is C.R.M.F. *Cruttwell's* definition in 1937. Peaceful change occurs in his mind simply when nations are ready to accept changes in the existing international order without wars. In fact the contingent threat of war is, Cruttwell says, the very reason why nations are ready to accept changes. Peaceful change thus takes place in the face of an ultimate threat of war.[18]

In its narrow meaning peaceful change is not only a substitute for war but also an exception from the rule in itself. Change through war is the major type of change in the international system which only under some specific conditions and circumstances may assume the form of a non-war change. The realist interpretation rarely shows an interest in motivations or matters of legitimacy. Claims for change are legitimate as such once they are made by nation-states, the only relevant and important actors of international relations. National interests for instance are legitimate reasons for demanding changes.

The realist interpretation identifies three major types or areas of change where peaceful models could be applied. They are territorial changes, modification of international treaties and the development of a collective security system. Demands for **territorial changes** are associated with sovereign states which are sovereign within certain territorial limits and, accordingly, most conflicts of interests touch territorial matters or the status of certain territories.

Territorial changes can be executed peacefully in a number of ways. Alterations of borders, changes in the status of territories or states and demilitarization of certain areas or states are examples falling under the narrow concept of peaceful change.[13]

A more abstract area of changes is the **international treaty system.** Treaty-making powers are also traditionally seen to be firmly entrenched in the heart of national sovereignty. Nations are the principal subjects of the international legal order. That was nearly an undisputable fact in the 1930s. The basic motivation for changing international treaties is that international obligations and norms should be brought to reflect the circumstances of change. The idea behind this argument is that a confrontation between norms and obligations and, on the other hand, realities of the international system create pressures in the direction of uncontrolled changes and increase the possibility of violent changes.[20]

The third area where models for peaceful change, in their narrow meaning, were developed in the 1930s was **the idea of collective security.** Peaceful change and collective security were in fact associated in many definitions and were seen primarily in terms of *status quo.* The close relationship between collective security and peaceful change was expressed by C.K. *Webster* as follows:[21]

> "Collective security and peaceful change are two aspects of all efforts to produce a more peaceful and ordered world and it may be said that each is impossible without the other".

Collective security rests essentially on the legitimate and natural security interests of states who, in principle, enjoy full sovereignty but who have, both in their common interest and in individual interests of each state, to agree on rules and norms of certain collective arrangements. In normal cases, collective security rests on non-binding and non-institutionalized measures, which for their essential parts reflect existing political and military considerations. *Status quo* is an ultimate measure of collective security. Hence peaceful change in most cases means changes in the *status quo.* This is expressed by Frederick *Dunn* as follows:[22]

> "The term 'peaceful change' then, refers simply to the alteration of the status quo by peaceful international procedures rather than by force. The 'status quo' is existing distribution of rights and possession as established or recognized by the legal system... Any peaceful procedure for altering either the existing territorial distribution or the status of any nation would be regarded as a procedure of peaceful change. In brief, peaceful change is concerned both with changes in the distribution of rights and possessions and changes in the laws which govern the acquisition of rights and possessions".

Dunn's basic argument calls for peaceful change within a certain international order so that existing rights and possessions are respected. Rights and possessions must, however, meet one condition: they must be legally recognized and respected and must be clothed in form of international treaties.

It is also evident that peaceful change and collective security were seen as intimately interconnected because of the international crises of the late 1930's. Arnold J. *Toynbee* noted this relationship during the Abyssinian war by arguing that "...the association of peaceful change and collective security is a common feature of many different approaches to the international crisis".[23] Peaceful change as a method of changing international relations without war became topical when "normal" means of guiding international relations did not work: peaceful change was invented largely as a last-resort tool in preventing war.

The major problem of the then existing international security system was seen to be individuality: collective security in fact was not collective but individualistic. Although a certain system of *status quo* prevailed, it rested on the individual security interests and measures of each participant nation. The result was an increasing destructive power of armies and an arms race.[24]

An individualistic security concept by necessity leads to an interpretation of security on the basis of objective factors: a nation can feel secure only when it can count on objective military power which is measurable in quantitative terms. What peaceful change could add to the existing international situation would logically be that international security should be developed more on the lines of collectivism by increasing collaboration and that measurable objective security should be replaced by subjective security elements, i.e. by a common sense of security.

But objective security issues cannot be set aside in international politics. Therefore, the prevention of wars is a parallel method in strengthening collective elements of security policy. More abstract principles of collective security are thus supported by concrete measures in preventing wars. Such are, for instance, legal possibilities of preventing intervention and limitation of armaments.[25]

Alongside the realist definition, a broader view developed. This implied **a restructuring of the existing international order through a peaceful dissolution of that order.** Trends to see change in this broader framework were gradually developed, but were in a minority position in the 1930s.

The broader framework of peaceful change is well illustrated in C.K. Webster's typology. He expands the concept to cover three types of change:[26]

1. peaceful change in order to avoid war;
2. peaceful change to produce justice or better, to remedy justice;
3. peaceful change to produce a world order better adapted to the material and mental processes.

Webster argues that the two first categories are based on the idea that sacrifice must be made by some country or a group of countries. The third type of peaceful change stresses the idea of expediency or efficiency because in such a change all can gain materially as well as morally by such a process.

In Webster's argumentation **peaceful change in order to avoid war** is a viable method because of the development of armaments. This reasoning is even more valid in the nuclear age than it was during the 1930s. But in any event, peaceful change as avoidance of war easily leads to a very narrow definition of peace as absence of war.

Webster's second argument, **peaceful change to produce justice,** should also be seen as a type of non-war change rather than as change producing positive peace. Webster himself refers to the settlement of the First World War which gave Germany a reason to claim remedy to justice. An international order as a peace order is essentially made by the winners of a war and it therefore always leaves claims for remedy.

Webster's third type of change, **change to produce a new world order,** which reflects the realities of international relations better than the existing one, obviously belongs to the category of peaceful change in its broader meaning. In this view peaceful change must offer a framework of appeasement within which nations can meet their basic security needs without the use or even threat of use of war as an ultimate method of change. Bryce *Wood* puts this idea as follows:[27]

> "Peace is peaceful change. Otherwise it is not peace since changes can be made in only two ways. In summary, then, peaceful change may be defined as a regularized process for effectuating modifications in law and policy of the economic and political relationships between nations, which will be so satisfactory to the dissentient elements that the threat of war's breaking out through their agression may be removed, but which will not be so distasteful to the defenders of things as they are that these will make their agreement contingent upon the outcome of a trial by battle."

Wood's main argument is that the establisment and functioning of peaceful change actually is peace: peace is not a state of affairs but a regularized and controlled process of modification of international relations in such a way that wars are prevented and the international order meets in an optimal way the needs of the international community.

Peaceful change as a process of regularized acts of modification of the international order comes close to the philosophical foundations of traditional functionalism. David A. *Mitrany* bridges the two schools. As an eminent representative, if not a founding father, of functionalism he defines peaceful change thus:[28]

> "The important thing is not merely to get a change. The important thing is to get changes through common agreement and to get them in due relation to factors and conditions affecting the life of several peoples, as ascertained impartially and realistically. That, more than pacts and protocols and sanctions, will provide a basis for an international society to assure the protection of its members".

Peaceful change in its broader meaning is primarily a model of social progress which must be safeguarded by suitable political arrangements. These arrangements appear as a function of the dynamism of social progress. For the international society to be a "civilized" society, the same general rules are applicable as to other human organizations: "first, to establish the rule of law and then, under its protection, to advance gradually but securely the reign of social justice".[29]

In conclusion, three models of peaceful change can be identified in the foregoing discussion. The first on is **the avoidance of war** -type of peaceful change where the sovereign rights of nation states are by no means hurt. Nations may accept methods of peaceful change if they can thereby avoid war. Sovereignty is also the key concept in applications of the procedures of peaceful change: either through territorial changes or through the international treaty system and in particular through the revision of international treaties. The avoidance of war -type of peaceful change is undoubtedly very much bound with the power structures of the international system: changes are made peacefully as far as they do not threaten the existing balance of power.

The second model of peaceful change consists of the **procedures of collective security.** Above, references were made to a way of thinking where peaceful change and collective security were seen as parallel concepts. In this view changes are made in the interest of a working international system, legally or at least respecting the treaty system governing international relations. Changes should also have a respect for *status quo:* they may not threaten the stability of international relations.

The third model is the **restructuring of international relations** peacefully. It deals with deep and qualitative changes which aim at changing also the rules of the game of international relations. The model questions traditional state sovereignties at least in the long run. Fundamental and structural change in the international society challenges traditional loyalties and obligations of citizens as well and will at the end produce changes where traditional power relationships are eroded.

The European Security Order and Peaceful Change

Our classification of models of peaceful change and Clark's typology of international orders are overlapping. An international order based on the recognition of the role of force as a concept seems to suggest that avoiding war as a method of peaceful change is closely associated with it. In a similar way, constraining force as the basic organizing principle of an international order comes very close to the category of peaceful change as a system of collective security. Finally, the rejection of force could be understood as an organizing principle for an order which is open to peaceful change in the sense of restructuring the existing international order. The next question obviously is, how these models and conceptualizations of order could be applied to the European security system.

We suggest the categorization in **Table 1,** in which the European security dimension is added to the previous argumentation.

Quite obviously, the European security order has gradually transformed from the phase of the pure recognition of force in the years immediately following the Second World War into an order where states are ready to accept constraints to the use of military force. The method of transformation has accordingly approached a collective security system from the crude and simple policy of a balance of power.

The transformation which has occurred has undoubtly been peaceful in the sense that an open use of violence has been minimized. An avoidance of war -type of peaceful change has taken place in Europe. Transformation from one security system to another has not affected very much the premises of security resting on arms and the ultimate

Table 1. The relationship between the principles of orders, models of peaceful change and European security orders

Organizing principles of order	Methods of peaceful change	European security orders
Recognition of force	Avoiding war	Alliance systems
Constraining force	Collective security	The CSCE -system
Making force disappear	Restructuring of order	Functional security system

threat of use of violence. For instance, the alliance system has not been eroded and it still is the basis of stability in Europe.

As essential elements of a security order which rests on the use of force, Clark names the balance of power, stability and deterrence. In many ways, the alliance system is in the centre of all these elements. It guarantees the quantity of order, it employs the doctrines of the actual use of nuclear weapons and it makes the doctrines of the use of force politically effective. In many ways, military alliances are the most outstanding examples of the premises of the European security order.

If we apply the terms of the foregoing theoretical discussion we must conclude that although certain elements of collective security are present, the European order still is based on **individual and objective elements of security.** Or, in Claude's terms, the European security order does not deny the use of force as such but seeks constraints in order to make its use difficult and unattractive. Attempts to create a mechanism of confidence-building measures are examples of creating constraints.

If the transformation of the European security order is to be advanced, and if models of peaceful change have any relevance in guiding our perspectives, the strengthening of **collective and subjective elements** in the current collective security system should be made more visible. In this particular context of transformation the CSCE process may show its relevance.

In transforming the European security system towards a more advanced collective security arrangement, the mere drafting of the ten basic principles of the Helsinki Final Act is an achievement as such. But during the ten years after the Helsinki Accords, the European security system has transformed into a more effective collective security arrangement only modestly. Obviously the very basis of that system, the military alliance system, has been under certain stresses and there are indications of certain tendencies of erosion. That, in addition to trends outside the state system, like the advance of peace movements, the formulation of Europeanist models of security policy as well as ideas of

common security, shows that new ideas are emerging and that the
basic model with a strong emphasis on the role of force is not un-
questioned.

But very little response is recognizable within the CSCE system itself.
In fact, it has often been said that the continuation of the CSCE process
as itself is its greatest achievement. Naturally the progress in the field of
peaceful settlement of disputes should be mentioned as a positive exception from the general picture. A standard argument in explaining this
somewhat gloomy situation is that unfavourable Great Power relations
prevent any advance and that, in fact, the positive evaluation of the CSCE
should be stressed by pointing out that in spite of Great Power relations,
the process has been kept alive.

Keeping alive the CSCE process under unfavourable Great Power
relations has loaded it with unfavourable stresses and expectations.
Sometimes it has been seen as "the only game in town", as a forum which
should carry on problems not directly associated with it or, at least, not
contributing to the realization of its principal aims. Since the CSCE is a
process and includes four distinct parts as indicated by the structure of
the diplomatic work within it, there now seems to be an unfavourable
balance between the different elements. The introduction of direct
military issues to the CSCE is counterproductive to the wholeness of
the process.

Our argument has been that there are tendencies in the European
security system which suggest than constraints to the use of force are
currently sought for and that the CSCE process has basic propensities
which might furnish the idea of peaceful change in its ideal type of
collective security. A further transformation of the European security
order towards the restructuring of that order seems to be a remote ideal
and one could seriously doubt whether that aim is achieved if the current
philosophy of the CSCE is to be maintained.

However, if structural changes in the European order are sought for
and if the role of force in inter-state relations in Europe is ever to be made
disappear, a strategy of further transformation must be developed. The
future development of the CSCE process must then be re-evaluated.
Accepting Martin Wight's idea of transformation from the quantity of
order to the quality of order, a strategy from collective security to the
restructuring of the security order is of greatest importance. Its formulation is not a matter of distinct future: the CSCE as a flexible process
can and should cope with elements of different nature and space.

A Functionalist Challenge

The first step from the collective security system of Europe ten years
after the Helsinki Final Act should be, in Inis Claude's terms, to increase
the subjective elements of the system, i.e. to strengthen positive commitments of participating nations to that process. It is highly questionable
that the current balance between the elements of the CSCE process
can contribute to that adherence. Therefore new ways to further subjective commitments must be found.

An appropriate theoretical framework for this type of development is **classical functionalism** or **Mitranian functionalism.** Its major theoretical contributions were made to sketch the new European order in the post-war period.[30] Mitranian ideas did not survive the results of the war but as ideas they still have relevance. Part of them have been realized in functionalist integration although practical results have been less favourable for the all-European security. We may regard the European Community as a security community between its members but for out-siders it has remained a closed bloc.[31]

The basic idea of the classical Mitranian functionalism is that inter-national cooperation should be based on needs: once there are obvious needs for cooperation, they should be fulfilled and necessary institutions should be established to make these processes workable. Mitrany him-self was very much bound to welfare issues: welfare is the motive why nations are ready to give up their sovereign rights in a long run and engage in cooperative efforts. Says Mitrany:[32]

> "The real sense of peaceful change, therefore, can only be so to facilitate the necessary changes in economic, social and cultural relations by timely and continuous adjustments that the need and desire for political-territorial changes shall dwindle and vanish. A frontier is obnoxious in social life because it is a frontier and it does not become less obnoxious because it is moved ten or a hundred miles one way or another".

It is obvious that the Mitranian definition of functionalism in its basic meaning is not very accurate as a part of the CSCE process. The basic problem in Europe is not how to bring about welfare through all-European cooperation but how to transform military confrontation into collective security along the lines which were established in the Final Act. The principles of cooperation, for instance, stress the sovereign rights of the participant nations while functionalists basically see state sovereignty working against the welfare interests of population.

Although we cannot apply classical functionalism as such to the future development of the European security order, its basic logic is helpful. Its logic can be described, in Chadwick *Alger*'s way[33], as a process where learning and institutionalization go hand in hand. The first task is to identify the areas of cooperation which should be as much free from high politics as possible; then establish permanent procedures in these areas, wait for favourable results which demonstrate the fruitfulness of the strategy adopted and, finally, if the model creates new functionalist processes in other issues, create methods and institutions to concrete functional cooperation schemes.

What Wight called transformation from the quantity of order to the quality of order is very close to what Mitrany said about collective, inter-national security arrangements in 1944:[34]

> "All talk about a new organization for security 'with teeth in it' is futile unless we follow one of the two possible lines of action. We might set up an autonomous international authority with power and means to keep the peace. Or we might develop joint economic

arrangements sufficiently comprehensive and far-reaching to prevent a split between the participating Powers".

Mitrany's idea is simply that instead of concentrating on establishing international security institutions with autonomous powers, an emphasis should be put on creating cooperative efforts in economic matters in order to increase interdependence and joint efforts between the Powers concerned.

For the future development of the European security system, this model is workable and worth of interest. No doubt such elements can be seen in the CSCE process. But at least up to now functionalist cooperation measures have not developed to the extent that they would add new blood to the security concepts which prevail in Europe. Functional cooperation in an ideal Mitranian sense could increase security in constraining force because of economic and cultural interdependencies and, in demonstrating success in areas where they have been applied, it may have a model effect.

If we study the CSCE process since the Helsinki Final Act from a functionalist perspective, we see astonishingly few achievements. Cooperation in trade for instance is almost non-existing: only some 4 per cent of the foreign trade of the EC takes place with the CMEA countries.[35] In fact, East-West economic relations have been subordinated to crude cold-war policies including sanctions and black lists. Among the sectors of the CSCE process only environment is typically a functional attempt. Functional cooperation could, however, in an important way strengthen subjective elements in the emerging collective security system.

In the strengthening of subjective elements of security, economic cooperation is a typical functionalist area. In the Final Act of Helsinki much of its content was passed to the Economic Commission for Europe (ECE). From a functionalist perspective this solution was not perhaps an optimal one. ECE has its disadvantage in being a body of many types of activities within which relevant items from the point of view of European security often are crushed.

Economic cooperation in the mid-1980s could become a take-off sector of the CSCE process at least for three important reasons. The first factor is **Europe's decline** in economic performance. In particular, this is seen in comparison with the emergence of Japan and the United States in new so called growth sectors, i.e. high technology and electronics. It has been often argued that Europe, which gave birth to two first industrial revolutions, has lost the third revolution. The relative decline is not only a problem for the EC but for the whole of Europe.

A common European problem is also the second factor pointing to the need of economic cooperation. We might call it the **Second Reconstruction of Europe.** Both in the East and in the West of Europe today processes of industrial reconstruction are under way. The European Community has launched the *ESPRIT* high technology programme and the *Eureka* project is in its initial stage. In a similar way, Socialist countries, the Soviet Union included, have initiated economic reform policies which aim at modernization. Both parts of Europe could benefit from cooperation. The CSCE process could be a forum where the second reconstruction of post-war Europe could strengthen security and not strengthen the division of Europe like the first reconstruction at the end of the 1940s.

The third reason indicating the strategic role of economic cooperation in the CSCE process is that **progress is underway.** In particular, the dialogue between the Soviet Union and the EC has reached its initial steps. This could mean that the need for cooperation is breaking down barriers created by the two closed economic groupings. The conditions for all-European economic cooperation are favourable: the further development of functionalist cooperation could be possible in spite of the chilly climate of Great Power relations.

On the basis of the foregoing discussion we may modify the main problem of this study into the following statement: how the existing security order and the established norms of the Helsinki Final Act could be so interconnected that a transformation into a qualitatively more stable, more egalitarian and a less force-dependent order could be established and the quantity of order transformed into a quality of order. A functionalist answer to that question is that a **two-tier speed system** should be established and accepted, where the hard core of national security issues, i.e. the questions of immediate military security should be let to live their own dynamics, and functionalist cooperation should have the main emphasis in the immediate future of the CSCE process.

The reason is twofold. For the first, military matters of the European security order are so much subordinated to the still superior role of the Great Powers that the factual contribution of the CSCE in the near future in these matters can be only marginal. It might be even desirable that the CSCE, in the contrary, should be more disconnected from the Great Power confrontation.

For the second, a major emphasis on matters of military security may even strengthen the elements of military logic in the whole of the CSCE. An example is the conference in Stockholm. Its work is intimately bound to the delicate power balance between the two Great Powers. That work may indeed contribute to the stability in Europe but emphasizing solely military aspects of stability. By referring again to Martin Wight's distinction, the quantity of order may be strengthened but its contribution to the quality of order is less visible. In fact the confidence- and security-building measures (CSBMs) have a great emphasis on crisis management which traditionally has enhanced military considerations and military aspects of nations' security policies by convincing that constraining force can be done technically and on a high force level.

The two-tier strategy would certainly not indicate a wishful retreat from the facts of life. A functionalist approach to security would only mean the choice of an alternative strategy before a traditional military approach. It assumes that in a long run the vital issues of national security can only be solved through creating new types of relationships between nations and thus at the same time setting constraints to the use of force. The major principle in the CSCE process should be that functional cooperation should start from areas where high politics is less visible and detrimental and where objective conditions for advance are at hand.

A two-tier system is therefore basically a new form of engagement: it gives space to advancement in sectors where it is feasible and possible while setbacks and stagnation in other areas do not lock up the process totally. But it also means that the speeds are parts of a same totality and that progress in one space might contribute to the other. It would be almost inevitable, however, that this type of a totality needs to be administrated and monitored in a more effective way than what is the case today in the CSCE process.

Notes

1. Recent works of Robert Gilpin and George Modelski serve as examples of debates on war cycles in the international system. See Robert Gilpin, *War & Change in World Politics*, Cambridge 1981; George Modelski, "The Long Cycle of Global Politics and the Nation-State", *Comparative Studies in Society and History*, Vol. 20, 1978.
2. The concept of *'vicious circle'* was introduced by Modelski when he described the logic between the nature of nation-states and wars in his *Principles of World Politics*, N.Y. 1972, pp. 253—266.
3. Martin Wight, "Balance of Power and International Order", in *Bases of International Order*, Alan James (ed.), Oxford 1973, p. 110.
4. *Ibid.*, pp. 110—111.
5. E.H. Carr, *Conditions of Peace*, London 1943, pp. ix—xv.
6. Hedley Bull, *The Anarchical Society*, Oxford 1977, p. 8.
7. *Ibid.*, pp. 16—20.
8. Ian Clark, *Reform and Resistance in the International Order*, Cambridge, Mass. 1980, pp. 19—28.
9. Charles R. Beitz, *Political Theory and International Relations*. Princeton 1979, pp. 35—63.
10. Clark, *op.cit.* 1980, p. 21.
11. Kenneth N. Waltz, *Man, the State and War*. New York, 1969, p. 205.
12. Geoffrey Goodwin, "International Institutions and International Order", in Alan James (ed), *The Bases of International Order*, London, 1973, pp. 167—177.
13. Kenneth W. Thompson, "Collective Security Reexamined", *American Political Science Review*, vol. XLVII, 1953, pp. 758—761.
14. Inis Claude, *Swords into Plowshares*, New York, 1959, pp. 255—256.
15. *Ibid.* pp. 257—264.
16. *Ibid.* pp. 264—269.
17. E.H. Carr, *The Twenty Years' Crisis*. New York, 1964, pp. 222—223.
18. C.R.M.F. Cruttwell, *A History of Peaceful Change in the Modern World*, London 1937, p. 19.
19. *Ibid.* pp. 4—5.
20. These ideas were debated in particular in the Tenth International Study Conference in Paris in 1937. See *Peaceful Change: Procedures, Population, Raw Materials, Colonies*. Proceedings of the Tenth International Study Conference, Paris, June 28 — July 3, 1937. Paris, 1938.
21. C.K. Webster, "What is the Problem of Peaceful Change" in *Peaceful Change*, ed. by C.A.W. Manning, London 1937, p. 3.
22. Frederick Sherwood Dunn, *Peaceful Change. A Study of International Procedures*, New York 1937, pp. 2—3.
23. Arnold Toynbee, "Peaceful Change or War? The Next Stage in International Crisis"; *International Affairs*, vol. XV, 1936, pp. 26.
24. See Maurice Bourquin (ed), *Collective Security: a Record of the Eight International Studies Conference*, Paris 1936, pp. 443—444.
25. *Ibid.* pp. 444—446.
26. Webster, *op. cit.* p. 5.
27. Bryce Wood, *Peaceful Change and the Colonial Problem*, New York 1940, p. 26.

28. David A. Mitrany, *The Problem of Peaceful Change*. United Kingdom Memorandum No. 3, Eight International Studies Conference, London, June 3—8, 1935, p. 364.

29. *Ibid.*

30. The basic philosophy of functionalism of that time is expressed by David A. Mitrany in *A Working Peace System*, Chicago 1966, which edition has some other articles of the same author. The first edition was issued in 1943.

31. This has been stressed in particular in the Socialist Countries of Europe, see for instance *Western Europe Today. Economics, Politics, the Class Struggle. International Relations*, Moscow 1980.

32. David A. Mitrany, "How can We Develope a Method of Peaceful Change", in *The Functional Theory of Politics*, London 1975, p. 170.

33. Chadwick F. Alger, 'Functionalism and Integration', *International Social Science Journal*, Vol. XXIX, 1977, pp. 77—78.

34. Mitrany, "International Security", in *The Functional Theory of Politics*, op. cit. p. 182.

35 Peter Marsh, "The European Community and East-West Economic Relations", *Journal of Common Market Studies*, Vol. XXIII, 1984, pp. 1—13.

5

SDI and European Security: Does Dependence Assure Security?

Hans-Henrik Holm

Is independence of the Super-Powers the way in which Europe can achieve security? Does the political quest for European security have any prospect of success or is European security tied to and dependent upon the respective Super-Powers?

European security has since the conclusion of the Second World War in many respects been a mere function of the relationship between East and West. To some the European problem is in itself a contributory cause of the adverse relationship between East and West. The Second World War, whether by design or by default, created a Europe divided between East and West, and in Germany created a symbol of the new division. In this context European security was nothing but reflections of policy and perceptions on either side of the superpower divide.

To the individual European states, security policy was based on a choice between a non-aligned stance and Super-Power alignment. Non-alignment was chosen by the non-combatants in World War II (Sweden, Switzerland) or by the countries neutralised by the Super-Powers (Finland, Austria and to some extent Yugoslavia). To the great majority of the European countries, Super-Power dependence was the way to achieve security. In Western Europe, massive arms aid and the creation of the NATO alliance instituted this dependence. In the East, ideological control secured the same objectives and later resulted in the creation of mirror image institutions (the Warsaw Pact, the CMEA).

European security could not be achieved in isolation and the security policy of the individual states revolved around the ensuing dilemma: How do you reduce dependence (and increase your freedom of action and self-determination in security policy) without jeopardising your security? The true irony of the situation is that the same situation exists for the superpowers. The institution of the East-West conflict in

Europe meant that the Super-Powers became hostages to their own clients. Confrontations and differences between European countries in East and West immediately became objects of Super-Power conflict, and this automatic escalation in itself endangered Super-Power security.[1]

Some fundamental questions arise from this dilemma and they appear in many of the debates on changes in security policy. The latest example is the proposal for a fundamental change of strategy as envisaged by President Ronald Reagan in the Strategic Defense Initiative or otherwise known as 'Star Wars'. The proposal to create a defensive system has once again brought up the issue of Europe's role in the East-West relations and posed the question to European governments and publics: Does dependence assure security?

The Quest for European Security

How may the European states (East and West) individually and collectively provide their own security? Around this fundamental question a number of security policy debates have revolved since the institution of the fundamental division of Europe between East and West.

Though many shades can be found in this debate, it is obvious that there are two fundamentally different positions confronting each other: Some argue that Europe needs the Super-Power commitment — European security is the Super-Power guarantee. The security policy of the aligned states must try to uphold and strengthen that commitment in the face of the other Super Power's attempt to break it down and in the face of centrifugal factors created by the economic, technological and politicall development within the countries.[2] Others (the independence movement) argue that the Super-Powers no longer provide security for the European countries. On the contrary, they inject instability into the European system. The Super-Powers are the ones that prevent East-West trade from developing its natural course. They are the ones clamping down on internal movements towards reforms that could produce tension-reducing changes in the individual countries. And they are the ones to introduce new weapons into the already overarmed Europe.

The fundamental threat to European security, it is argued, emanates from the Super-Powers and their conflict. Europe must achieve independence in order to increase its own security.[3] These two views are so fundamental that they merit a closer look.

European Security is the Super-Power Guarantee

This school of thought argues that without the security guarantee from the United States and from the USSR, both Eastern and Western Europe would exist under the constant threat of blackmail, intimidation and even invasion from the other superpower. The US nuclear umbrella and its extension over the NATO members of Western Europe is seen as a cornerstone in the security policy both of the Western European countries and of the US. This 'coupling' between the US and Western

Europe has consequently been a fundamental problem for the security policy relationship between these countries.[4]

The nuclear guarantee fundamentally rests on the willingness of the US to initiate a nuclear war with the Soviet Union over the defence of Western Europe. This commitment obviously is a worrisome policy both to the Europeans and to the Americans. To the Americans it means, first, that the United States may be drawn into a conflict with the Soviet Union that is not of its own making, and, second, that the US puts its own population at risk in order to couple its security to that of the NATO countries. To the Europeans it is a worrisome policy in that it has required the introduction of US nuclear weapons on European soil. Coupling requires the European countries to tie their security policy in with that of the US, and consequently reduces their freedom of action.

The limitations have been accepted due to the perceived beneficial effects for the European countries. The nuclear guarantee has introduced an element of stability into the post-war world, and has helped reduce the internal disagreement between the various Western European countries by moving fundamental security policy decisions out of Europe. The problem of German rearmament, for instance, would have been a major conflict, had it not been for the US presence and influence. European security dependence has also reduced the pressure for conventional armaments and made it possible for some of the NATO countries to keep the Super-Powers arms race at arm's length.[5]

The European policy choice to base security on the US nuclear guarantee, however, has not been the result of a weighing of advantages and disadvantages of coupling, but rather the result of a perceived lack of alternatives. In the face of an aggressive and powerful Soviet Union, the Western European nations have not considered themselves capable of providing their own defence. In the immediate post-war years the American guarantee was needed to counter the powerful Red Army, which never demobilised to the same extent as it was done in the West. Following the development of the Soviet nuclear capabilities, the nuclear guarantee was needed to prevent the Soviet Union from using their power to put pressure on the Western European countries. With the advent of nuclear parity between the Super-Powers, new nuclear weapons are perceived to be needed in Europe. The new intermediate-range nuclear force (INF)-weapons threaten the Soviet Union directly from European soil. Thus the Soviet Union is prevented from driving a wedge between the US and her Western allies due to the reduced credibility of the US-based strategic forces. In this argument for coupling between the US and Western Europe lies the rationale of introducing the new INF systems into Europe: the Pershing II and the ground-launched cruise missiles (GLCM).[6]

The fundamental political rationale of introducing these weapons was based on the necessity of providing a coupling between the strategic American forces and the European theatre. To the proponents of the INF decision, that is also what has been achieved. The alliance is now claimed to be in a better shape than ever, and the INF decision and its implementation are seen as contributing to the present favourable state of affairs within the alliance.[7]

This school of thought argues that to Western Europe there is no viable alternative to the dependence on the US nuclear guarantee, and despite the costs associated with this guarantee, coupling is necessary and provides Western Europe with a security that it would be difficult, costly and maybe even impossible to achieve in any other way. These arguments have increasingly been challenged by the movement for a more independent Europe.

European Security: The Independence Movement

Concurrently with the development of the NATO alliance the reinforcement of the US commitment to Europe, the inherent tensions and costs associated with being dependent on US security policy and interests created the motivation for the growth of support for a more independent European security policy. Moreover, the existence of the non-aligned Europe (Sweden, Finland, Austria, Switzerland and Yugoslavia) meant that an independent security policy was present as an alternative. To a number of the European countries, the choice was between an alliance with the US and some sort of independence, either alone or together with others. The negotiations over a Scandinavian defence pact in 1948—49 is a case in point. But even after the individual European countries made their choice of alignment (our discussion is limited to Western Europe — the situation of the Eastern European countries is quite different and will not be discussed here), the impetus was present for a more independent European role in providing for their own security.

The construction of the Brussels treaty (and the subsequent transformation of it into the Western European Union (WEU) was to some of the participating countries one of the first vehicles for the expression of an independent European security policy. The plans for a European Defence Community (EDC) (1951—54) were ambitious attempts to create an independent security forum corresponding to the economic forum created through the European Coal and Steel Union. However, the plans for the EDC fell, first and foremost because of the reluctance of the major European countries to relinquish national control (especially France, but also Great Britain). Later attempts to reinvigorate the security cooperation within Europe proved no more successful than the failed EDC.[8]

None of these policy attempts had much success in creating independent European security policies until the advent and consolidation of détente strengthened the Europeans' feeling of increased freedom of manoeuvre vis-à-vis the US. Détente, US involvement in Vietnam, Watergate and US economic decline reduced the US hegemony and allowed the growth of an independent European security policy in embryo. The breakdown of détente from the end of the 1970s increased the pressure for an independently formulated European policy. The US demands for alliance solidarity clashed with the interest created in Europe during détente for a more peaceful relationship with the Soviet

Union and Eastern Europe. The foreign policy differences over Iran, the Middle East, Afghanistan and Poland occurred together with the difficulties created by the INF decision and created strong and consistent demands from both left and right of the European political spectrum for an independent European security policy. The political consultations under the European Political Cooperation (EPC) were used by the European countries as a mechanism for voicing their collective concern with developments in US policy deemed detrimental to European interests. The revival of the WEU and increased bilateral contacts between West Germany and France are current examples of this tendency. Finally the growth of the peace movements in many of the Western European countries, and the involvement of new groups in the security debate meant that an independent European security policy was a constant and major demand in the revitalised national security debate.

Fearful of this new tendency, the European governments in the allied countries have made demands for increased consultation between the US and her European allies, for increased participation of the European defence industries in NATO procurement, and for an independent European voice in dealings with the Soviet Union. Despite agreement on this, the difficulty in achieving European agreement on matters of substance means that a European security policy is still a dream. Nevertheless European security independence is a powerful dream, and the political forces supporting policies aimed at making the dream come true seem to be growing in strength.

There are several different versions of independence within what I have here labelled 'the independence movement'. Independence in the least radical form is to see Europe as unified within an Atlantic framework. Europe has to be one pillar of the alliance, and the US the other. In order to achieve true interdependence between Europe and the US, Europe needs to be more unified than it is today. This conception of independence is one that conforms easily to American plans of reducing European reliance on the US, thus alleviating some of the burden that the United States is carrying today.

The other version is to see an independent Europe as a counter to Super-Power control and dominance. This version has been a long concern ot the French, and also a driving force behind many European integrationists.

Finally some regard an independent Europe as a delinked, all-European system where Western Europe is detached from NATO and Eastern Europe from the USSR. This Europe has been enjoying widespread support among the peace movements, and among politicians, but has had less support on the state level.

In terms of the debate on single issues like the debate on the SDI, these different versions of independence become mixed. Here I shall concentrate mostly on the state, as the SDI debate is a debate on the policies of the various European states, either one by one or coordinated in common policies.

Central to many of the proposals aired for an independent European security policy, is the notion of Europe as a Third Force in the antagonistic relationship between the US and the USSR. Europe has to play the role as a balancer that can reduce the antagonism between East and West and create an all-European security system.[9]

According to some, Europe has become a battlefield of the hegemonial conflicts of the Super-Powers: Consequently, the allies have to reconsider their policy of 'subordinance to American supremacy'. This subordinance no longer guarantees European security, either to the allies or to the non-aligned. Western Europe has to play the role of the mediator, both in political terms and in developing a different defence posture in Europe through a non-provocative conventional defence. The goal is an all-European security system based on cooperation and mutual acceptance of the adversaries' right to exist.[10]

A number of institutional suggestions and proposals have been aired. Some argue for the reconstitution of the EPC and others think that the WEU is the best forum. Finally, some regard the German-French cooperation as the best possibility of increased European cooperation.

In all of the issues that form the substance of the present security debate in Europe, the parameters of the debate are determined by the discussion between the proponents of relying on the guarantee of the Super-Powers and the independence movement. The differing views on the Geneva arms control negotiations, on the CSCE negotiations and even on trade and technology policy are reflections of the different views on how European security is best achieved. This debate takes place between the different states in Europe, but, perhaps more importantly, within the various states. This internal and external debate over the costs and benefits associated with dependence and independence in the European context is very clearly visible in the debate over the proposed new Strategic Defense Initiative. This new programme will fundamentally affect the debate on the costs and benefits associated with European security dependence. Two questions need to be raised here: How does the SDI affect the European security dependence, and does the SDI enhance or reduce European security?

SDI: What Is It?

President Reagan's speech on defence spending and defensive technology of 23 March, 1983, introduced a new initiative into the strategic discussion. The Strategic Defense Initiative has since then grown in importance both in the priorities of the Reagan administration itself and consequently also in the international security debate.

When the SDI was introduced it was as much of a surprise as the feared 'bolt from the blue'. Very few in the administration was aware of the initiative before they saw the President on TV, and experts, allies and adversaries alike were taken by surprise.[12]

Certainly the SDI had antecedents, but they were of little importance and virtually unnoticed both by the strategic community and by the public at large. Research into Anti-Ballistic Missile (ABM) technology had been going on in the US for quite some time. In the Joint Chiefs of

Staff's United States Military Posture for the fiscal year 1983, the ASAT (Anti-satellite) programme was described as 'vigorously pursued'. The Ballistic Missile Defense was described as heading toward a decision on providing options for the defence of ICBMs through "Low Altitude Defence (LoAD), future systems and overlay defence". The research was claimed to be conducted within existing treaties and purported to be a hedge against Soviet treaty abrogation and as a counter to specific Soviet threats (e.g. against American satellites).[13]

Lobby groups existed who tried to argue for an increased use of space and high-energy technology to create a 'High Frontier' that could give the US a strategic advantage in the competition with the USSR.[14]

Very few, however, took any of this seriously. The potential economic and political costs and the technical difficulties associated with the schemes marketed in Washington, together with the failure of the previous ABM scheme (the Safeguard ABM system was dismantled in 1976 due to cost effectiveness considerations) meant that very few anticipated that strategic defense would be the new focus of the strategic debate.

Yet, that is exactly what Ronald Reagan proposed in his March 23 speech. Reagan in his own words "launched an effort which holds the promise of changing the course of human history. There will be risks, and results take time. But I believe we can do it".[15]

What is it that is to change the course of human history, one may ask. What are the goals of this new initiative and what are the envisaged means to achieve it?

The SDI Goals

The goals as they were seen by President Reagan and explained to the public in his March 1983 speech, were all ultimately directed towards rendering nuclear weapons "impotent and obsolete", and this should be done by "eliminating the threat posed by strategic nuclear missiles". In his inaugural speech in 1985 he had the further goal of totally eliminating the threat of nuclear war. Considering the important roles played by nuclear weapons, ICBMs and nuclear war planning in present US policy, this certainly is an ambitious goal. However, the mere utterance of long-term goals of this type would probably not in and of itself have produced a major reaction, since it might be regarded as yet another example of political hyperbole and hypocracy when at the same time more nuclear weapons were constructed, deployed and used as threats.

Removal of Offensive Nuclear Weapons

But the SDI contained other goals. The goal was also to do away with offensive weapons. As the technology for the new defensive systems is developed and deployed, the offensive nuclear weapons may be dismantled so that a stable balance is maintained between offensive and defensive weapons with a final goal of removing all offensive weapons.[16]

Secretary of Defense Caspar Weinberger was even more explicit and presumed that a move in the direction of defence on the part of the US would create a corresponding move in the USSR: "I would hope assume that the Soviets with all the work they have done and are doing in this field, would develop a similar defense, which would have the effect of **totally and completely removing these missiles from the face of the earth".**[17]

In the later statements on the SDI, the removal of offensive weapons has, however, been stressed less and mentioned only as a result of potential arms control, arms reduction talks between the two Super-Powers.[18]

This reinterpretation of original goals is in the process of radically transforming the SDI from what it was originally conceived as and into something quite different. This is especially evident in the overall goal that the President raised of doing away with deterrence as the basis for US and allied security. The President in his speech stressed that it is necessary to break out of a future that relies solely on offensive retaliation. "Wouldn't it be better to save lives than to avenge them?", asked Ronald Reagan, and a number of his senior counsellors and advisers echoed that question in speeches and statements of their own since his speech. Secretary Weinberger expressed it very clearly when he said that the SDI "...is an attempt to devise a system that protects our people instead of avenging them", (speech to Pittsburg World Affairs Council, 30 October, 1984).

A lot of his advisers, however, have also begun to question this assumption of their President. Undersecretary of Defense Fred Iklé, for example, has asserted that blaming the SDI for overturning the existing policy of strategic nuclear deterrence, is just plain wrong. The SDI would not scrap a policy of deterrence, on the contrary, it would enhance deterrence by making it harder for the Soviet Union to reach its goal. To prevent the split between the different views of the role of deterrence within the SDI, the argument has been developed that by destroying attacking missiles the deterrent (e.g. the US' own ICBMs) is protected and at the same time the population is protected because a Soviet first strike becomes impossible. The protection of the US is of course the central goal of the SDI.

A 100 Per Cent Effective Defence

Protection is the ultimate goal of the SDI, but also a very elusive goal. What is it that is going to be protected? To the President it is "our own soil and that of our allies". It is the goal of total defence against strategic ballistic missiles, since the removal of fear in the population is the underlying political objective.[19] Technology should be developed that would make it feasible to achieve a high degree of defence against the threat of a nuclear strike from the Soviet Union or anybody else. The ultimate goal, is a 100 per cent effective defence. "The defensive systems the President is talking about are not designed to be partial. What we want to try to get is a system... that is thoroughly reliable and total. I don't see any reason why that can't be done", said Caspar Weinberger, (NBC's 'Meet the Press', 27 March, 1983).

Even as a goal this is not realistic. The perfect defence is not possible. Even disregarding the problem of circumvention, the SDI system as presently imagined would not be capable of shooting down all the missiles directed at the West. Director of the SDI office, Lieutenant General James Abrahamson has stated several times that a perfect astrodome defence is "not a realistic thing", *(Science,* 10 August, 1984). But a defence which is less than perfect (e.g. 90 per cent success rate) would all the same be beneficial, it is argued, compared to the situation that we are in now where there is no defence except through deterrence by the posing of counter-threats. The sheer fact that a 100 per cent population defence is an unrealistic goal, however, distracts considerably from the political benefits associated with the original vision of the President. As critics have pointed out, a system with a 90 per cent success rate would still leave enough missiles coming through to inflict unacceptable damage on the US (e.g. the destruction of the 10 major US cities).[20]

Combination of Offence and Defence

Consequently, more attention has focussed on the ability of the proposed systems to achieve point defence. The objective here is to defend the US ICBMs or other essential military targets from incoming missiles, and thus it is a continuation of the already ongoing research on BMD. Achieving this goal is technically more realistic, it is argued, and it would restore the credibility of the land-based ICBM-deterrent. Especially it is argued, that it is necessary to protect the Minuteman 3 with the Mark 12 A warhead due to its capability of destroying hardened Soviet targets (both missiles and leadership bunkers). Even this goal is probably difficult to achieve due to the foreseen Soviet countermeasure (overwhelming the defence etc.). But, it is argued, the defence will be beneficial anyway by complicating Soviet planning and making a Soviet first strike more difficult to achieve.[21] The defensive system would 'complicate and frustrate aggression' and would thereby enhance the US deterrent. The "window of vulnerability" would be closed by this combination of offensive and defensive forces.[22]

Edward Teller illustrates this argument clearly in outlining the necessity for a combination of offence and defence.

> "...Their (the US and the USSR) armaments at present include only swords. A combination of swords and shields represents a considerable improvement, which would increase with the proliferation of shields. Such a situation does not make it possible to throw away swords, but if shields are much less expensive than swords, peace will tend to become more stable".[23]

Disregarding the cost considerations — on which there is considerable uncertainty — this is a far cry from the President's goal of changing the course of human history.

Goals of a less ambitious nature include considerations on creating **a thin defence** against small attacks. An ABM defence constructed to handle nuclear missiles launched by accident from the USSR or missiles launched by one of the smaller nuclear capable states. The construction of a 'thin' defence either in the terminal or in the boost phase would, however, require the same technology needed to develop a full system and therefore be very cost-inefficient. Furthermore, terrorist nuclear attacks through other means of transporting nuclear bombs (suitcases, freightships, etc.) could not be prevented with such a system. The problem of dealing with accidental launching could be solved much simpler in other ways. The goal of a thin defence has, however, not been a central one for the administration even though it does figure in certain arguments advanced for the current research expenditure.[24]

The Interests of the Allies

Apparently, a central goal of the SDI has been to ensure that the allies should also be covered by the new defensive system. The protection should cover also their soil. Even though the concern for the allies was added on in small sentences in the original drafts of the President's speech it does nevertheless figure in there, and a major preoccupation of the administration since the launching of the initiative has been to calm allied fears of this new initiative. The President underlined that: "Proceeding boldly with these new technologies, we can significantly reduce any incentive that the Soviet Union may have to threaten attack against the United States or its allies." The protection envisaged for the allies is based partly on a protective shield and partly on reducing Soviet ability to threaten with the use of nuclear weapons. SDI is supposed to develop a capability to provide a shield against theatre weapons like the SS 20.

But more important than the theoretical ability to defend against the SS 20, is the postulated effect the SDI will have on increasing Soviet uncertainties in planning an ICBM attack on the US. If the USSR is no longer certain that it can penetrate US defences, the credibility of the US deterrent force is enhanced. This should then increase the credibility of the extended deterrent. This, it is argued, is in the interest of the allies.[25]

As the SDI has developed and been elaborated, other goals have evolved, and more are sure to come. Most of these are arguments constructed to support the development of the SDI and are not central goals to the programme. It is argued, for instance, that the advent of the powerful peace movements underlines the need to find an alternative to deterrence. Policy cannot be executed unless there is some element of public support. "Policies have to be in harmony with what is commonly held as proper behavior."[26] If nothing is done to ensure greater harmony, unilateral disarmament may present itself as a solution, and that, it is argued, should be avoided. Others have stressed that even though the SDI could not provide a perfect defence, it could ensure that the number of nuclear explosions in a nuclear exchange could be reduced down to a number that would not trigger the climatic catastrophes associated with the so-called nuclear winter. In any case, it is argued, damage limitation is in itself a more moral goal than the threat to retaliate.[27]

An Almost Complete Confusion

All of the goals of the SDI program are present in the ongoing discussion in a highly confused and mixed manner, and the inherent contradictions between many of these goals are papered over by claims that what appears as contradictions are merely differences between short-range and long-range objectives. By claims that there are multiple objectives, or by saying that so far it is only research and nobody will be able to foresee what is going to be discovered tomorrow, the inconsistencies are disregarded.

The debate over the various goals of the SDI has been going on within the US administration and has created confusion and uncertainty as to what the SDI constitutes. SDI seems to exist in at least different versions within the administration:

The first version stresses that the SDI is only a research programme. The "object is to provide the basis for an informed decision, sometime in the next decade, as to the feasibility of providing for a defense of the United States and our allies against ballistic missile attack.", (Paul H. Nitze, Special Advisor to the President, Speech to the IISS, London, 28 March, 1985). According to this view, deterrence is and will continue to be the basis of US-USSR strategic relations for the foreseeable future, and the preservation of the ABM treaty is very important according to this point of view.

The second version also underlines that the SDI is a research programme, but here the goal is to create the perfect defence. *The Defensive Technology Study* under the chairmanship of James Fletcher concluded in their first study that "the scientific community may indeed give the United States 'the means of rendering' the ballistic missile threat 'impotent and obsolete'". Through a 10—20 year research programme with emphasis on detection programmes and boost-phase programmes, the study foresees a final, low-leakage system created.[28] This conception of the SDI is supported by i.a. George Keyworth, the President's Science Advisor, and by Ronald Reagan.[29] This plan will only involve testing permitted by the ABM treaty, and the decisions on complience and deployment are pushed into the future. The demonstration test necessary will of course, despite what the advocates of this form of SDI say, subject the ABM regime to severe challenges.

The third type of SDI enjoying support within the present administration places the emphasis on intermediate defences. The idea is that research is conducted on all aspects and that deployment is undertaken as you go along and discover new possibilities in the various phases of defence. The fundamental assumption is that some defence is better than none. Deployment of an intermediate defensive system is useful because it will solve the security problem while full systems are being developed. This argument is presented in the so-called 'Hoffmann Report on Ballistic Missile Defenses and U.S. National Security'. This study was undertaken at the request of the President to assess the role of defensive systems in security strategy. It thus complemented the Fletcher report that reviewed the technological feasibility of the SDI programme. The study advocated concentrating on the ABM option, the development of sensors (CONUS) and a limited boost-phase intercept option. These options if chosen and pursued now will "contribute to reducing the prelaunch vulnerability of our offensive forces".[30]

Finally **the fourth version** of the SDI presently discussed sees SDI as a programme to protect missile silos, and reduce the vulnerability of the ICBM. Consequently, terminal defences that may intercept incoming warheads should be deployed now. Either under the ABM treaty ceiling of a hundred launchers, or through a reneging on the ABM treaty. Neither Caspar Weinberger nor Richard Perle is an ABM supporter, and through stressing Soviet non-compliance with the treaty some observers see the administration as gearing up for termination of the ABM regime. "I am sorry to say it (i.e. the ABM treaty) does not expire. That is one of its many defects", (Richard Perle, House Armed Services Committee Hearings, 23 February, 1982). According to reports, this option of deployment of terminal defences is now supported especially in the US army.[31]

A Unifying Strategic Concept

With all of these differing versions of the SDI being advocated by different branches of the administration, the confusion was complete. Everybody had their own favorite version of the SDI, and a need was felt for **a central unifying strategic concept** that could tie all these many versions together in one formula.

Formulated by Paul H. Nitze, four sentences summarized the common SDI concept:

The Strategic Concept

"During the next ten years, the US objective is a radical reduction in the power of existing and planned offensive nuclear arms, as well as the stabilization of the relationship between offensive and defensive nuclear arms, whether on earth or in space.

We are even now looking forward to a period of transition to a more stable world, with greatly reduced levels of nuclear arms and an enhanced ability to deter war based upon an increasing contribution of non-nuclear defenses against offensive nuclear arms.

This period of transition could lead to the eventual elimination of all nuclear arms, both offensive and defensive.

A world free of nuclear arms is an ultimate objective to which we, the Soviet Union, and all other nations can agree."

As a result of this strategic concept, three criteria were developed that have become fundamental criteria for the administration when outlining the case for the SDI. The defensive technologies must be **effective,** they must be **survivable** (the Soviets can not easily shoot them down or render them ineffective in some other manner), and finally they must be **cost-effective at the margins.** As Nitze put it in his speech to the Philadelphia World Affairs Council: "...that is, it must be cheap enough to add defensive capability so that the other side has no incentive to add additional offensive capability to overcome the defense".[37]

According to Nitze, these criteria are demanding and deployment is conditioned upon meeting these standards.

SDI: How to Do It

The SDI programme is premised on the technological ability to destroy ballistic missiles before they reach their target. The flightpath of the ballistic missiles may be divided into four phases: The boost phase where the first and the second stages of the engines are burning. In the post-boost phase the 'bus' (the projectile of the missile, containing guiding systems, fuel and MRV (individual nuclear warheads called multiple reentry vehicles (MRV)) has separated from the engines and launches the MRV on their separate flight paths. The mid-course phase describes the now individual flight paths of the warheads. The final phase is the terminal phase where the warheads and decoys along with them re-enter the atmosphere.

The SDI is designed to engage missiles in all phases of its flight (a four-layer defence). Attacking the missiles in the final phases of the flight involved wellknown technology and corresponds to existing ABM technology. The new aspects of the SDI have primarily to do with the capability to hit missiles in the boost and post-boost phases. However, technological development have been underway for some time that may enable the development of new systems in all of the phases.[33]

The SDI programmes require global full-time surveillance (the increased importance of satellites has put ASAT programmes on the SDI agenda) and defensive technologies of its own to prevent the new battle stations from being hit. Furthermore the programme also aims for defence against shorter range ballistic missiles whether ground or submarine launched.

The development of a defensive system should produce an incentive for states to do away with nuclear weapons presently in their arsenals. It should also make it possible for arms control to succeed because the threat of destruction is reduced in importance. In presenting this argument (during the election campaign), Ronald Reagan proposed that the US should share the result of the development of these new technologies with the Soviet Union so that they, too, would do away with the offensive weapons.

Obviously, in a situation with no offensive weapons and no threat, there is no need for or basis for a nuclear deterrence policy. However, this situation is certainly not right around the corner, the technology is not even developed yet, the Soviet Union has not accepted the idea and the costs of getting there are unknown.[34]

The interim period is therefore of more immediate importance. This was also underscored in the President's SDI speech:

> "As we proceed we must remain constant in preserving the nuclear deterrent and maintaining a solid capacity for flexible response."

This, according to the President, requires continuing modernisation of the present offensive strategic forces, both ballistic missiles and bombers and other missiles. In Europe in particular, it requires an increase in conventional armaments. In terms of arms control policy it means that negotiations from a position of strength is still the favoured US arms control approach.

Apart from some of the more esoteric technology, the SDI does not in the foreseeable future change the present arms, defence, and strategic policy of the US nor of the alliance. The original version of the President was at best futuristic, and even he saw no change in the short or medium term. The subsequent presentation of the problem underscores the SDI is more an expanded and updated ABM program than a fundamental revision of Mutual Assured Destruction (MAD). Even in terms of funding, the $ 26 billion requested for SDI for the period 1985—1989 is only an increase of $ 9.5 billion of what the outlay for this research would have been anyway, (Report to Congress, 1985, p. 77).

Why then spend so much time discussing the SDI as if it was something totally revolutionary, and why bother with the importance that these changes may have on the US-European relations? The SDI shows the fundamental problem in the security dependence of Western Europe on the US in that the SDI is internally generated, but with strong external effects. The mere fact that the US proposes a system like this has political and strategic effects. It changes the arms control negotiation situation between the US and the USSR and it changes the situation between the US and its Western European allies.

The question is how.

SDI and Europe

The presentation of the SDI was certainly also to the allies a bolt from the blue. Nobody had been informed beforehand, they were not even given the usual advance notices that the President was going to present a major new policy. The presentation of the SDI decision was a clear example of what is usually a major gripe from the Europeans: The US does not treat the rest of the NATO alliance as equals. It expects support for US policies, but does not bother to consult with the allies before making major decisions that affect their security. As Helmut Schmidt expressed it once: A major problem in US-European relations is that the Americans' understanding of consultation is to say to the Europeans: "Do as we ask — and please do it within the next two days".[35]

The President's speech mentioned the need for closer consultation with the allies, but also said that "I am directing an effort..." This is what the Europeans resent. Asking the Europeans to back something they had not been part of conceiving is to create scepticism and resentment in Europe at the outset. Some argue, as indeed administration officials have done, that this new initiative is 'a generous offer'. The President offered a new programme to achieve the protection of not only the US but also the soil of the allies from London to Tokyo. The research programme is offered with no demands for allied financing and no demands that the allies should do anything active to receive this generous offer from the US. Their safety and ours are one, the President said, and hoped presumably to alleviate any fears that the US was retreating into a fortress America position.[36]

The way the President presented the SDI created questions and fears among allies that the concern for allied safety was an add-on more than an integral part of the initiative. The President said that he wanted to eliminate the threat posed by **strategic** nuclear missiles, thereby excluding tactical, theatre, cruise missiles and bombers. These are the types of weapons which are of primary concern to the Europeans. How is the President going to render nuclear weapons obsolete, if the programme concentrates on the strategic missiles?

In the period following the President's speech, his advisers had tried to explain these contradictions in two ways: One argument is that the SDI system — concentrating on boost-phase defence — would offer global protection against strategic missiles. There is no way to detect the target of a launched missile, and consequently all launched missiles would be shot down. His advisers have further said that in reality the President meant that all ballistic missiles would be covered, and through this, improved air defence and terminal defences in Europe, the SDI could offer protection of European soil too. This is, however, far beyond the scope of the SDI, and would certainly involve huge European costs.

The other main argument used is that if the US ICBM force is protected, deterrence is enhanced because the US threat to use them becomes credible. The reduction of the vulnerability of the land-based leg of the strategic triad will itself increase strategic stability because, the administration argues, the risk of being pushed into a 'lose-them-or-use-them dilemma' is reduced. According to Iklé, SDI 'envisages and would include deterrence against threatre-range missiles targeted on Europe'. Arms control negotiator Max Kampelman argued that a two-tier strategic defence capability would protect the US missiles, thereby making the US counter-threats more credible to the Soviets. Thus, the credibility of the deterrence would be enhanced, which would be of value to the Europeans.[37] Even if we regard the goal of providing population defence both for the US and for the allies as unrealistic, the SDI could, according to administration arguments, increase the security of Europe by reducing the counter-force threat and by making the US capable of retaliating by protecting their ICBM force from a Soviet first-strike.

An unstated, but it seems increasingly important goal of the SDI vis-à-vis the alliance is to strengthen the alliance by demonstrating unity on the SDI. The 'generous' offer from the President to the allies becomes a symbol of alliance cohesion and solidarity. As the programme matures and develops in the American system the arguments for cost-sharing, for sharing of responsibility and the sharing of political obligations will undoubtedly be raised on both sides of the Atlantic; in Europe, by the ones that fear the effects any differences in view between the US and Europe may have on the alliance; in the US demands for solidarity may be raised both by the right wing advocates of a strong leadership and strong military, but certainly also by the isolationist liberals that accept commitments unwillingly and have a low tolerance for upholding US commitments and programmes that are unwanted. The Nunn, Glenn, Roth and Warner amendment to the FY-86 defence bill is a case in point. The amendment provides incentives for cooperative research and development projects between Europe and the US on defence equipment. As part of this incentive, Senator Nunn stressed that it is required that "the Europeans are prepared to cooperate with us using their own funds".[38]

It has been argued that the SDI is being marketed with so much fervour and commitment that it is turning into an implicit alliance-loyalty test. Allied governments are becoming obliged to pledge their support to the initiative since any expression of doubt connotes contempt. Terence A. Todman, the U.S. Ambassador to Denmark, expressed it in terms of coupling. He referred to the European criticism of the SDI programme for decoupling the US from Europe, and said that when invited to participate in the research some of the European countries refuse. "Noting some of the allied reaction one might ask who is decoupling from whom?".[39] The presentation of the SDI, furthermore, came in the midst of the deployment of the INF missiles in Europe. That decision also had turned into a test of alliance solidarity and mutual purpose. The decision is of course still in the process of being implemented, but the difficulty in getting everyone — or at least almost everyone — in the alliance to back this decision, means that the absorptive capacities within the alliance for disagreement and disunity have been spent to the limit. The US demands for new symbols of solidarity through the SDI present the alliance with new and grave challenges at a time when it is not very well equipped to handle them. European reactions should be seen in this light.

A central argument in presenting the SDI to the Europeans has been that the SDI at its present stage is a guard against a Soviet breakout from the provisions in the ABM treaty. The treaty allows (Article VII) modernisation and research on ABM systems, and as such the new US programmes are presented as hedges against sudden Soviet breakthroughs in technology that would present the West with a *fait accompli*. The SDI is claimed to be consistent with the obligations contained in the ABM treaty, and even though this is disputed by some with reference to violations on both sides, the central problem with the SDI in relation to the ABM treaty is that the envisaged deployments certainly will undermine the ABM regime and possibly create an offensive-defensive race among the superpowers.[40]

It is this possibility that itself is the basis of the other argument that the SDI is useful because it provides the allies with leverage over the USSR in arms control negotiations. The present ABM treaty was not concluded, despite USA offers to negotiate ABM systems in the sixties, before the US started developing its own ABM systems. In the same way, it is argued, is the SDI today a major force behind the Soviet willingness to negotiate in Geneva. The SDI is then presented as a bargaining chip that may eventually be negotiated away in the Geneva talks between the US and the USSR. Even though the bargaining chip argument certainly is disputed — among the critics you find Ronald Reagan — it is used especially in the American marketing effort in Europe. The statement that Caspar Weinberger made to the *Christian Science Monitor,* 29 October, 1984, is illustrative: "It's not a bargaining chip. If we can get it, we would want to have it, and we're working very hard to get it. It is not a chimerical thing out there on the margins to try to influence them to make reductions in offensive systems". Compare this with the statement made by Abrahamson the same day: "We may even do some trading. We might say, OK, we won't put something up for three years if you take out 500 warheads".[41] European support for the programme is becoming a priority US concern, and consequently the US has offered the Europeans participation in the research programmes under SDI. Cooperation will assume the form of cooperative scientific research and allied bidding on SDI contracts and political consultations through existing mechanisms.[42]

The SDI would, it is argued by the proponents, increase coupling between the US and Europe. The gradual reduction of American strategic vulnerability would make the US threat of nuclear retaliation more credible, because strategic defence would solve the problem of choosing between Boston and Bonn. The USSR would be deterred from attacking the US by the existence of the defensive systems, and the threat to answer any Soviet attack on Europe with a blow against the USSR would be more credible.

Some have argued that the SDI might eventually require some sort of basing in Europe (laserground stations etc.), which would in itself be an expression of commitment to Europe parallel to the basing of inter-mediate-range nuclear offensive systems. To provide the needed pro-tection for Europe, the deployment of a modernised air defence system (the Patriot) to defend missiles stationed in Europe has been mentioned, but the costs and effectiveness of this system is still unknown.[43] Station-ing of modernised versions of air defence missiles to hit incoming miss-iles is, however, a likely future prospect. This will reopen the entire debate on Europe's defensive-offensive role and the debate on the coup-ling between Europe and the US. The SDI proposals have already stirred a controversy both within Europe and between Europe and the US. So much so that an observer has argued that the political costs associated with getting the SDI accepted and implemented by far would outweigh the military and strategic benefits that it may eventually produce.[44]

The SDI as a new transatlantic strategic concept has created yet another discussion over the relative costs and merits of equating basing NATO policy with US policy and US conception of interests.

The SDI programme may potentially further increase Europe's dependence on US policy. The technology of the programme would have to rely heavily on US developments, and the strategic rationale and even the arms control policy use of this new programme would underline European dependence.

European Reactions: Should Dependency Be Welcomed?

When the Strategic Defense Initiative was presented to the world on 23 March, 1983, the initial European reaction was one of disbelief. The traditional US supporters maintained an embarrassed silence and maintained that the SDI was just something for domestic US consumption and had nothing to do with strategy between East and West. The Soviets reacted immediately and denounced the US initiative. Because it would violate the ABM treaty they argued it would lead to a new arms race. It reflected the US ambition to achieve superiority through a first strike capability. The USSR followed on with a series of proposals for bans on weapons in space, and a declaration of no-first-deployment on the part of the USSR. 18 August, 1983 General Secretary Yury Andropov said that the USSR would not place ASAT weapons in outer space before the US did so, and he also proposed a mutual ban on deployment and testing of all space-based weapons.[45]

The Super-Power public negotiation game was regarded as yet another indication that the SDI was a propaganda ploy, and there was no need to take it seriously. German newspapers called it "Ein Traum — kein wirkliches Programm". Other papers warned that this would complicate the arms control negotiations and make it more difficult to get public support for NATO's ongoing modernisation. Others, however, evaluated the US initiative on its moral goals and expressed approval of the underlying ambition to do away with MAD and the preference for defensive technologies. Furthermore, it was seen as a counter to perceived Soviet dominance in ABM and ASAT research and technology. The first reactions from Europe were *in toto* based more on Pavlovian reactions and there were few that considered it necessary to enter into more reflective analysis of the new proposal.[46]

Allied Endorsement in Short Supply

The US, however, slowly began detailing the programme and began pressuring the Europeans for political support. When the NATO nuclear planning group met in Cesme on 3 April 1984, Caspar Weinberger asked the Europeans for some sort of political support for the programme, but was met with opposition from several countries, including the Federal Republic of Germany. The communique from the meeting registered allied agreement, but later in public both Defence Minister Manfred Wörner and Chancellor Helmut Kohl voiced their opposition. At a series of meetings in 1985, the United States tried to get allied endorsement, but except for the NATO defence minister meeting in Luxembourg in March, common endorsement was not forthcoming.

The criticism also came from the German opposition where both the SPD and the Greens voiced strong resistance to the plans. Towards the end of 1984 and in the beginning of 1985 the US launched, as a consequence of this criticism from the allies, a major effort to convince the Europeans about the merits of the US proposal and added a carrot to the package: European participation in the SDI research programme.[47]

The results were increased awareness on the European side of the priority that the US accorded this programme and also that the Europeans began to give their reluctant support — support that was filled with fine print and double meanings, but these could and were disregarded by the US administration. The SDI programme began acquiring a major role in Western discussions.

The European reaction can be exemplified through an analysis of the four points agreed upon by Ronald Reagan and Margaret Thatcher at their Camp David meeting in December 1984. The agreed points were:

One: The purpose of the West is to maintain balance. It is not to achieve superiority. Two: The new strategic defences cannot be deployed without negotiation in view of existing treaty obligations (i.a. the ABM treaty). Three: The overall aim is to enhance and not to undermine deterrence. Four: The aim of negotiations between East and West is to reduce the arsenal of offensive arms on both sides.

In presenting the agreement Thatcher stressed that she supported the SDI plan, that is as a research plan and not as a deployment plan, and that it is a long-range programme.[48] The support is qualified with a lot of fine print, and the four points of 'agreement' reflect some of the fundamental worries that the Western European governments have.

The first point reflects the worry that the US will use the defensive systems to press for superiority as indeed some US commentators have been arguing that the US should.[49] The SDI as an ABM defense plan to protect the ICBMs will increase the Soviet fears that the US is planning a first strike and therefore induce them to either increase their offensive arms or create their own ABM and we would have a new arms race as a result.[50]

The second point illustrates the fear that the SDI would increase the already existing pressure for abrogating the ABM treaty. The research and the testing will in itself create pressures for Soviet actions that will be taken to constitute violations of the treaty and there will be a race in order to prevent the other part from breaking out.

The third of the agreed points was that the purpose is to enhance deterrence, and the underlining of this reflects the Europan fear that the research on SDI will destroy deterrence. People will be deluded into believing that we are moving away from MAD and into a situation of MAS (mutual assured security). In the transition period, first strike is a very likely policy — indeed perhaps the only possible one. Furthermore, the French and the British deterrent will be reduced in effectiveness. The flexible response strategy of NATO would be impaired in that the nuclear deterrent would be incredible against a conventional Soviet attack.

Finally, the building up of defence increases the incentive to increase offenses and the fourth point of the agreement, that offensive armaments should be reduced, reflect this. The Soviets have already made clear that they will increase their offensive weapons as a result of the proposed plans. Since no limitations on offensive nuclear arms are in place in Europe they may do so most easily here. Furthermore, the SDI would create a race between creating new space systems and systems to hit these systems, and systems to defend the defensive systems etc., etc.[51]

Underlying the presentation of these 'agreed' four points were fears that arms control will be impaired rather than helped by this new plan, and that the economic consequences will be so great that the Europeans will be left in the cold because they cannot afford it. The costs will also increase the already existing domestic pressure in the US to reduce its military presence in Europe.

Behind the agreement between the US and the allies, serious and wide-spread concern about the proposal linger on. Sir Geoffrey Howe, the British Foreign Secretary, in a speech to the Royal United Services Institute, 15 March, 1985 outlined the concerns quite explicitly. He said that the concerns about not fuelling a new arms race should be brought into consideration during the research stage, rather than after. He also voiced concern over the defensability of these new systems, and the ability of politicians to maintain control over important peace and war decisions.[52]

Finally, he said, as members of the Atlantic Alliance, we must consider the potential consequences of this unique relationship. "We must be sure that the United States' nuclear guarantee to Europe will indeed be enhanced not at the end of the process, but from its very inception."[53]

Western European Cooperation on High Technology: Eureka

The misgivings and fears presented by the British reflect wide-spread sentiments in Western Europe and are with minor differences also present in France and West Germany. The French have worried in particular over the credibility of their own deterrent, and have been working on the possibility of developing their own space defence, either developed alone, or in cooperation with other European nations. Mitterrand explicitly spoke about a European space community as the best answer to tomorrow's demands and military realities.[54]

The French have reacted negatively to the American SDI proposal. Due to the enticing effect that the promise of participation in a high technology programme might have on the European states, France has proposed a cooperation programme designed to strengthen European technological capability in the areas where SDI will also concentrate. The programme named *Eureka* (ironically also the motto of California) has met with support both from Britain and from the FRG. Owing to the strong pressures in Europe and especially among the WEU countries for a common European position on the SDI offer, the French proposal has met with general approval. The US has recognised this and is trying to stress the compatibility between the SDI and the Eureka programmes. So far, however, the Eureka proposal seems to be doing what the French intended it to: reinforcing the strong scepticism against the SDI in Europe. The French have been very outspoken in their criticism of the SDI proposal. Defence Minister Charles Hernu called it dangerously destabilising, and France proposed to the Conference on Disarmament that a treaty banning the militarisation of space should be adopted. This should limit ASAT systems, prevent energy weapons, whether deployed in space or on land, and guarantee that each state may use and orbit satellites without fear of them being taken out.[55]

Solidarity by Saying Yes to 'Research Cooperation'

It could have been expected that the West Germans would react more favourably than Britain and France since they do not have a deterrent of their own to protect. And indeed the FRG has expressed support with the SDI plans on several occasions. Defence Minister Wörner has said that "Wir unterstützen das SDI-Forschungsprogramm", and Chancellor Kohl has on several occasions expressed support for the SDI programme. He has stressed that Western Europe should not be "technologically decoupled" from the United States. At the same time, reservations are expressed by Hans-Dietrich Genscher and his spokesmen. Jürgen Möllmann (State Secretary in the Foreign Ministry) has said that "Die Bundesregierung nimmt eine abwartende Haltung ein".[56]

Despite the obvious differences in view within the present CDU-FDP government, even the CDU has qualified its support for the SDI programme with a number of provisions: SDI research should be seen as an attempt to deter a new research competition between the US and the USSR. The research should not replace deterrence. Europe must have full insight and full participation in the programme, and the effects on the ABM treaty must be carefully considered. Given the fact that these considerations come from the CDU caucus, they highlight the widespread scepticism against the SDI in the Federal Republic.[57] Defence Minister Wörner said as an early comment to the SDI plan: "Schutzschirm oder Falle für Europa. Das ist das Thema der nächsten Jahre. Dadurch sei eine Destabilisierung des Ost-West-Gleichgewichts, eine Abkopplung Westeuropas von den USA und sogar eine Spaltung der westlichen Allianzen zu befürchten."[58]

Despite the present ideological compatibility between West Germany and the US, and despite the fact that nobody wants to create another INF débâcle within the Alliance, the Kohl government has in fact reacted quite reluctantly to all but the suggestion that mutual research is done. The reluctantly favourable response to the US research proposal may be explained by pointing to the fact that this is the only way to gain some influence over the programme. Since research in itself may create potential benefits for Europe economically or technologically, the Europeans have satisfied the US demands for solidarity by giving a positive response to the research cooperation proposal.[59]

It does not mean, however, that the SDI programme is supported. The West German government fears public reaction to this new proposal, and they fear that détente between East and West will be destroyed as a consequence of this new initiative. It may also lead to decoupling as Wörner pointed out. Both in the sense of the nuclear guarantee but also in the sense that economic and research competition between Europe and the US would be intensified as a result of the SDI.

Worries and Scepticism Remain

The European reaction has been critical, and even on the proposals for research cooperation sceptical voices now appear, in part from some of the smaller European countries: Norway, Holland, Denmark, but also from groups within the major European Powers. Who is going to cooperate on this new research — corporations, scientists or governments? (The United States rejected an offer from the Soviet Union to have a team of scientists from both countries work out the potential consequences of the new technologies by arguing that such an evaluation had to be done through governmental negotiation.) What sort of influence will the Europeans be accorded if they enter into this research? Does this mean that they will have an independent voice in the determination of strategy?[60]

What will it all cost, and how is it to be financed? If through public financing, is the money going to be diverted from other arms programmes or are additional funds needed? Finally, some Europeans worry whether the cooperation would actually involve any transfer of knowledge. The cooperation between Europe and the US on the Columbus project have lead many to regard US offers about mutual research with a high degree of suspicion.[61] The critical voices have, however, so far not prevented the Europeans from entering into agreements with the US on space research projects. The Germans and the Italians have concluded agreements with the US on the Columbus project, and have left the French standing in the cold with their proposal for a common European effort. Some French commentators have speculated that this is a case of the losers of the Second World War trying to gain influence over nuclear weapons through the backdoor and without the participation of France and Great Britain.[62]

Far-fetched as this may be, it does reflect the divisive influence that the SDI initiative already has had on the Europeans. The differences in relationship of these countries to the US and their differences in national security policy seem to be exacerbated through the SDI proposal and the US research offer.

This in and of itself has made it increasingly difficult to reach the compatibility in goals which is the substance of coupling between the US and Western Europe. The SDI proposal has increased and sharpened the debate in Europe on whether to follow along with the American initiative in order to reduce its negative effect and to ensure political coupling, or to fight the SDI plans since they will endanger European security.

By highlighting the European dependence on the US in the field of security policy, the SDI proposal has strengthened the wish for an independent European policy. Independence as a set-off to increased dependence, as a counter-attempt to reduce the divisive influence that the SDI has on the inter-European relations, as a necessary foundation for a domestic consensus on security policy in Europe, and in order to prevent the SDI from placing further obstacles to the development of a better relationship between East and West.

SDI: Security - Dependence or Independence?

The SDI fundamentally focuses on defensive weapons. The object of the research programme, the interallied consultations, and the long range vision of the US President: All focus on defensive weapons. Simultaneously the US is modernising its offensive weapons: The MX is, in the President's own words, "a long overdue modernisation. We are sitting here with our land-based missiles out-dated by anything and any comparison with the Soviet Union."

We are in a situation where the US and the Soviet Union are modernising their offensive missiles and other types of offensive weapons (the cruise missiles, the stealth bomber etc.), and a future consisting of a mix between offensive and defensive systems resulting from the new research seem the most likely prospect. Ronald Reagan obviously envisages this situation too. In an interview with *Newsweek,* 18 March, 1985, he was asked:

> "Is there anything that suggests to you that the Soviets will not try to build up offensively while we are researching Star Wars, or that they will not try to match the program?"

He answered:

> "Oh, I think they're trying to match it, and as I say, I think they started ahead of us. If we're right in our suspicions that they are expansionist and they already outnumber us greatly in the offensive weapons, and then they alone developed a defensive weapon before us, then they wouldn't have to worry about our deterrent — a retaliatory strike. Then they could issue the ultimatum to the world. So if there's any thought of that, then it would make it all the more necessary that whave a defensive weapon, too."

Obviously the Soviets will have an identical view of US intentions behind the SDI and consequently we are likely to enter into a defensive-offensive arms race. What are the consequences for Europe of this situation? What happens if defensive systems are developed at different paces in the different countries? Four scenarios are imaginable: Defence is developed 1) only in the US; 2) only in the US and Europe; 3) only in the Super-Powers, but not covering either of the allies; 4) only in the USSR.

Defence Only in the US

Development of the defensive systems to cover the US alone (not giving total security but at least enough to make the leaders feel more confident about the ability to withstand an all-out nuclear attack) is in essence for what the SDI is first and foremost designed, and the political add-ons about extending it to cover Europe and sharing it with the Soviets are political commitments that may change from one situation to the next.

If the defensive systems protected the United States, two situations might occur: One is that the US would decouple itself from the European scene. Their interests, economically, politically and strategically, in preventing others from dominating Europe would naturally be the same as they are today. But with the existence of a defensive shield, the Soviets would have only Europe to direct a retaliatory blow against in a situation of nuclear exchange between the Super-Powers. However unlikely this situation may seem in military terms, the political realities of foreseeing such a situation are more than enough to produce strategic instability and alliance insecurity. European governments will worry in such a situation that the US may be more prone to reckless behaviour vis-à-vis the Soviet Union, because of its own feeling of security against attack.[63]

The opposing argument is that since the risk to the US of fighting a war in Europe is reduced as the American homeland is protected, the threat to retaliate with offensive nuclear weapons against the USSR becomes more credible. As a result, deterrence is enhanced. Consequently, one could argue that increased strategic stability will result. This situation, besides assuming perfect defences and political leaders willing to risk their populations to achieve political ends, also foresees limiting war to Europe — which, of course, is completely contrary to any definition of European security, and therefore no marketable alternative in Europe.

Defence Only in US and in Europe

The SDI initiative contained from the start a stated commitment to extend the 'shield' to cover the allies. In Europe this will involve a combination of boost-phase defences from the overall systems and a series of terminal defences based in Europe. The political coupling problem that besets the present relationship between the US and Europe will remain the same. The European reliance on US decisions will even increase. The employment of the defensive systems would involve a US decision, and the US may be reluctant to make this decision in a situation where the attack is directed only against Europe. Furthermore, the European feeling of security under the defensive shield, however unrealistic, may itself create problems in the relations between the US and Europe. The final element keeping European and US security interests on line has been the common threat from the Soviet Union. Furthermore, internal differences within the European countries will resurface, and we are already seeing the beginning of this in the French fears of German and Italian participation in the SDI research.

Defence Covering Only the Super-Powers

A scenario that brings out fear, insecurity and political anxiety is the prospect of both of the Super-Powers having some sort of defensive shield covering themselves but nobody else. In this situation deterrence between the Super-Powers is devoid of meaning, British and French nuclear deterrence will be useless against the Soviet Union and the demands for conventional deterrence will increase dramatically. Security in Europe will be tied to the possibility of Europe to defend itself against conventional attacks, and it will be impossible to do anything about a nuclear threat. Europe will in this situation become a hostage to the Super-Powers' differences, and will be the true theatre for confrontation. The Super-Powers will feel secure and accordingly play out policy differences openly in the European scene. The situation will be highly unstable and will involve strong pressure towards an independent European security policy and probably European attempts to devise their own defensive systems.

Defence Only in USSR

Finally, one could imagine the unlikely, but possible situation that only the Soviet Union possessed a defensive system. Obviously this scenario is part of the motivation behind the present American effort. In this situation, the relationship between Europe and the US will be under a strong pressure for change. The present US guarantee and escalation dominance will be reduced, and Europe will have to provide for its security more independently. The situation will be highly unstable. Given the composition of the strategic forces, a Soviet capability to destroy incoming ICBMs would be less of a threat to the US nuclear force than the US threat is to the USSR strategic force. The USSR strategic forces have 70 per cent of their warheads on ICBMs whereas the corresponding US figure is 21 per cent. The possibility of the West placing Eastern Europe at risk and the possibility of circumvention plus the vulnerability of the USSR to embargo means that a Soviet defensive system would not in itself give the security background for achieving political goals through intimidation. The demands for substantial rearmament in Europe would, however, present themselves very strongly. Furthermore, the devise effects on the NATO alliance would probably be very serious.

These scenarios are relevant to the present discussion in so far as they explain the fear that motivates discussions between the Europeans and between Europe and the US. A defensive scenario with the continuing existence of offensive weapons is more unstable than any other scenario imaginable including one where offensive weapons are continously developed and deployed.[64]

Evaluating the effect of the SDI on European security would include an assessment of the effect the SDI proposal has on the present East-West climate. How does the SDI affect the arms control negotiations and the mutual attitudes between the Super-Powers? How does the SDI proposal affect the European perceptions of US interests and commitments vis-à-vis Europe, and what is the reaction from the public at large in the face of these prospects?

The research programme that is started will have effects on the direction of research. The research funds allocated for other purposes will decrease or other governmental expenditures will suffer. The research programme and the discussion of the SDI plans in itself also affects the relationship between different groups internally in the different states. The internal discussion within the US e.g. between the various branches of the armed services over the SDI proposals is a case in point. Similar cleavages will develop in Europe. Finally, the costs of the SDI proposal has already presented itself in terms of putting strain on the domestic consensus that was slowly being rebuilt inside the European countries, and between the US and Europe. The potential benefits are at present more imaginable than real, seen from a European perspective. It is possible that the SDI proposal induced the Soviet Union to return to the negotiation table in Geneva, but it will not induce them to arms control agreement when the SDI is non-negotiable. The political costs of the SDI are clearly seen. The benefits are hard to find. The SDI has already made Europe more dependent on the US and that in and of itself is part of the problem with the proposal.

Is, as many Europeans are now arguing, European independence an alternative to this situation?

It may appear more attractive to opt for European independence than it actually is. In the present situation the possibility for the Europeans to influence the direction of the strategic development between East and West is very small. The increase of European independence may further decrease European possibilities to influence the East-West debate. There is not a third way, and there is no such thing as regional European security in an insecure world.

However labourious and difficult the process may be, the only true solution to the European security problem is through common global security. The only definition of European security interest which will in the end be able to increase European security, is a definition building on global security. Europe can not achieve its security without involving itself directly in the security of other regions and first and foremost in the East-West relationship.

One of the possible ways that Europe may follow is the assertion of pressure that reduces Super-Power confrontation, and such a possibility may exist in firmly rejecting the SDI offer. The rejection itself will be difficult in that it runs counter to a long tradition. But acceptance will, as pointed out, increase Europe's dependence and increase strategic instability. The offensive-defensive race is not on yet, and may be stopped. Europe has a responsibility to the security of other regions, to the security of the global system to help stop a new arms race. The Nordic countries may be the place to start such an initiative due to the different affiliation of the Nordic countries. Since part of the rejection of the SDI obviously involves refraining the USSR from pursuing a similar type of research and development, the Nordic countries may also present a bridge between East and West. The SDI at present is a stumbling block for arms control and confidence-building discussions, and if Europe removed itself from the SDI, the enthusiasm in both of the Super-Powers for an enormously expensive and probably ineffective space defensive system would probably wane.

What Europe should not do is to choose dependence once again.

Dependence does not assure security, but neither does isolated independence in a strategically interdependent world.

Notes

1. See Michael Smith's excellent overview in his book, *Western Europe and the United States, The Uncertain Alliance,* George Allen and Unwin, London 1984.
2. See Andrew J. Pierre, "Can Europe's Security be 'Decoupled' from America?", *Foreign Affairs,* 1973, pp. 761—777; and Alan Ned Sabrosky, "NATO: A House Divided?", *Atlantic Quarterly,* Vol. 2, No. 2, Summer 1984, pp. 97—118.
3. See for one of many expressions of this Horst Ehmke, Eine Politik zur Selbstbehauptung Europas, *Europa-Archiv,* Folge 7, 1984, pp. 195—204.
4. See Hans-Henrik Holm, *U.S. and European Security: The Troublesome Coupling,* mimeo 1984.
5. Defence expenditure as a percentage of GNP varies substantially within the NATO alliance. In 1982 Canada, Denmark, Italy, Luxembourg and Spain spent under 3 per cent of GNP; Belgium, the Netherlands, Norway and Portugal send between 3 and 4 per cent; France and FRG spent between 4 and 5 per cent; Britain, Greece, Turkey and the USA spent more than 5 per cent of GNP on defence. See *The Military Balance 1984-1985,* IISS, London 1984.
6. See Hans-Henrik Holm, Nikolaj Petersen (eds.), *The European Missiles Crisis: Nuclear Weapons and Security Policy,* Frances Pinter Publishers, London 1983.
7. Secretary of State George Shultz in his speech at a Rand Conference, October 19, 1984 made this point. He said that harmony and confidence has been restored. Increasing consensus and widening agreement is what characterises the alliance today.
8. The US provided a strong external pressure for European independence. From the Marshall Aid and through the Atlantic partnership of the Kennedy administration to Kissinger's year of Europe various US administrations have themselves pressed for a united Europe. See Michael Smith, *op.cit.,* pp. 103—116.
9. For a list of various of the proposals see *Bulletin of Peace Proposals,* Vol. 15, No. 1, 1984.
10. See Peter Schlotter, "Reflections on European Security 2000", loc.cit., pp. 5—6.
11. See Hors Ehmke, *op.cit.,* p. 199.
12. Laurence I. Barrett gives in *Time,* 11 March, 1985 an account of 'How Reagan Became a Believer'. According to this story it was the combination of Robert McFarlane and Edward Teller that made Reagan a believer.
13. See *United States Military Posture for FY 1983,* Washington D.C., 1982, p. 77. Accounts of the development of defensive technologies may be found in Union of Concerned Scientists, *The Fallacy of Star Wars,* Vintage, New York 1984. And in David Baker, *The Shape of Wars to Come,* Stein and Day, New York, 1984.
14. See Daniel O. Graham, *We Must Defend America and Put an End to Madness,* Conservative Press, Chicago 1983.
15. President Ronald Reagan's speech on Defense Spending and Defense Technology, 23 March 1983.
16. See testimony before Senate subcommittee 22 February, by the Director of the Strategic Defense Initiative, James Abrahamson.
17. Caspar Weinberger, 27 March 1983. (Emphasis added).
18. A good example is the interview with Ronal Reagan published in *Newsweek,* 8 March 1985.
19. Ronald Reagan's 23 March, 1983 speech.
20. See MacGeorge Bundy, George F. Kennan, Robert S. McNamara, Gerard Smith, "The President's Choice: Star Wars or Arms Control", in *Foreign Affairs,* winter 1984—85, Vol. 63, No. 2, pp. 264—278.
21. See Zbigniew Brzezinski, Robert Jastrow, Max M. Kampelman, "Search for Security: The Case for the Strategic Defense Initiative", *International Herald Tribune,* 28 January 1985.

22. The window of vulnerability debate refers to the critique against the SALT II accord that it gave the Soviets an advantage in landbased-ICBMs. President Reagan started his term by arguing for the necessity to change this. However, the START proposals and the Reagan approval of the Scowcroft commission report closed the window — until it resurfaced in the SDI-debate. See Strobe Talbott, *Deadly Gambits*, Alfred A. Knopf, New York 1984, pp. 304—305.

23. Edward Teller, "The Role of Space and Defense in the NATO Alliance" in *NATO's Sixteen Nations*, Nov. 1984, pp. 14—16. Gen. Edward Rowny, American START negotiator, in his fight against the ABM treaty used the same metaphor: "Two adversaries arm themselves with shields and spears, then agree to throw away the shields. But if one side starts making more and longer spears, then sooner or later the other side has to think seriously about retrieving its shields". Here quoted from Strobe Talbott, *op.cit.*, p. 319. He points out that the trouble with this analogy is that shields can never deflect nuclear spears, and given the absence of limits or the number of spears the development of shields become fruitless.
The reuse of old analogies reflect that the SDI has turned into a continuation of the old ABM debate.

24. See Sidney D. Drell, Philip J. Farley, David Holloway, *The Reagan Strategic Defense Initiative: A Technical, Political and Arms Control Assessment*, A Special Report of the Center for International Security and Arms Control, Stanford University, 1984, pp. 70—72.

25. See Lawrence Freedmann, "NATO and the Strategic Defense Initiative", *NATO's Sixteen Nations*, Nov. 84, pp. 17—20. See also *Report to the Congress on the SDI*, April 1985, p. A—7.

26. See Edward Teller, *op.cit.*

27. See Paine and Gray, "Nuclear Policy and the Defensive Transition", *Foreign Affairs*, vol. 62, pp. 819—42, in particular p. 840.

28. See The Strategic Defense Initiative, *Defensive Technologies Study*, DOD, March 1984.

29. See George A. Keyworth, *The Case for Strategic Defense: An Option for a World Disarmed*, Issues in Science and Technology, Vol. 1, No. 1, pp. 30—44, and Ronald Reagan, *Remarks of the President to the National Space Club Luncheon*, 19 March 1985.

30. Fred S. Hoffman, *Ballistic Missile Defenses and U.S. National Security*, FSSS, 1983, quote from p. 3.

31. IISS, *Strategic Survey*, 1984—85, London 1985, p. 14.

32. Paul H. Nitze, *On the Road to A More Stable Peace*, Speech to the Philadelphia World Affairs Council, 20 February 1985.

33. See Holger H. Mey, "Technologie der Raketenabwehr", *Osterr. Milit. Zeitzchrift*, Heft 6, 1984. See also a series of articles in the *International Herald Tribune: Weapons in Space*, March 1985.

34. For a technical assessment see Sidney Drell et al., *op.cit.*, pp. 39—63. The conclusion of this study as well as that of others like the Scowcroft Commission is that we do not know how to build an effective defense against strategic ballistic missiles, and a truly effective system is not conceivable.

35. See Helmut Schmidt, "Saving the Western Alliance", *The New York Review of Books*, 31 May, 1984, pp. 25—27.

36. Lawrence Freedman, *op.cit.*

37. See Zbigniew Brzezinski et al., *op.cit.* The argument that deterrence is also protection and therefore there is no difference between the two views is false. Obviously Ronald Reagan by protection means a protective shield covering the 'soil' not just the weapons.

38. The NATO debate is summarised in the following articles: Stanley R. Sloan, "In Search of a New Transatlantic Bargain"; William Wallace, "European Defence Co-Operation: The Reopening Debate" both *Survival*, Vol. 26, No. 6, Nov. 1984. And Phil Williams, "The Nunn Amendment, Burden Sharing and US Troops in Europe", in *Survival*, Vol. 27, No. 1, Jan. 1985.

39. See Joseph Kraft, "Observe the Fine Print in the SDI Support", *The International Herald Tribune*, Feb. 23—24, 1985. And Terence A. Todman, *The Reality Behind "Star Wars"*, Address to the American Club, Copenhagen, 8 May 1985.

40. *Arms Control Today*, Vol. 14, No. 6, July-August 1984. See also Report to the Congress: S.D.I., 1985, App. B. Here it is stressed that the US may withdraw

form the treaty, and that an agreement on offensive arms limitation is a precondition for maintaining the ABM-regime.

41. *Loc.cit*, pp. 8—9.
42. See *The Economist*, Feb. 16, 1985, "Europe is reluctant to reach for the stars". See also *Rapport to Congress: SDI*, 1985, *op.cit.*, App. A.
43. See *The Economist*, "A Patriot for Europe", Jan. 12, 1985.
44. Lawrence Freedman, *op.cit.*
45. See *Keesing Contemporary Archives*, 1983.
46. See the account in Jürgen Scheffran, "Schutschirm oder Falle für Europa? Zur Debatte in der NATO über Weltraumsrüstung und Raketenabwehr", *Blätter für deutsche und internationale Politik*, No. 6, 1984, pp. 657—677.
47. *The NATO Communique*, NPG, April 4, 1984.
48. See *International Herald Tribune*, Feb. 22, 1985.
49. Colin Gray, Keith Payne, "Victory is Possible", *Foreign Policy*, No. 39, 1980, pp. 14—28.
50. The defensive system capability obviously increases if command and control facilities and ICBMs are hit in a first strike. This makes the SDI provocative and therefore increases the incentive of the USSR to preempt in a situation where war is likely. See Bernd Greiner, "Zwanzig Argumente gegen den "Krieg der Sterne"", *Blätter für Deutsche und Internationale Politik*, 1985, Nr. 3, p. 275, and Peter A. Clausen, "SDI in Search of a Mission", *World Policy Journal*, Vol. II, No. 2, pp. 249—270.
51. See Peter Jenkins, "Star Spangled Banner", *The Guardian*, Feb. 27, 1985.
52. The warning time will be so short that the defensive systems will have to be triggered automatically without any political decision-making.
53. See *The International Herald Tribune*, March 16, 1985, and *The Guardian*, March 16, 1985.
54. See Mitterrand's speech to the Parliament in the Haag, Feb. 7, 1984. See also Jürgen Scheffran, "Die Europäische Weltraumsgemeinschaft — Aufbruch in die Zukunft", *Blätter für deutsche und internationale Politik*, No. 2, 1985, pp. 169—185.
55. See *Politique Etrangère*, no. 2, 1984, pp. 377—380.
56. See *Der Spiegel*, Nr. 15, 1985, pp. 21—23.
57. See Jonathan Dean, *Will NATO survive Ballistic Missile Defense?*, mimeo, Washington, March 1985, pp. 13—15.
58. See Jürgen Scheffran, *op.cit.*
59. See Kohls statement in his speech to the Annual Congress of the Christian Democratic Party, March 20, 1985.
60. See Theo Sommer, "Der Wink mit dem Raketen-Zaunpfahl", *Die Zeit*, 22. Feb. 1985. See also E.P. Thompson, "The Ideological Delirium which strikes chords in the worst traditions of American Populism", *The Guardian*, Feb. 18, 1985.
61. See Jürgen Scheffran, "Ist die Militarisierung des Weltraums noch aufzuhalten", *Blätter für Deutsche und internationale Politik*, No. 10, 1984, pp. 1167—1183. And *Der Spiegel*. 1985, Nr. 15, p. 21.
62. See Pierre Lellouche, "The Star-Crossed Star Wars Plan", in *Newsweek*, 4 March 1985.
63. See Sidney Drell et al., *op.cit.*
64. See Charles Krauthammer, "Will Star Wars Kill Arms Control", *New Republic*, Jan. 21, 1985, pp. 12—16. In Paul E. Gallis, Mark M. Lowenthal and Marcia S. Smith, *The Strategic Defense Initiative and United States Alliance Strategy*, CRS report 85—48F, Washington 1985, three different scenarios are discussed: A U.S. lead in SDI, a Soviet lead in SDI, and a close mutual cooperation.

6
Nuclear-Weapon-Free Zones and Confidence-Building Measures

Lars B. Wallin

My assignment is to discuss some aspects of European security from the point of view of a European neutral, more specifically prospects for disengagement in Europe.* I do not believe that it is possible to give a neutral point of view, if this is taken to imply something which is more or less representative for **all** European neutrals. Although the neutrals, in many respects, have much in common, and in several cases have been able to act together to help find constructive solutions in international fora, the conditions for and the expressions of their neutrality nevertheless show significant differences.

Austrian neutrality became part of the Austrian Constitution in an amendment voted on the day after the signing of the State Treaty which re-established Austrian sovereignty in 1955. Swiss neutrality has a long history and is part of the Swiss Constitution. It is characterized by a strong defence and a very restrained foreign policy, and supported by a favourable geography. Although both countries are geographically close to the centre of the potential battlefield in a war between the two major Power blocs, their strategic situation is rather dissimilar, with Switzerland being, in a way, behind the lines.

The main motivations for Ireland's policy of neutrality should probably not be sought in the context of an East-West conflict. Anyway, Ireland being practically undefended and situated very much to the rear of continental NATO, Irish neutrality is very different from the neutrality of the other North European neutrals.

Finland's security policy is based on a neutrality policy aiming at promoting good relations between the various powers in the region, friendly and neighbourly relations with the Soviet Union as expressed by the Treaty of Friendship, Cooperation and Mutual Assistance, and it is supported by a military defence which is generally looked upon with great respect. Finland, like Sweden, has traditionally set great store at keeping the northernmost part of Europe an area of low tension. The neutrality of the latter country, finally, is neither prescribed by its Constitution nor guaranteed by any foreign power. While supported by a defence which is strong for a state of its size, foreign policy is given a prominent place in underpinning Swedish neutrality.

A Neutral Perspective on Disengagement

To the extent that I am able to give a neutral perspective on disengagement in Europe it will therefore be a Swedish perspective. Furthermore it will not be **the** Swedish perspective, i.e. the official view, but **a** Swedish perspective, i.e. it must be seen as the views of an individual, albeit heavily influenced by his environment. A few words about the security policy environment of Sweden might thus be appropriate.

One lesson of the Second World War was **the importance of a sufficiently strong defence** as a foundation for a policy of neutrality. The task of the military forces is to deter attacks on Sweden in case of a war in Europe, and active defence if Sweden nevertheless is attacked. Thanks to circumstances of geography, Sweden has been able to avail itself of an effective defence with a very defensive profile. This is one reason why we believe that our military defence is a stabilizing factor in the Nordic area. So long as both sides are confident that Sweden will fulfil the obligations of a neutral state, they should be able to keep a low military profile in the North, and the risk of a war starting there as a result of unforeseen developments in a crisis is minimized. The existence of Sweden and Finland between the power blocs is in itself a measure of disengagement.

However, it is clear that, when supreme interests are at stake, as in an armed East-West conflict, whatever the intentions of the belligerents be *vis-à-vis* a neutral state, the time might come when they would feel compelled to breach its neutrality, defended or not. Modern technology contributes to this, as it probably has made more difficult the geographical limitation of military operations. A nuclear war in Europe virtually ensures that even states which had succeeded in staying out of the war would suffer at least some of its effects on their own territory. And this may still be only a marginal addition to the sufferings both belligerents and non-belligerents would be exposed to as a result of the disastrous breakdown of the industrialized societies of Europe, brought about by any large-scale war in the area, and particularly by a nuclear war.

Measures and initiatives aiming at alleviating the East-West conflict, preventing its deterioration into an armed conflict in or around Europe, and reducing the risk of nuclear war must be important and legitimate parts of the security policies of any European state, aligned or not. Accepting one of the basic assumptions of Swedish security policy, that a possible armed conflict in Europe most likely would arise out of deteriorating East-West relations, a corollary to this is that **the military and political strategies of the major power blocs in Europe are legitimate concerns also of the European neutrals.**

This conviction is certainly an important motive behind various expressions of Swedish foreign policy, and although its implementation could, perhaps, be discussed, the principle itself can hardly be questioned. Traditionally this aspect of Swedish security and foreign policy has been strongly oriented towards **disarmament measures** (and measures aiming at bringing about a better international climate), while, it seems to me, problems of **crisis management** have, in the past, not got the attention they merit. Nevertheless, the three cases which will be examined here, a Nordic nuclear-weapon-free zone (NNWFZ), a battle-field-nuclear-weapon-free corridor (BNWFC), and possible confidence-and security-building measures (CSBMs) arising from the Conference on Disarmament in Europe (CDE) are all influenced by crisis management and tension reduction considerations.

A Nordic Nuclear-Weapon-Free Zone

Several proposals for nuclear-weapon-free zones in Europe and otherwhere have been made during the past 30 years.[1] A European zone was proposed by the Soviet Union in 1956. In 1957, the Polish foreign minister Adam Rapacki suggested a plan for the establishment of a nuclear-free zone consisting of East and West Germany, Poland and Czechoslovakia, a plan which was subsequently revised several times over the following years. From the same year dates a proposal for **a Balkan zone,** last time revived by Greece in 1984. The Adriatic, the Mediterranean, the Pacific, the Indian Ocean, Africa, and South Asia have also been discussed off and on, but only in the case of Latin America has there been any real progress.

A specifically Nordic zone was suggested for the first time in 1958 in a letter from Soviet Premier Bulganin to the Norwegian and Danish Prime Ministers. The proposal was rejected by both countries, the Norwegian answer interestingly enough drawing attention to the fact that also part of the Soviet Union belongs to Northern Europe. A similar proposal in the following year by Nikita Khrushchev (referring to Scandinavia and the Baltic area) was returned by the Swedish foreign minister Östen Undén, who observed that the only power around the Baltic possessing nuclear weapons was the Soviet Union. Undén himself, in 1961, suggested the creation of a "Non-Atom Club", but although the Nordic states certainly were supposed to join it, it had a much wider, both geographical and political scope.

The "modern" debate on a Nordic zone stems from a series of initiatives by the former Finnish President, Urho Kekkonen, first in 1963, and lastly in a lecture at the Swedish Institute of International Affairs in 1978. From having been rather much a Finnish monopoly, the debate on a Nordic zone developed explosively in Norway and in Sweden around 1980, and has since become closely associated with Swedish policy.

The Swedish View

The official Swedish position on a NNWFZ has recently been summarized in a Foreign Ministry pamphlet.[2] According to the pamphlet, a

NWFZ can be defined as follows:

1. States which are part of a nuclear-weapon-free zone are not allowed to have, receive, or directly or indirectly gain control over nuclear weapons, nor to manufacture or in any other way come into the possession of nuclear weapons.

2. The member states are not allowed to have, or to accept the existence of nuclear weapons on their territories.

3. The nuclear weapons states must respect the nuclear free status of the zone and are not allowed to take measures contrary to this obligation. They must also give assurances not to use or to threaten the use of nuclear weapons against targets on the territories of the member states.

These conditions should be fulfilled in peace, in times of crisis, as well as in war. It is also noted that the Nordic countries fulfil condition (1) by adhering to the Non-Proliferation Treaty; condition (2) is fulfilled in peacetime; while condition (3) is not fulfilled.

The above definition has been proposed i.a. in the reply by the Swedish Government to an enquiry by the UN Secretary General in 1976. At the same time it was noted that the obligations of the Nuclear Powers towards a NWFZ being integral to the concept, the establishment of such a zone is likely to require negotiations with these Powers.

The reply also suggested that nuclear weapons deployed in the proximity of a NWFZ should be retired, to the extent that they were destined or suitable primarily for use against targets within the zone. That these observations are still valid can be seen from the Swedish Prime Minister Olof Palme's speech at the Paasikivi Society in 1983. In his speech Prime Minister Palme defined the geographical extent of a Nordic nuclear-weapon-free zone as comprising, at a minimum, the territories, including the territorial seas and the air spaces, of Denmark, Finland, Norway and Sweden. Although the Baltic, being international waters, cannot become part of a zone by a decision of the Nordic states, he nevertheless firmly stated that a NNWFZ must be combined with obligations concerning a nuclear-free Baltic.[3]

According to the Swedish view, the fundamental purpose of the NNWFZ is to improve the security of its members (although it is recognized that a NNWFZ cannot entirely eliminate the nuclear threat against the Nordic countries). It is also suggested, however, that by the restraint required, as well by its members as by the Nuclear Powers, for the creation of such a zone, it could constitute an important CBM. It is furthermore suggested that a zone would increase stability in crisis situations and reduce the risk of misjudgements. So far the official view.

Discussion

The following observations are not meant as an exhaustive analysis of the consequences of a NNWFZ. They are proposed as points of departure for a discussion.

Technically, an obligation not to **introduce** nuclear weapons on the territories of the Nordic countries does not seem to imply any significant restraints on military options in the area. An obligation not to **use** nuclear weapons **against** targets in the zone would, in theory, be a restraint. Unfortunately, a NWFZ is not likely to be respected in a general nuclear war, particularly if forces of nations engaged in such a war are present on the territory of states belonging to the zone, so the restrictions would mainly apply to first use of nuclear weapons taking place in the Nordic countries. However, I doubt it very much that this area would be regarded important enough to "merit" escalation to nuclear war. After all, its importance mainly derives from its role in a long **conventional** war.

The case of the Baltic is a bit different, in that it is used as the basing area for some Soviet "eurostrategic" SLBMs. In view of the age of these submarines, and the very large number of land-mobile missiles covering the same targets, the military cost of giving up these old submarines would seem to be very modest, if indeed it should be seen as a cost.

Still, a nuclear-free Baltic would pose several difficult problems, for example with respect to verification. A minor matter might be that it would require the Nuclear Powers to change their policy of neither affirming nor denying the existence of nuclear weapons aboard their ships. However, it is an open question how long they will be able to maintain this policy anyhow, and for what purpose.

All difficulties notwithstanding, a nuclear-free Baltic would be one of the few tangible gains of a NNWFZ, and, as noted above, has long been and remains a Swedish condition.

Concerning "thinning-out" zones, it appears, as suggested by the Swedish defence minister (at the time under-secretary at the Ministry for Foreign Affairs), Anders Thunborg, ten years ago in *Ulkopolitiikka*[4] and by Prime Minister Palme in his Paasikivi Society speech, that the retirement of weapons suitable (primarily) for use against targets in the zone is a natural consequence of the establishment of a zone. The establishment of such **a thinning-out zone** ought to be rather straightforward in areas adjoining Finland, Norway and Sweden; however, in the neighbourhood of Denmark problems of definition, for example, might make it quite difficult to agree on concrete measures.

The introduction, in a crisis, of nuclear weapons in Norway or Denmark would be a highly escalatory measure and most likely a seriously destabilizing one. A NNWFZ would constitute an obstacle against this. Still, the difference compared with a situation without a zone would probably be marginal, both because the military reasons for introducing nuclear weapons in Norway and Denmark are probably not very strong, and because of the divisive effects it might have internally in these countries.

Obviously, a NNWFZ is not a military problem. Its military implications would be minor, if any. It is a political problem. The fundamental objections against a zone are of a political nature — partly having to do with alliance politics — and so are the main concerns of its proponents. The latter have, however, probably less to do with the effects of the very **existence** of a NNWFZ, for example in promoting détente. In fact, it is not evident to me that a NNWFZ would change the present situation very much in this respect. Détente is, after all, something that can only exist in peacetime, and in peacetime the Nordic countries are nuclear-weapon-free already. They have rather more to do with the **process of establishing** a zone.

With the very strong reservations in NATO against a zone, and the essential role the Nuclear Powers must play in the creation of a zone, it is quite clear that it can only come into being if both blocs, and all Nuclear Powers with a stake in the area, judge it to be in their interest. It is quite common to assert that a (much) better international climate is a precondition to any substantial East-West agreement. This may well be so, but then the problem is how to create this better climate. Assuming that there is a will to find ways to do it, a process of discussion and negotiation aiming at creating a NNWFZ **might** be used as a vehicle for confidence building.

A Battlefield-Nuclear-Weapon-Free Corridor

In its report of April 1982, *the Independent Commission on Disarmament and Security Issues* (the Palme Commission) proposed the establishment in Central Europe of a corridor free of battlefield nuclear weapons.[5] As a follow-up to this proposal, the Swedish Government in December of the same year addressed a note to the member nations of the NATO, the Warsaw Pact and a number of European neutral and non-aligned nations, asking for their views on the proposal. Comments were received from all nations which had received the note, with those of the NATO members generally arguing against the proposal, the Warsaw Pact members in favour and suggesting extensions of the proposed corridor, while the replies from the neutral and non-aligned states were, with some notable exception, positive to the idea. A summary of the replies[6] and a commentary[7] have later been made public by the Swedish Government.

The Proposal

The Swedish note (which has never been made public by the Swedish Government) did not give a very detailed definition of the proposed corridor. Evidently the respondents were supposed to refer to the Palme Commission report for this. In fact, a main purpose of the note was to draw attention to the report and act as a catalyst for discussions of its proposals.

Briefly, the corridor should consist of a strip 150 km wide (although the width, like most of its more detailed characteristics, might be subject to negotiation) on each side of the dividing line between the military-political blocs in Central Europe. No nuclear warheads for battlefield weapons systems or exclusive battlefield nuclear weapons were to be allowed within the corridor. The corridor would, however, not affect other kinds of nuclear weapons, nor, it is important to note, would there be any prohibition against using nuclear weapons against targets within the corridor. It would thus **not** constitute a **nuclear-weapon-free zone.**

A BNWFC would, according to the Swedish documents, constitute an important confidence-building measure which should contribute towards reduced tensions in Europe **and** reduce the risk of an immediate recourse to battlefield nuclear weapons were an armed conflict to break out. In fact, the Swedish aide-memoire is somewhat ambiguous, stating that the corridor should mainly be regarded as a measure aiming at the latter goal, and that it should mainly be regarded as a CBM. In the latter connection, it suggests that "a corridor... — with, for instance, verification measures comprising on-site inspection — would by its very existence increase confidence and transparency and, in this way, reduce the risk of a conflict breaking out."[6]

This may well be so, such on-site inspections probably having to include not only nuclear storage sites but also nuclear capable (dual capable) weapons systems, e.g. nuclear capable aircraft and, in particular, artillery pieces of a calibre larger than 15 cm or thereabout. On-site inspections including such weapons systems certainly would have the potential of substantially increasing transparency. The other side of the coin is, of course, that such verification measures would be extremely difficult to agree on.

Objections to a BNWFC

Some objections to the idea had the appearance of being based on misunderstandings of the proposal and will not be discussed here.

Incompatibility with NATO Unity

A political argument against the corridor proposal was that it would not be compatible with the principle of NATO unity — equal protection and equal risk. Strategically it was said to increase the risk of a conflict. By heightening the nuclear threshold, a corridor would weaken deterrence and increase the risk of war (and, thereby, the risk of nuclear war would increase, too). Militarily, it would allow the conventionally stronger side to concentrate his forces, allowing him better to exploit his superiority, but it was also claimed that nothing prevented the reintroduction of nuclear weapons into the corridor in a crisis or targeting the corridor from outside its limits. It was also suggested that a debate on a BNWFC would be harmful by diverting attention from (then) current negotiations on intermediate range weapons (INF), and generally complicate such negotiations.

I do not propose to discuss the argument about the unity of NATO. It has a strong flavour of holy writ and its correspondence to reality is not too convincing. It should be sufficient to remind of the Danish and Norwegian base and nuclear policy, and that the most likely battlefield in a conventional or tactical nuclear war (if such a war is conceivable) is Western Germany, while the territories of the United States and Canada are at risk only if the war were allowed to escalate to intercontinental nuclear war.

The Real Role of Battlefield Nuclear Weapons

Perceptions of the role of battlefield nuclear weapons in a war in
Europe are in many ways critical to any evaluation of the objections
against a corridor, as well as of the assumptions motivating its proponents. It is difficult to imagine that nuclear weapons can be used as a
weapon in the close-in battle or that, for example, the West Germans
would accept the conduct of a battlefield nuclear war on their territory.
The task of keeping at risk the forces of the other side could presumably
be fulfilled by weapons based outside the corridor, e.g. air delivered
weapons, or tactical missiles of longer range.

Furthermore, present trends within NATO seem to point towards
stressing targets in the deep rear of the Warsaw Pact as the ones most
likely to be attacked in a first strike. It seems to me that, whereas short-
range systems like nuclear artillery and some battlefield missile systems,
available on the divisional level, would have a place on a hypothetical
dynamic nuclear battlefield, they hardly have a place in a deterrence
strategy based on an ability to escalate to nuclear use, absent an
intention to carry on an extensive nuclear battle.

If I am right in this, there would not seem to be any compelling reason
to expect a BNWFC to have much of an impact on the so-called nuclear
threshold. The contrary assumption is advanced by the corridor proponents, however. One reason for their belief might be the idea that it
could be easier to take the political decision to escalate to nuclear use
with short-range weapons and on one's own territory. As indicated
above, NATO thinking seems to be going in a different direction. Another
very common argument, to be found for instance in the Palme Commission report, is the one of "use-or-lose". In critical situations there might
be pressures to authorize use of battlefield weapons, or commanders
under heavy strain might use weapons available to them on their own
initiative, it is suggested.

I will briefly discuss three putative use-or-lose situations. The first one
concerns a low level commander initiating nuclear use on his own initiative when facing the risk of having his unit destroyed. Quite apart from the
question of the rationality of such a decision, he would not, if available
information on the control of nuclear weapons is correct, be able to do it.
The nuclear warheads are not necessarily in the same location as the
firing unit, they are guarded by special (American) units and are equipped
with locking devices which are supposed to protect against unauthorized
use until release has been granted.

A second possibility which, fantastic as it may be, has been suggested,
is that rather than losing a number of nuclear weapons to the enemy
when nuclear equipped units risk being overrun, authorization would be
given to fire the weapons. Why? The Warsaw Pact already has a large
number of nuclear weapons and would most likely not be able to use
NATO weapons anyhow. Nor would the loss of a fraction of its stockpile
put NATO in a position of significant nuclear inferiority, nor prevent it
from escalating. Besides, the warheads could fairly easily be moved out
of the threatened area.

In fact, closing the battlefield nuclear escalation option to NATO would require eliminating virtually all nuclear capable aircraft and nuclear capable army units. This, on the other hand, would require, or be equivalent to, a complete break-down of NATO's defence in Central Europe. A likely cause for nuclear escalation if any, not because of the loss of some nuclear weapons however, but because of NATO being about to lose the war.

The Confidence-Building Potential of the Corridor

If, as I argue, a BNWFC would on the whole be consistent with NATO strategy and would have no real impact on the "nuclear threshold", what about its confidence-building potential? There might be some similarities to the Nordic situation, in that the Easternmost parts of West Germany (on the situation in East Germany I must confess to an even higher degree of ignorance) might already be more or less nuclear-weapon-free in peacetime. The dispersion in a crisis — or the reintroduction in the case of a corridor — of nuclear weapons within the area of the proposed corridor could be a destabilizing measure. On the other hand, it would possibly only be a marginal addition, if any, to the impact of the alerting of other nuclear systems in the region.

We are therefore back to the possible CBM value of a **negotiation process.** While I do not want to exclude all possibility of negotiations aiming at a Nordic NWFZ serving a confidence-building purpose, I tend to do so in connection with a BNWFC in Central Europe. This is because such negotiations would be inextricably linked to negotiations on all kinds of nuclear systems **and** conventional forces, would have to consist of a mixture of inter-and intra-alliance negotiations extremely difficult to manage, and most importantly, would force deepgoing differences of interest and perception of the role of nuclear weapons inside NATO into the open.

This goes, I believe, together with an unwillingness to accept the legitimacy of the interests of neutral and non-aligned states in military-political issues in Central Europe, a long way towards explaining the reactions in NATO to the Swedish note.

Mutual Advantages and Unilateral Measures

Lest what is written above give a wholly negative view on a BNWFC in Central Europe, I should add that I believe that such a corridor, or rather the elimination or reduction of short-range nuclear weapons would be a positive development, and that it would also be in NATO's own interest (that the Warsaw Pact considers it to be advantageous is evident in the replies to the Swedish note). Looked upon from the NATO point of view, the battlefield nuclear weapons steal resources from the conventional forces, not only capital, manpower for guarding and handling them as well as training time, but also, and perhaps most importantly, they divert attention from the planning and organizing for a conventional battle. Significant gains in conventional capability might result from greater clarity regarding the roles of conventional forces in NATO's strategy.

Despite my pessimism relative to negotiations on a BNWFC, I can still see some cause for optimism regarding the battlefield nuclear weapons situation in Europe. I believe, for example, that we will see some unilateral steps being taken by NATO in the direction of reducing the number of such weapons. A decision was taken to retire 1000 nuclear warheads in connection with the December 1979 agreement on the Eurostrategic weapons, and the retirement of an additional 1400 was agreed on in 1983. The opinion for reducing the role of tactical nuclear weapons in NATO's strategy seems to be gaining in strength, also in policy making circles. In fact, I tend to interpret the insistent demands by General Bernard Rogers and others for increased conventional strength as being moti-vated, not only by a wish to reduce the dependence on the threat of nuclear escalation, but on the realisation that it is unlikely that political authorization to use nuclear weapons will be obtained.

Clearly, visible reductions of nuclear weapons in Europe could have a significant value in improving the East-West climate. It is therefore un-fortunate that the Soviet Union appears to have introduced nuclear artil-lery in Eastern Europe over the past few years, and that it could not resist a politically motivated counter-deployment to NATO's deployment of Pershing II and ground-launched cruise missiles.

The Stockholm Conference

When the Conference on Confidence- and Security-Building Measures and Disarmament in Europe began its work in Stockholm in January 1984, it did so accompanied by great public interest and high hopes for significant disarmament results. The part of the public entertaining such hopes is likely to feel deceived with the results that will have been accomplished by the time the CSCE follow-up meeting opens in Vienna in the autumn of 1986. Disarmament measures are, in fact, not part of the mandate of the Stockholm Conference. Such measures might be the subject of a future, post-Vienna phase of the CSCE process.

But if the CDE does not reach an agreement on disarmament measures, it may still accomplish valuable results. The CSCE process, of which the Stockholm Conference is an outgrowth, can be seen as a new departure in international security negotiations. Instead of attempting to find solutions to major issues of disarmament, as has been the purpose of many negotiations in the past (some of which are still going on), the CSCE could be seen as an attempt at getting a dynamic process going, by starting with easier problems and trying to get agreements on a step by step basis.

After a long introductory period, during which the two alliances[8] and the N+N-states (as well as Rumania and Malta) tabled their proposals, the Conference has settled down to serious negotiations. I will not discuss the various proposals in any detail. Briefly characterized, the Eastern proposal is strongly flavoured by political-declaratory measures — e.g. non-use of violence, which is, in fact, already subscribed to in the UN Charter — and proposals which are of a global nature and/or under consideration in other fora, for example related to defence budgets, a complete test ban, a chemical weapons ban, nuclear-free zones etc. It also contains a proposal for limiting the size of military exercises and for the notification of exercises and military movements.

Also the Western proposal contains one measure which might be seen more in a political perspective — information exchange about the organization and location of major formations — but is otherwise giving quite detailed proposals for the notification, observation and inspection of military activities.

The N+N proposal has similarities to the Western one. It is less detailed, however, and envisages the possibility of certain geographical limitions and, in particular, constraints on the size of military activities.

With the adoption of a negotiating procedure in December 1984, the conference has entered a phase of highly technical work.

Outlines of an Agreement

What, then, might be the shape of the agreement which hopefully will be negotiated in time for the Vienna follow-up meeting in November 1986? Clearly, the likelihood of anything resembling disarmament measures, zones of disengagement, or any other measures that would appeal to a public anxious for more dramatic signs of reduced military potentials in Europe, is very low. What is being discussed are exchanging annual calendars for military activities, expanding the categories of military activities which should be notified in advance (from manoeuvres only, as in the Helsinki Final Act, to movements, redeployment, alert and mobilization activities), lowering the thresholds of notification (25 000 troops in the Final Act), increasing the notification period (21 days in the Final Act), establishing binding rules for the invitation of observers and for the procedures and conditions of their participation, measures of verification and inspection, and communications and complaints arrangements. The principle of non-use of force is likely to figure in some way in an agreement, and the prospects of some measures of constraint being included appear to have increased.

While according to the Madrid Mandate the measures to be negotiated should apply to all of Europe (and adjoining sea and air space), matters of geography and of defence organization, for example, mean that some measures will have different implications for different states or alliances.

Looking at available statistics it is evident that low ceilings on the size of military manoeuvres would be of greater consequence for NATO, with its large multinational exercises concentrated to a few periods of the year, than for the Warsaw Pact. Constraints on military activities have several purposes, of which a general reduction of the level of military activity is one, and the limitation of particularly threatening activites is another. The threatening aspect of an activity has to do, among other things, with its size and with the amount of warning time provided. It might thus be possible to accept a higher ceiling on activities that are announced in an annual calendar than on those that are notified perhaps a month or so in advance. Still lower ceilings might be applicable to activities which by their very nature and purpose cannot be notified in advance, such as alert exercises. Low ceilings are desirable also for activities with a potential for rapidly developing into a threatening direction, such as airborne and amphibious exercises.

The provision of adequate verification and inspection procedures obviously becomes more important the more militarily significant the measures agreed. This is one area where the problems might be particularly difficult for the N+N-states. Their national technical means of verification are much more limited than those belonging to members of the two alliances, but their main problem might lie elsewhere. These states all rely on sensitive mobilization procedures for their military defence, and would therefore have difficulties allowing some forms of observation and inspection.

CSBMs, of course, become particularly pertinent in crises. Fear that a CSBM regime might be exploited for deceptive purposes, or that it will make timely counter-measures more difficult to decide on, increase the reluctance to accept the inclusion e.g. of restraints and amplifies the need for efficient consultation and complaints procedures. These must be designed so as not to allow their exploitation neither for delaying tactics nor as a means of exerting political pressure.

The Stockholm Conference is an important meeting ground for political and military experts from all of Europe and North America. Even if the work of the conference should be aimed at negotiating as militarily significant CSBMs as possible, I believe that its main importance maybe lies in this political function. To some extent it might also contribute to a greater sophistication in the debate on the military balance and military threats in Europe, by forcing more attention to factors other than purely numerical comparisons of forces. Should it succeed in reaching agreement on some significant CSBMs too, so much the better. For the N+N states, which do not participate in an alliance exchange on security matters or in bloc-to-bloc negotiations in other fora, the work in the CDE has provided new insights in European security problems and has generally stimulated an interest in such matters, this, at least, is the conclusion drawn from looking at the Swedish experience.

Credo

In one version of the programme of the seminar for which this paper was written, it appears under the title of Prospects of Military Disengagement in Europe. Neither of the three cases I have discussed above contains any significant measure of military disengagement. But then I do not see any appreciable prospect of this happening within a timeframe of concern to me.

While I certainly agree that military forces should be reduced and all efforts made to reduce the possibilities of using military power for political gain, it is my opinion that what is most urgently needed is efforts to greatly improve **crisis management** capabilities. Ultimately we must achieve a fundamental reduction in East-West tensions. Efforts towards this goal must be pursued with high priority and in parallel to those oriented toward improved crisis management. As a means of lowering the risk of war one has to accept, however, that the reduction of political tensions can have a significant impact only in the (very) long term.

It is not obvious to me that efforts to bring about military disengagement promise the highest pay-offs when it comes to our ability to control and prevent crises. Nor do I believe that military disengagement can lead to a reduction of tension. What I do believe is that we must strive for increased contacts in all fields over all of Europe. Negotiations on military and other security issues constitute one such field, and a very important one at that.

Notes

*) The article expresses the author's own opinions. It should in no way be regarded as representing the views of the Swedish Government, nor of any of its agencies.

1. A very useful study, unfortunately only available in Swedish, is Johan Tunberger, *Norden - en kärnvapenfri zon? Historik och problem*, Folk & Försvar, Trosa 1982.

2. *En kärnvapenfri zon i Norden*, UD informerar 1984:4, Stockholm 1984.

3. For the text in English, see "Security and Stability in the Nordic Area", Speech by the Prime Minister of Sweden, Olof Palme, to the Paasikivi Society in Helsinki on June 1, 1983 in Kari Möttölä (ed.), *Nuclear Weapons and Northern Europe*, The Finnish Institute of International Affairs, Helsinki 1983, pp. 83—86.

4. Anders Thunborg, "Nuclear Weapons and the Nordic Countries Today — A Swedish Commentary", *A Nuclear-free Zone and Nordic Security*, a special issue of *Ulkopolitiikka*, March 1975, pp. 34—38.

5. *Common security - A Programme for Disarmament*, Pan Books, London 1982.

6. *Reactions to the inquiry by the Swedish Government on the proposal by the Independent Commission on Disarmament and Security Issue regarding battlefield nuclear weapons in Central Europe*, Aide-memoire I 1983-12-09, Swedish Ministry for Foreign Affairs.

7. *Swedish Views on the proposal for a corridor free from battlefield nuclear weapons in Central Europe*, Aide-memoire II, Swedish Ministry for Foreign Affairs.

8. Although formally a Soviet and not a Warsaw Pact proposal the Soviet proposal is commonly treated as a Warsaw Pact one.

7

Global Perspectives of European Security

Leo Mates

Introduction

In this article, we shall present and examine briefly only a few points of the complex problem of linkage between European and world security. In particular, we shall examine the following aspects of the problem: 1. The world-wide significance of European security, 2. Outside threats to European security, 3. Non-alignment and European security.

Before passing on to the examination of these specific points, it must be clarified that for the purpose of this examination Europe is understood, or rather European security is understood, including all those countries which participated in the Helsinki Conference which then led to the signing of the Final Act in 1975. At the same time we do not forget that the area on the European continent lying in between the two major World Powers is a distinct region and represents Europe in the more narrow sense.

Hence we are obliged in examining the issues of security to apply in the same argument both definitions of Europe. This will introduce some complications, but they are unavoidable in the present situation of close links and interdependence in the world as a whole, and in particular in those parts of the world which are closely connected with Europe, as it was known in the last few centuries, that is, as a continent attached to Asia and surrounded by high seas on all other sides.

We must, however, also not forget that Europe was and still is the centre and birthplace of a civilization which has spread far beyond its boundaries and deeply influenced the rest of the world. This role of Europe appears to be in a deep crisis as well as its security and general role in world politics.

As it was said, we must examine European problems of peace and security in the wider framework of the membership of the Helsinki Conference. This means, including all of the Soviet Union in the East, and North America in the West. The specification in some agreements arrived at during the Helsinki Process, specifying that they apply only to the European parts of the Soviet Union, do not contradict this assumption.

In fact it only proves that such limitations were necessary since normally an agreement with a government covers the whole territory of the given country.

The Indispensable World Powers

The extension of the boundaries of Europe for the purpose of examining and safeguarding its security are the results of the Second World War. The two major World Powers gained such a thorough and durable influence over Europe, that it became unthinkable to discuss problems of cooperation and security in Europe without including them in the debate and in the agreements resulting from the debate. We can see without difficulty that by the elimination of either of the two, the United States of America, or the Soviet Union, the equation becomes unbalanced.

The overwhelming military might of these World Powers is an essential component of whatever precarious equilibrium is thinkable in and around Europe. Their presence in Europe is not only a strategic fact, made visible by the presence of their troops in some of the countries of the area lying between them, but they are also linked with key states of Europe by the two alliances. In these alliances, they play the role of leading partners and their military potential exceeds several times the total potential of all the other allies.

On the other hand, by the elimination from the equation of both of them, no balance can be attained either. In Europe, as it stands between the two World Powers, the western part is in all respects, superior. This is so, even if we ignore that within Europe in the narrower sense, there are also two nuclear powers, and both in the West. In other words, the western part of Europe is more developed, and has a larger population, and is militarily superior, even if we do not count the nuclear arsenals of Great Britain and France.

Europe must therefore be regarded, for strategic purposes, as one whole and indivisible area including the North American Continent, and extending in the East to include the Soviet Union. This had been fully recognized when the Helsinki Conference was finally convened. Earlier objections by the Soviet Union to a full participation of the United States and Canada were dropped, and they both became full members of the Helsinki process.

The convening of the Helsinki Conference reflected thus the understanding and general acceptance of two important foundations of European security. First, the recognition that the wider framework, including both of the major World Powers, was the only sound basis for securing a reliable peace within Europe. Secondly, the realization that the destructive power of the nuclear arsenals on both sides could in a war lead only to a total devastation and no victory of either Power.

The Conference, however, was not only the reflection of the realities in Europe and in the world, but also an attempt of influencing these realities. If a major nuclear military conflict in the future was to be ruled out, there still remained the necessity of organizing peace so as not to produce revivals of tensions that might lead again to the dangerous threshold of war. Hence the main concern was the strengthening of security and cooperation in Europe, of course, Europe in the wider framework including all states which participated in the Conference.

The World-Wide Significance of European Security

In the Final Act, in several places, the concern was expressed of applying the principles and agreements agreed in Helsinki also to relations with other countries in the world. The linkage with peace and security outside the enlarged European zone was in the Conference fully understood. This was in those years reflected also in bilateral agreements between the United States and the Soviet Union. Briefly, there was no doubt at the time of the debates in Helsinki and in Geneva, during the drafting stage of the Conference, that stability in Europe should not lead to exporting the rivalry and hostility to other parts of the world.

There were two ways of striving for the main objective of securing peace and cooperation in Europe itself. One was **a bilateral agreement** between the two alliances, or rather the two major World Powers. The other, advanced by the neutrals and the non-aligned of Europe, was a strictly and fully **multilateral approach,** a truly collective agreement among all states participating in Helsinki. Formally, the Final Act was conceived as a multilateral document and an understanding reached among all participating states individually.

Under this cover of multilaterality, however, the bipolarity could be clearly seen in a great number of compromise solutions. This character comes out still more clearly in the records of the Geneva phase, where bilateral controversies were dominant, and solutions frequently attained on the basis of compromises between the two sides. In the praxis after the Conference, this was still more prominent, both in the treatment of the Conference and the Final Act in the media and in statements of politicians and statesmen on both sides.

The alternative view of the group of the neutrals and the non-aligned was in fact not taken as the basis for security and cooperation, because of the internal divisions in the European security zone. Yet, the increasingly single-handed actions of the major Powers affected gradually also the cohesion within the two alliances, although this process did not develop symmetrically on both sides. The most important consequence was the bilateral treatment of practically all important problems that came up between the two major Powers.

The recognition of the dangers of continuing the Cold War, as an unrestained confrontation, however induced them to seek agreement or moderation in all controversial situations. In Europe, détente was the outcome of this restraint. Europe became thus the most stable region in the world. This stability in the very centre of controversy, where the Cold War originated, did, however, not prevent aggressive policies in other parts of the world. The fact remains that bilateral agreements regarding other areas were during the 1970s increasingly disregarded. Tensions and clashes in different parts of the world produced retroactively ever more hostile relations between the two major Powers and in East-West relations in Europe.

Détente Limited to Europe

The stabilization in Europe did not lead to the extention of the European détente to areas outside Europe. In fact, the European stabilization developed soon into a controversy, restrained only by the fear of a nuclear holocaust, which might easily develop out of any war between the two sides in Europe.

This same restraint did not work in the Third World, where already in the past numerous wars where fought without the use of nuclear weapons. The stabilization in Europe, based on the fear of a nuclear war, in fact, reinforced the belief that it was likely that nuclear weapons would not be used in a war in the Third World. Hence, the Helsinki Conference, in spite of all efforts made in the formulation of the Final Act, did not durably influence conditions in the Third World.

The strategic significance of the area covered by the Helsinki agreement, in particular the overwhelming power of armaments deployed there and the involvement of the two major Powers in problems in all regions of the world, give it nevertheless a dominant significance for peace and security. The Helsinki Final Act, by the importance of the contracting parties, the members of the Helsinki Conference, and the continuing follow-up process and negotiations, is still crucially important for peace and security in the world.

It is most likely that in the future also, Helsinki will, as long as the process started there is alive in Europe, play an important role restraining the major Powers in all aspects and on all places where they confront one another. The determination to avoid an open breakdown and clash in Europe will continually induce them to refrain from rush actions in other regions. They will, however, hardly discontinue efforts of damaging the positions of the opponent and enchancing their own influence in different parts of the world.

The significance of Helsinki, as much as it may be decisive for the maintenance of peace in Europe and the prevention of a general war, can hardly be expected to prevent regional clashes, including those in which states belonging to the Helsinki process participate. Most of all, it cannot prevent the urge of major Powers to be involved in all critical situations wherever they may develop.

Outside Threats to European Security

The widening of the boundaries of Europe has tied Europe inseparably with the rest of the world in a way unknown in the earlier European history. Whilst Europe used to be the centre of the world, and the breeding ground of world powers, it became now an object of contention of the two major World Powers and greatly dependent on them. Europe in the more narrow sense became also vulnerable in many respects to developments in the outside world.

We have seen how the area covered by the Helsinki Conference influences conditions in the world. Now we must turn to the reverse flow of influence. Current developments and experience of the past induced the major Powers to modify their relations in and outside Europe. The increasingly tense relations produced by conflicts in the Third World, affected negatively also the behaviour of those two Powers in Europe. In the first place, it destroyed temporarily the dialogue on strategic arms. Then, it affected also other negotiations and contacts between East and West in Europe.

Briefly, the exacerbation of American-Soviet relations in various areas of confrontation in the Third World were gradually transferred into the European region. This became soon visible when the Belgrade follow-up meeting failed to attain any substantial results, and furthermore, when the Madrid meeting hovered for almost two years over the abyss of complete collapse. Yet, the spirit of Helsinki, based on the essential necessity of preserving peace in Europe, saved the situation from deteriorating beyond control. The result was a continuous conflict between the tendency of abandoning the détente altogether and disregarding the Final Act, and the realization that there was no alternative indeed to the continuation of the debate opened in Helsinki.

The dominant form of confrontation between the two major Powers could no longer be directed to the effort of intimidating the rival by the destructive capability of nuclear weapons. This had to be eliminated because of the mutually recognized inability of winning a major nuclear war, but also because of the parity in practically all forms and types of strategic and tactical weapons.

The post-Cold-War and post-Détente form of confrontation between the two major Powers turned into attempts of **eroding the opponent's alliance.** The most conspicious example of this new type of strife is the controversy over the build-up of nuclear weapons in Europe. They were presented to the public as military threats, although it is an undeniable fact that the deployments were politically inspired, and that they could not be put into action without causing irreparable and uncontrollable damage to the whole of Europe by direct, and still more by secondary effects of radiation and fall-out.

The deployment on both sides produced instability within the one and the other alliance; moreover serious divisions and strife within individual nations emerged. In the process the controversy affected negatively also relations between the two major Powers and stopped temporarily the process of cooperation and jeopardized security in Europe.

As a matter of fact, negative impulses, introduced into the intra-European process from outside by means of the two major Powers, could not destroy the historical significance and the durability of the early period of the détente and of the Helsinki spirit. We are now again witnesses of significant efforts to overcome the damage done during the late 1970s and the early 1980s.

Another way in which European security was and is influenced from outside is the dependence of Europe on supplies from the Third World. In particular on the supplies of crude oil from sources situation in regions rife with conflicts and major power clashes of Europe's economy developed in the past relying greatly on secure supplies from dependencies of European colonial powers. With the loss of the colonies and also in the power of influencing events in critical areas, the European countries became dependent on situations and developments which they could not control.

However, irrespective of direct European interests and their direct relations, major power controversies in the Third World affect decisively the stability in Europe in a most immediate way. Both the major Powers are so deeply and inextricably involved in a series of conflicts and tense situations in various continents, that serious military clashes could break out at any time involving their military forces. As a matter of fact, one-sided direct involvements have already occurred in more than one case, and it is realistically possible to think of direct clashes also.

In the case of a direct involvement of units of both the major Powers in whatever place in the world, it would still be possible to keep this clash in a regional framework. Nevertheless, the security in Europe would thereby always be affected. Furthermore, developments of this kind are likely to affect internal relations in Europe, as well as inside the two alliances and within individual countries.

Finally, it should be made clear that destabilization within the two alliances, and divisions within individual countries, are not necessarily leading towards a diminishing role of the alliances and a harmonization of relations across the political divide in Europe. In fact, we could observe the contrary in connection with the divisions caused by the deployment of euromissiles, and by other development creating intra-alliance frictions.

Non-alignment and European Security

So far, only the aligned countries of Europe were mentioned. Their role regarding problems of security is most important, and they played leading roles in most of the developments after the war. Yet, even in the divided continent of Europe the division is not absolute. Neutral countries of past conflicts continued their neutralistic policy, and new ones joined them. The real novelty for the European pattern is the formation of a group of non-aligned countries in Europe.

Thus, a zone was formed in Europe which stood outside the great confrontation between the two alliances. It assumed the more structured character of a special group only in connection with the Helsinki Conference. Already in the early stages of the almost two years long debate of the committee phase of the CSCE in Geneva, the N+N Group was formed, comprising the neutrals and the non-aligned. This group played a rather important role during that long debate and helped substantially in the attainment of consensus on the text of the Final Act of Helsinki. They continued to be an important element in all the follow-up meetings and are still functioning as an independent actor producing original ideas and proposals, as well as helping in bridging differences between the two alliances.

The role of those countries should not be underestimated, but they still cannot be taken as a decisive factor of European security. As much as these countries can help to achieve consensus whenever the two opposed sides are ready and willing to do so, they cannot prevent a clash, or even serious tensions, in periods of deteriorating relations between the East and the West. Hence, they are mostly important in periods of détente and efforts to control the conflict.

Fortunately, the realization of catastrophic and uncontrollable results of an open conflict within Europe makes the task of the N+N countries easier and more effective. Furthermore, the danger to peace in Europe comes primarily, if not exclusively, from conflicts and clashes in the world outside the European security zone. Hence the role of the non-aligned in the Movement of the Non-Aligned Countries has also an important role in regard of European security.

The Threat of Spreading of Regional Conflicts to Europe

A strictly realistic appraisal of the current situation in the world, would indicate that the spread of regional conflicts to Europe, or their development into world-wide conflicts, is not an immediate threat, but it cannot be excluded either. There have been tense moments during the long conflicts in the Middle East, but at no time did the danger of spreading become really acute. The most tense incident including real danger occurred however in the final stage of the Arab-Israeli war of 1973. The United States declared an alert for a large part of its armed forces in reply to certain reported movements of Soviet units which could be brought to the battlefield at the Suez Canal.

Another form of extending war to Europe would be a more or less direct involvement of the two major Powers in conflicts or situations in the Third World. There are more examples of extremely dangerous tensions which could have led to serious armed conflicts. Korea, Cuba and Vietnam are only some of the best known instances. Therefore the danger of conflicts originating in the Third World for peace and security in the world, and that means also in Europe, cannot be taken lightly. Yet, one can assume that the inhibitions referred to earlier would function also in the future.

The main task of this article is, in fact, the examination of the real and possible roles of the non-aligned acting against this threat. Quite obviously, the non-aligned countries in the world outside the European zone do not possess material forces which could restrain or control the activities of major powers if inhibitions against war should fail. It might, therefore, appear that their role could not be more important than the role of the N+N Group within Europe. We shall see that this is partly true, but that there are still important differences between the two cases.

First of all, we must define more precisely what is non-alignment and what is the aim and the methods of acting of the movement of the non-aligned. Frequently the gathering of the non-aligned in the Movement is understood as an agreement to conduct certain current foreign policies,

such as not joining the one or the other alliance. This is indeed a requirement for admission, although not the most important one and certainly it
is not enforced very strictly. Furthermore, the laxity in regard of associations of members with the one or the other major power is not a recent
development, as many observers wish us to believe.

Already at the first summit of the non-aligned in Belgrade in 1961 Cuba
was present, although Havana had then as close relations with Moscow
as she has now. On the other hand, we can find among the statesmen
assembled in Belgrade in 1961 also some close friends of the United
States, for instance the representatives of Saudi Arabia. The records of
this first summit give us a solid basis for the understanding of the aims
and intentions of the countries there assembled. These fundamental
aims did not change, and efforts made to that effect in Havana in 1979,
failed.

In the first place, the Movement is an association of the Third World
countries. The presence of Yugoslavia is the result of the experience of
that country in the early post-war years. Yugoslavia came into a bitter
conflict with the Soviet Union and at the same time had very bad relations
with the Western powers over the Trieste problem. On a more durable
basis, it turned out that Yugoslavia, although a socialist country, could in
principle not accept a close association with the East, and remained
unwilling to join the Western associations. The other two non-aligned
European countries are Cyprus and Malta. They are also exceptional
cases, politically as well as geographically.

The Third World character of non-alignment should however not be
taken as a geographical definition of the Movement. The two essential
elements of the platform on which non-alignment stands are, first, the
striving for a more rapid development of the more or less underdevel-
oped societies. The other is joining efforts with the aim of changing
conditions in the world so as to make it easier to overcome the handicap
under which they are labouring on the world scene, to secure their
autonomy and identity as new nations.

Hence a more or less openly expressed and pursued friendship or
affinity towards one or the other major powers can be tolerated as long as
the country in question remains ready to act jointly with other non-
aligned countries towards the attainment of the main aims. The critical
moment in Havana, regarding Cuba, was not her closeness to the Soviet
Union, important was her readiness at the end of the Conference to accept the final document although it was purged of the pro-Soviet bias
included by Cuba in the draft. The acceptance of the final document,
reiterating the main principles and aims of the Movement, was the
decisive test.

The Moral Power of the Third World

The main ways and means of the non-aligned are massive actions in the
United Nations and in specialized meetings. The aim is usually the
strengthening of the position of Third World countries as a whole or
checking actions, interventions or other forms of undue interference

from outside with the rights or interests of Third World countries. The main way of acting is moral pressure and influencing public opinion in the world.

All this may sound rather irrelevant in comparison with forceful actions based on military or economic might. However, the moral power of the Third World, incorporated in the Movement, has until now produced quite remarkable results. Let us only mention the fact that in most conflicts of Third World countries with industrialized powers, including wars fought with impressive armed forces and equipment, the Third World countries have won their goals. The result has been the disappearance of colonial empires and the withdrawal of foreign forces which were introduced to impose certain solutions.

These results, one may object, were not the result of specific actions of the Movement of the Non-aligned, and many of them happened even before it came into being. This is, of course, correct. The Movement does not claim to be, nor would it make sense of interpreting it as a separate entity, as an independent actor in current affairs. The Movement has not an autonomous will, it is in fact the expression of the collective will and aspirations of the awakened Third World nations. This explains also its ability to survive setbacks and internal conflicts about current national interests, and even wars between members.

As can be seen, we do not speak of the Movement preventing this or that violent action or threat to peace and security, but of creating a general atmosphere and conditions which make it more difficult for any power, which might wish to disturb peace in the world.

In conclusion, we must accept that Europe and its problems no longer determine the future of the world, but also face the fact that there is an inevitable linkage between European and world security. Europe, although no longer a generator of peace or war in the whole world, is a sensitive region and is in the centre of the major contention between the two most powerful states of the world. It can play a constructive role in world affairs only inasmuch as it can assert its own will and interests, mollifying the rigidity of the controversy of the major Powers. Europe can thus lower the tensions in the centre of the field of controversy.

The non-aligned in the Third World on the other hand have no way of influencing directly relations in Europe, but they can in the long run strengthen peace and security in the Third World. As a matter of fact, they have done so in the past. If not by other means, this was done by preventing the major powers from spreading the military alliances more in the Third World. A zone of non-alignment covering most of the Third World certainly can be called an important contribution to the control of tensions between the two major Powers. Thus, security in Europe had the indirect benefit of the activities of the non-aligned in the Third World.

8

The Political Role of the European Community in the CSCE

Philippe Moreau Defarges

At the Conference on Security and Cooperation in Europe, the European Community was able to assert itself internationally for the first time as a "distinct entity with a common security policy"[1]. Both the Economic Community (second basket) and Europe of Nine with its humanitarian goals would, it seemed, become a political force which would be able to mediate between East and West. Eight years later, after the meetings in Belgrade (June 1977— March 1978) and Madrid (November 1980 — September 1983) and before that of Vienna (1986), Europe of Ten seems generally to have lost its particular character. Could it be that the meeting at Helsinki — Geneva was just an exceptional, limited effort, the result only of special circumstances?

The change in East-West relations since 1975, the questioning of détente, the 1979—83 crises (Afghanistan, euromissiles, Poland, the South Korean plane disaster) were very revealing. They pinpointed the Community's weaknesses and its only partial unity, a unity constantly questioned by member states.

The Initial Factor: The Emergence at Helsinki of the European Community as a Separate Force (July 1973 - August 1975)

The Helsinki conference came at a specific historical and political time. Détente was at its height, albeit brief and precarious. The United States was going through "years of upheaval" as Henry Kissinger put it. The Vietnam war which had finished with the fall of Saigon in the spring of 1975, the Watergate affair and the resignation of President Richard Nixon (8 August 1975) all threw doubt on the ability of the US to lead the Western world.

At the same time, the EC found itself faced with contradictions. On the one hand, Europe at this time seemed to be a real success, almost a model of its kind. Since 1970, political cooperation — a system of

diplomatic consultation — increased and reinforced economic integration, although it was not itself part of this integration. In 1971 and
1972, the first steps were taken towards an economic and monetary
union. Finally, on 1 January 1973, the Community welcomed into its
ranks Great Britain, Denmark and Ireland.

In short, the Community, the biggest commercial union in the world
bringing together three of the oldest nations (France, Germany and
Britain), might then have been a third force in the world, becoming, in the
confrontation between the Super-Powers, "a force for peace, reason and
freedom" (André Fontaine). In the early 1970s, talks with the Eastern
bloc developed and expanded regularly, first through Gaullist diplomacy
and then through Chancellor Willy Brandt's *Ostpolitik*.

And yet in 1973, a key year in every respect, this unity was in fact
flawed. Henry Kissinger, who became Secretary of State on 22 August
1973, launched his "Year of Europe": "While recognizing the structure
of Europe, the US does not consider it to be an end in itself but rather a
means of strengthening the West as a whole, a basic element in a wider
Atlantic association" (speech on 12 December 1973). In fact Kissinger's
vision of a tiered system, encompassing the Community, met with reservations from the French and general indifference from the rest of Europe.

However, if Kissinger met with partial failure, Europe itself proved to
have neither unity nor will-power. This was clearly revealed during the
Yom Kippur war with restrictions in petrol supplies from the Organization
of the Arab Oil Exporters. Unity was shattered. France, protected from
the worst effects through its Arab policy, was accused of being selfish.
But above all, the lack of unity was evident in Washington in front of
Kissinger at the Energy Conference (11—13 February 1974) when eight
member-states of the Community decided to adopt a joint energy policy
(the International Energy Agency) with France alone refusing to join.

Even towards the Eastern bloc, in particular the USSR, the EC found
itself in a dilemma. The USSR rejected the idea of official contacts with
what it considered to be an "imperialist war machine". And yet "both
politically and economically the EEC is a major factor in Europe... At
the end of the 1970s the European centre of the capitalist nations was
becoming increasingly independent of the other centre i.e. the United
States" (N.N. Inozemtsev)[2].

The existence of the EEC was at least accepted as a fact and several
East European countries — Rumania, Hungary... — set up specific
agreements with the Community.

These political events throw some light on the particular nature of the
EC at the time of the Helsinki conference. At Helsinki, the discussions
were mainly on statements and principles. The interests of the individual
nations were not challenged. Similarly vis-à-vis the Israeli-Arab conflict
— the second field about which the Community adopted a common
political stand in the years 1977—80 —, it was a question of setting up
guidelines, of adopting resolutions, and not of negotiating. In the first half
of the 1970s, it seemed that responsibilities were divided in Europe of
Nine between bilateral and multilateral diplomacies; the nations, first the
Federal Republic of Germany, worked out their individual problems with

the Eastern bloc, while the EC as such set out general policy.

The Two Peculiarities of Europe at the Helsinki Conference

In fact, the Nine were present in **two forms**. On political questions (first and second baskets), it was the Europe of political cooperation and joint diplomatic action. The EC as an economic organisation was only concerned with the second basket.

Since the EC was not legally recognised by certain participants (in particular the USSR), its views were put forward through one of the national delegations, that of the Community's president.[3] On economic matters the Commission within the president's own national delegation became the spokesman. On political questions the president's national delegation expressed the opinions of the Nine after, of course, having discussed the questions together previously: "The convenient division of subjects within the framework of the Conference on Security and Cooperation in Europe (CSCE) into political and economic baskets, each serviced by separate working groups, fitted this organizational division fairly well; although there were occasions, during the Community's first discussions about contacts with Comecon and a concerted policy towards the East European countries, when Council committees consisting of representatives from national foreign ministries' economic directorates came close to conceding points which were being held firm as bargaining counters in Helsinki or Geneva".[4]

Finally, at Helsinki, since the US was only there as a kind of observer, the Nine emerged as an independent body. There was some friction between the United Kingdom, the FRG and France. The last one systematically supported European independence. However, "Instead of dividing the Nine, as some had feared, the CSCE managed to bring them together in one very important area of foreign policy. The signing of the Final Document of the CSCE by the Italian Prime Minister in his role as President of the Council of the European Community must also be considered to be the actual recognition of the Community by the East. Cooperation between the Nine and the USA has considerably revitalized within the West".[5]

This was soon to appear as a rather overoptimistic view.

The Basic Situation Changes Completely

Unity at Helsinki was in a way overestimated. It had come about through a set of circumstances which, already at the time of the conference, were about to change radically.

Obviously, the greatest change was in the disintegration of détente — the arrival of the "cool war" (Brezhnev) — in the second half of the 1970s. The Community's room for manoeuvre and self-assertion was restricted.

On the one hand, tension between the EC (joined by Greece in 1981) and the United States meant that the European entity hesitated between support for the West and its own desire for independence. The crises in Afghanistan, Iran and Poland showed a US firm in its resolve and a

Europe anxious to compromise. The US viewed détente as nothing but a stratagem to the advantage of the USSR whereas Europe wanted to keep alive talks with the Eastern bloc.

In addition, faced with these stumbling blocks to improvement in East/-West relations, the European nations reacted nationally. The member nations in their relations with the Communist bloc "opted in varying degrees for bilateral competition rather than more effective means of cooperation, or even a delegation of their powers to the Commission. It would appear that whenever governments have to face urgent internal or external problems they have less and less confidence in institutional machinery".[6]

Afghanistan, (Warsaw meeting between Leonid Brezhnev and Giscard d'Estaing, 19 May 1980), or the question of euromissiles (Chancellor Helmut Schmidt's visit to Moscow, July 1980) showed just how deeply the bilateral reflex was ingrained. The EC's ability to mediate through parliamentary-type conferences seems to dissolve in a crisis, especially when crises come in rapid succession.

Finally, the growing recognition of the Community which Helsinki seemed to have established did not continue to develop or was indeed perhaps just an illusion. The *de facto* recognition did not translate itself into law.

At the same time, talks parallel to those of the CSCE began between the EEC and the CMEA (Council for Mutual Economic Assistance) in August 1973 and became official in 1976 (the CMEA proposed agreement with the EEC on general terms of trade and co-operation).[7] Although the setting up of links between the two economic organisations was the logical outcome of détente between the two sides of Europe and of the CSCE, fundamental differences existed between the two institutions. The EC was the concrete symbol of a Western European force distinct from, and sometimes opposed to, the US and one which would become the basis of future confederation, whereas the CMEA, dominated by the USSR, was an integral part of the Eastern bloc.

Furthermore, the commercial and economic integration of the EC was complete and irreversible whereas the CMEA was only reluctantly supported by most of the Eastern European nations (trade is three times as great within the EEC as in the CMEA). So, the nature of the EEC/CMEA talks was distorted from the start. The EEC wanted to encourage and support Eastern Europe's hopes for independence whereas the very fact of mutual recognition between the EEC and the CMEA reinforced the idea that there were two separate identities and therefore two separate Europes. There have been occasional talks between the two organisations but as yet there have been no results...[8]

The impossibility of reaching an agreement throws light on the ambiguity which lay at the heart of the EC's action at Helsinki. The objective was the recognition of Europe as a plurality of nations and the key to this lay with the USSR. The stand taken by Europe as a whole, as well as individual nations, was marked by the tension between the pressures of power politics and the desire to reconstitute a European space of freedom.

As for European political cooperation, the Nine, then the Ten, showed their unity over certain principles concerning Afghanistan and Poland but had to face Moscow's refusal of recognition. The Carrington proposals for a European summit conference on Afghanistan made in the name of the Community in July 1981 were rejected. An attempt to send a European emissary to Poland at the height of tension (the martial law proclamation on 13 December 1981) was aborted.

Finally, between Helsinki and Belgrade, then between Belgrade and Madrid, Madrid and Stockholm, the basic situation changed, forcing the European group to re-examine its position. At Helsinki the question of détente and the passive participation of the US aside, questions dealt within the second and the third baskets encouraged European initiatives. The Nine, then the Ten, were united on practical measures concerning individual rights (personal and professional contacts, family visits, etc.).

In Belgrade, because of stiffening attitudes, the Mediterranean problem (a subject already raised at the Helsinki Conference where several non-European nations, such as Morocco, Algeria, Tunisia, Egypt, Syria and Lebanon gave statements) was one of the few questions that gave rise to some debate. Only France put forward the idea that there should be a meeting of only those countries bordering the Mediterranean (Mediterranean Working group, November 1977). But more significantly, the question of security in Madrid became so important that it considerably reduced the role of European concertation as distinct from that of the Atlantic nations. In Stockholm (the Conference on Disarmament in Europe), the question of disarmament and its military implications in particular, was left to member states, political cooperation being concerned only with regard to "certain important foreign policy questions relating to aspects of security policies".[9]

The Role and Contradictions of the European Community in the Helsinki Process

The deterioration in international relations, the Eastern bloc's recognition *de facto* but not *de jure* of the EC and a change in prospects, all altered the EC's position in the Helsinki process. Between Helsinki and Belgrade, and then between Belgrade and Madrid, the Nine then the Ten showed just how weak and incomplete their unity was.

Of course the institutions themselves, the infrastructure of the coordination between the Community matters and European Political Cooperation improved and unified between Helsinki and Belgrade. Within the Permanent Representative Committee in Brussels, a CSCE group covering the second basket was set up to prepare the Belgrade meeting. Thanks in particular to the Commission members, links between this group and that of political cooperation were strengthened. But the basic obstacles were not administrative but political. The CSCE process was just one factor in East-West relations. What détente had never dealt with, the renewed tension emphasised this.

The United Kingdom continued its close relationship with the United States while France considered it essential to maintain and to be seen to maintain its independence. However, there was then a change of events: in May 1981 François Mitterrand who was very much concerned with human rights was elected the President of France. Even more importantly, he gave his support to the installation of US missiles in retaliation to the installation of Soviet SS 20's. The FRG could not consider to withdraw from talks begun with the East, particularly with the GDR. But the changing nature of European unity was most apparent after Greece joined the EEC in 1981 and refused to condemn the USSR. (This was very obvious after the South Korean plane was brought down by a Soviet fighter on 31 August 1983).[10] National interests did not disappear despite the links between the Ten; and the chain of events 1979 seemed only to harden national attitudes. The crisis management guidelines set up by **the London Report** (13 October 1981) made no difference. Following the martial law in Poland, several EC nations opposed setting the crisis machinery in action.

In Belgrade the balance of power had changed. The US through their representative Arthur Goldberg was ready for confrontation. Within the EC, France tried in vain to mediate (on 17 February 1978, the French proposal for a final document was dismissed summarily by the Soviet delegation). Indeed, France's partners preferred to stress solidarity with the US. At Belgrade links were forged between countries of similar culture. Denmark became the intermediary for the EC and Scandinavia and an informal German-speaking group made up of the two Germanies, Austria, Switzerland and Liechtenstein, supervised on linguistic exactitude of the documents.

In Madrid, although the Ten remained united in their position on human rights and over what practical measures to adopt, they were separated by changing international events. After the martial law in Poland, Italy and the UK, together with the US felt that any agreement in Madrid was impossible whereas France and the FRG thought negotiations should continue. This is what happened. The Ten characteristically compromised — Europe does not know how to say no! Above all the importance of military questions (the French proposal for a European Disarmament Conference) switched the centre of concerted action to the Atlantic group.

So it is increasingly the neutral and non-aligned nations who play the role of mediator.

The Conference on Disarmament in Europe

The Stockholm conference on confidence- and security-building measures and disarmament in Europe, which began on 17 January 1984, was the result of a French proposal. At no time did it become a proposal made by the Nine. Thus, on 20 November 1979, the Nine gave their support to the guidelines which inspired the proposals made by the French in May 1978 to the 35 signatories of the Helsinki agreement. In Stockholm the generally united approach adopted by the West at the opening of the conference was remarkable. The identity of views held by the Atlantic Alliance seemed complete. After one week's work the

16 NATO memberstates put forward an official six point proposal subsequently referred to as a "package deal" in conference jargon.[11]

In the CSCE process as in other areas of diplomacy (the Israeli-Arab conflict, relations with the US), the EC was soon confronted with basic problems. Its aim remains the establishment of a political body. But at present it is still **an association of sovereign nations** which changes with every crisis and round of negotiations. Thus until Europe takes a major step forward which will transform it into a real power, this will remain the role of the EC.

The ambiguity which appeared between Helsinki and Madrid can only persist. With twelve member states in 1986, there will be even more differences and more contradictions. The Western summit in Bonn (2—4 May 1985), while emphasising that "the CSCE in which so much hope was invested for the improvement of human rights, should strengthen mutual trust, cooperation and security in Europe", underlined all the divisions of the Ten when faced with the US (particularly about the opening of the new trade negotiations inside the GATT and the Strategic Defence Initiative).

But, in the eyes of the EC, the CSCE process (even if the number of East-West meetings increases up to the plenary session in Vienna 4 November 1986) is only of secondary importance. The debate on West European — US relations, postponed after the euromissile crisis, was again renewed over the questions of trade and of "Star Wars." The arrival of Mikhail Gorbachev and his team at the head of the USSR will also result in some hard thinking within the Ten (then the Twelve) about the Soviet Union and the possibility of a European — Soviet dialogue.

Notes

1. Karl Kaiser, Cesare Merlini, Thierry de Montbrial, William Wallace, Edmond Wellenstein, *The European Community: Progress or Decline,* Royal Institute of International Affairs, Institut Français des Relations Internationales, 1983.
2. N.N. Inozemtsev, *The International Relations in Europe in the 1970's, Europe 1980,* Institut Universitaire des Hautes Etudes Internationales de Genève, 1972, p. 129.
3. First semester 1973: Belgium,
   Second semester 1973: Denmark,
   First semester 1974: Federal Republic of Germany,
   Second semester 1974: France,
   First semester 1975: Ireland,
   Second semester 1975: Italy,
4. William Wallace, "National Inputs into European Political Cooperation", in *European Political Cooperation,* ed. by David Allen, Rheinhardt Rummel, Wolfgang Wessels, Butterworths European Studies, 1982, p. 47.
5. Götz von Groll, "The Nine at the Conference on Security and Cooperation in Europe", quoted in (4), pp. 67—68.
6. Pierre Hassner, *Les politiques envers l'Est, rivalités et convergences dans "Les politiques extérieures européennes dans la crise",* the Fondation Nationale des Sciences Politiques, Paris, 1976, 74.
7. As from January 1st 1975, the negotiation and signing of trade agreements comes under the authority of the EEC. However, all agreements on cooperation and particularly industrial agreements remain under the control of member states.

8. At present, only Rumania among the CMEA nations has signed an agreement with the EEC.

9. Extract from the *London Report,* October 13th 1981.

10. Similarly, after the declaration of martial law in Poland on 13 December 1981, the European Council in its declaration on 30 March 1982 pointed out "that the situation in Poland continues to influence East-West relations and therefore affects the relations of the Ten with Poland and the USSR which is responsible for the situation". In another paragraph of the declaration, "the Hellenic delegation made a reservation concerning that part of the first sentence which states that the relationship between the Ten and the USSR is influenced by events in Poland".

11. Victor—Yves Ghebali, "The Stockholm Conference — Preliminary Perspectives", *Défense Nationale,* juin 1984, p. 58.

9

The CSCE as a Forum: How to Increase the Efficiency of Decision-Making

Rudolf Th. Jurrjens

Introduction

In the preparatory phase of the second CSCE follow-up meeting in Madrid the basis was laid for an effort to bring the meeting to its conclusion in March 1981, once more with a concluding document which, it was hoped, would have more breadth and content than the one of its predecessor of Belgrade. Finally, after a conference of unanticipated duration, crammed with debates that bristled with bitterly enunciated accusations and inculpations, the desired result was achieved three years later in September 1983. The atmosphere of the final session when the 35 foreign ministers adopted the concluding document reflected the increased tension between the participating states, which already played so drastic a role throughout the conference.

It comes therefore as no surprise to find that although the Madrid Concluding Document does have as a concrete result the pushing forward of the CSCE process in a further series of meetings mandated in the document, the text is largely limited to setting out a catalogue of the problems that exist without describing authoritatively how they should be solved.

It may be asked whether, with of without the increased tension between the participants, it might have been possible to reach a similar outcome in a more efficient way, or even perhaps whether a different approach to negotiations that were of such magnitude might not have led to markedly better results.

The personal feelings of relief experienced by more than one Madrid diplomat when the final consensus was reached deserve every sympathy. What had seemed to be a never-ending litany could at last be rounded off with an "Amen" even if one that was less than heartly, but for the future, they hoped that never again would they have to go through such an experience: Madrid never again.

On the basis of the conditions of the Madrid Meeting with regard to agenda, institutional framework and rules of procedure and the way these conditions affected the organization, course and results of the meeting in Madrid, an attempt will be made here to recommend modifications of an organizational and procedural nature which may lead to greater efficiency in the decision-making process of future meetings and also, hopefully, to the achievement of results of higher political value.

The series of recommendations, each followed by a discussion, which are formulated here,* respectively deal with the agenda, the follow-up system and the rules of procedure which reign the CSCE-meetings. The recommendations have been so designed that each one is capable of execution independently of the rest but they should also be regarded as interrelated and together constitute a package.

Agenda

Recommendation 1:

> Participating states should exercise the greatest restraint in putting forward proposals to be approved by the next follow-up meeting: a single political group of countries should contribute not more than one proposal per basket, focussed on the most important problem in the relations between the 35 states.

Recommendation 2:

> Neither a substantive concluding document nor any other comprehensive final document should be aimed at: the function of such a document can be performed by a small number of separate chairman's statements.

The Madrid Concluding Document is an extensive document representing nearly three years of negotiation on 87 proposals. The repetition of such an exercise is not to be recommended. Madrid, never again! The provisions contained in the Madrid document vary in importance. The most important Western and East European proposals occupy a disproportionate place. It would seem to be more efficient and less time-consuming if negotiations were concentrated only on proposals that are of essential interest in the relations between the 35 states. Whether such negotiations would be likely to achieve results would depend, as always, on the political climate of the moment, but it would at least become swiftly apparent what the prospects were for a useful outcome.

The Final Act does not require the follow-up meetings to produce a final document at all. Towards the end of the Madrid negotiations the mechanism of the chairman's statement proved to be an effective method of reaching consensus. The less text there is to be agreed the less time consensus takes to reach. On the other hand the consensus rule might still be used to veto one chairman's statement until agreement is reached on a different one; conditional linkages of this sort are unavoidable where the rule of consensus has absolute force. Therefore the pattern of negotiations would remain unchanged. As a result, the "balance" desired by the participating states would grow out of the negotiations themselves.

If follow-up meetings confine themselves in future to the approval of a limited number of chairman's statements, this is not to prevent any future Conference — say once every ten years — from attempting to achieve a balanced and substantive consluding document which might then include the chairman's statements from preceding years or use these statements as a starting point for negotiations.

The Follow-Up System

Recommendation 3:

> The Preparatory Meeting in Vienna should take a decision on the duration of the interval between the Vienna Meeting and the fourth Follow-up Meeting, one of say two years. The main Vienna Meeting should then decide on the periodicity and duration of follow-up meetings in the future (for example, biennial meetings of perhaps six weeks before and six weeks after a Christmas recess). The possibility of interim meetings between regularly scheduled follow-up meetings should be left open.

In Geneva, during negotiations on the Final Act, it was the East European countries that fought for an automatic succession of follow-up meetings; the West preferred to envisage the taking of a specific decision for holding each succeeding follow-up meeting. During the Preparatory Meeting in Madrid positions were reversed because the East European countries were not inclined to take a decision for holding a third follow-up meeting after Madrid, while the West, together with the N+N countries now laid great stress on it. The question of whether there would be a further follow-up meeting at all, a point sometimes hotly discussed in Madrid during the first two years, now appears to have been somewhat academic; which of the 35 participating states can afford, politically, to stop the CSCE follow-up process? The CSCE is here to stay.

There is nothing in the Final Act to prevent strengthening the institutionalization of the CSCE and regulating the follow-up process. Certainty on the question of whether there will be a fourth follow-up meeting after Vienna, would improve the climate of negotiation in Vienna.

The Executive Secretary (see Recommendation 13) should be given the right, during periods between follow-up meetings and at the request of one of the participating states, to call a meeting of CSCE ambassadors which could then decide to convoke an *ad hoc* CSCE meeting at the level of representatives of ministers of foreign affairs. This might be done in the event of sudden crises in relations between the 35 states in consequence of alleged flagrant violation of the letter or spirit of the Final Act. The rule-suprevisory function of the CSCE (or, in CSCE shorthand, the implementation discussion) would be strengthened in this way. Even if the meeting of CSCE ambassadors should be unable to decide on calling an *ad hoc* meeting of the normal follow-up type, because of lack of consensus, a rule-supervisory gesture would nevertheless have been made.

Recommendation 4:

> Every encouragement should be given to the efforts already begun by the Madrid Meeting to declare the existing rules of procedure, agenda, working programme and other modalities of follow-up meetings valid, *mutatis mutandis,* for future meetings as well. The Blue Book and the Purple Book should be recognized as regulating the conditions of all succeeding follow-up meetings.

The Madrid Concluding Document provides that "the agenda, working programme and modalities of the main Madrid Meeting will be applied *mutatis mutandis* to the main Vienna Meeting, unless other decisions on these questions are taken by the preparatory meeting...". This means that both the Purple Book and the Blue Book have been declared to apply to Vienna unless there is a consensus to depart from them. Thus no further consensus is required in order to formulate new rules of procedure. Recommendation 4 more or less comes down to changing the words in the quotation given above from "the main Vienna meeting" to "all other Follow-up meetings". This would palpably lighten the task of every preparatory meeting preceding a follow-up meeting and so increase the efficiency of preparation. The degree of institutionalization of the CSCE would be raised by this measure.

Recommendation 5:

> The Executive Secretary from the most recent host country should be held to be responsible for the CSCE secretariat up to the moment at the beginning of the succeeding follow-up meeting when the Executive Secretary from the new host country takes over the responsibility.

This recommendation follows the rule from the Blue Book that the retiring chairman remains responsible until the new session begins. The retiring Executive Secretary should be obliged to bear responsibility for his secretarial tasks up to the moment when he can hand over his responsibility to his successor by means of a symbolic handshake, a gesture that would then serve to underline the continuity of the CSCE.

In the interim period up to this moment the retiring Executive Secretary would carry out the tasks allotted to him in Recommendation 13.

Recommendation 6:

> The two jobs of a follow-up meeting, review of implementation of the Final Act and examination of new proposals, should not have to be done at separate times but could from the very beginning of the meeting go on simultaneously.

In Madrid the West wanted to follow the same programme as had been followed in Belgrade, devoting the first weeks of the meeting to discussion of implementation alone and only subsequently going on to examination of new proposals. In fact the implementation discussion continued in Madrid from first to last. Much time would be gained if new proposals were introduced immediately after the meeting's opening and their examination initiated in formal or informal working groups in parallel with the Plenary's discussion of implementation. The Purple Book's timetable would have to be adapted to this purpose, under the *mutatis mutandis* rule.

Recommendation 7:

> The trend begun in Madrid to make greater use of the possibility of organizing expert meetings, should be continued. Each succeeding follow-up meeting should pay more attention to the results of such interim meetings.

In Belgrade it was decided to hold one expert meeting on peaceful settlement of disputes, one on co-operation in the Mediterranean and also a Scientific Forum. Three expert meetings were decided on in Madrid together with one forum, one seminar, a commemoration of the tenth anniversary of the Final Act and a disarmament conference extending over a long period. This proliferation of expert meetings reinforces the multilateral CSCE follow-up process. Any tendency for such meetings to detract from the importance of the real follow-up meetings will be annulled if the follow-up meetings make fuller use of the results of the expert meetings, both in discussions and in the formulation of the concluding chairman's statements.

Recommendation 8:

> However unrealistic organizational links with UNO organs may appear to be, the practice of engaging certain of these organs in the CSCE process should be actively continued.

In the options for an institutional framework for the CSCE suggested by theorists in the early seventies, much attention was paid to the possibility of establishing organizational links with the UNO. Among the suggestions was one for a regional framework with links to the Security Council. The options as a whole are now of little more than academic interest because it is clear that consensus for their adoption will never be achieved in the CSCE, if only for the reason that various CSCE members, such as Switzerland and the Holy See, are not UN members and have no wish to be connected with it. In the Madrid Concluding Document the CSCE states issued one invitation and six recommendations to the ECE and on one occasion expressed their interest in UNESCO activity. The ECE came in for special mention because it is itself concerned with the same subjects as fall into the second basket of the Final Act, over the same geographical area. On the other hand, non-European members of UNESCO and other UN organs cannot be expected to interest themselves in purely European affairs. Yet where CSCE countries succeed in reaching agreement during follow-up meetings, to delegate certain responsibilities to UN organs, this should be encouraged in the interest of avoiding duplication. It is not the role of the CSCE to duplicate the activities of functional or regional UN organizations.

The Rules of Procedure

Recommendation 9:

> In the context of the application of the rule of consensus to both procedural and substantive matters, it would be more effective to attempt to reach an early consensus firstly by abandoning the effort to achieve an extensive concluding document and aiming for a small number of chairman's statements instead; secondly by going over to drafting in informal work groups at an earlier stage, and thirdly by giving the N+N co-ordinators of such work groups the right to frame Informal Single Negotiating Texts.

The desirability of changing the consensus rule with regard to procedural matters may well be open to question but what is certain is that the rule of consensus can only be replaced by consensus and this consensus will never now be achieved. The same is true with regard to whether in the case of substantive matters the consensus rule should be altered to allow some sort of voting procedure: consensus on this is no longer possible.

If the rule of consensus is there to stay in the CSCE, then what must be looked for is how to achieve results more quickly than was the case in Madrid. It is more difficult to get consensus for an extensive concluding document like that of Madrid than for a restricted number of chairman's statements. The lesson of the Madrid experience is that agreement can be reached in a reasonable time on the text of a chairman's statement because it has a concrete content which can be grasped from the beginning. If, in parallel with official treatment of the agenda, informal negotiation is started at a much earlier stage, considerable time is saved. During the informal negotiations the N+N co-ordinators might make use of Informal Single Negotiating Texts, at an earlier stage, as was the practice in UNCLOS III, in order to put forward their perception of a possible basis for consensus.

Recommendation 10:

> More intensive use of formal reservations and interpretative statements should not be encouraged.

Formal reservations and interpretative statements are necessary escape mechanisms which accelerate the decision-making process if adequate use is made of them. The only way of making them more attractive would be to give them a status equivalent to that of the decision to which they refer; this could be done by appending them to the decision itself together with which they would then be published. However, if it were known that such unilateral declarations would receive the same publicity as the final documents, other delegations would feel obliged to state their views on the subject as well. As a maximum result the concluding documents would be accompanied by 35 unilateral declarations.

It would therefore be better to continue the practice followed in Madrid and to regard this escape mechanism as a last resort enabling a delegation to avoid blocking consensus without losing face. An intensive use of unilateral interpretative statements and formal reservations would open the way for each state to dine *à la carte* and, in the end, rob consensus of its meaning as the ideal of the CSCE.

Recommendation 11:

> If the change-over to informal negotiation happens at an earlier stage (see Recommendation 9) there will be no need to interfere with the rule of daily rotation of the chairmanship; the provision for departure from this rule in the Blue Book should be used if a formal drafting group itself goes over to actual drafting.

Daily rotation of the chairmanship is an expression of the principle of equality of all the CSCE states which gives it an interest which far outweighs its drawbacks. The drawbacks themselves can be avoided by leaving the actual drafting to informal working bodies. In Madrid the one formal drafting group in which actual drafting was done was the one on co-operation in the Mediterranean where the East-West conflict had no role to play. In such a situation it is possible to revert to rule 71 (b) of the Blue Book and establish "a basis of rotation in accordance with practical arrangements".

Recommendation 12:

> In the absence of an extensive concluding document as an objective, this having been replaced by the ideal of a small number of chairman's statements, the Plenary should fulfil its role as central organ in the formally-prescribed procedure by establishing guidelines at an early stage, which should lay down the number of chairman's statements to be agreed and the areas they should cover, so that the bottom-up approach can function more effectively.

The bottom-up approach would be more efficient if the negotiators in formal or informal work groups had a general principle of reference at their disposal from the beginning. If the Plenary, which, according to the Purple Book, is the main body of the meeting, indicated the number and subject matter of the chairman's statements (for example one per basket) then the structure of the final result would already be established which would prevent a succession of events similar to the Malta phase.

Recommendation 13:

> The Executive Secretary for technical matters should be given the following additional responsibilities:
> a) before the Meeting: to formulate and distribute the Purple Book *mutatis mutandis;*
> b) during the Meeting: to report on any complaints about fulfilment of the Final Act received during the interim period; to provide technical support for co-ordinators in arriving at single negotiating texts;
> c) after the Meeting: to provide a clearing house for complaints about violation of the Final Act or the Madrid Concluding Document

and to call a meeting of the CSCE ambassadors if requested to do so by a CSCE state.

The last line of the Final Act reads: "The services of a technical secretariat will be provided by the host country". According to the Blue Book the Executive Secretary is to be concerned only with technical matters. Within such limits it is impossible to create an institutionalized permanent, international CSCE secretariat. The recommendations given above are only intended to increase the **permanence** and **degree of institutionalization** of the CSCE to the extent possible within these limits. As, in future, the Purple Book is only to be "adjusted" in order to serve for the next follow-up meeting, and these "adjustments" are considered to be merely of a technical nature, the Executive Secretary and his secretariat may properly frame and circulate a draft for the adjusted Purple Book. During the Meeting the Executive Secretary and his secretariat should be more actively and intensively involved in the N+N co-ordinators' efforts to produce their negotiating texts and made fully responsible, for example, for registration and distribution of proposals, amendments, textual changes and decisions on which agreement has been reached, or in other words given the job of archivist and registrar.

In the interim period, that is, after any one Meeting, the secretariat should act as **clearing house** for complaints put in by participating states on fulfilment of the Final Act and the Madrid Concluding Document by other CSCE states. These complaints would be published and distributed by the secretariat. If any state so required, the secretariat would call a meeting of CSCE ambassadors, empowered to decide to convoke an *ad hoc* CSCE meeting following a consensus (see Recommendation 3). This new function for the secretariat would lay stress on the importance of the multilateral CSCE follow-up process.

Recommendation 14:

It should not be automatically considered necessary for every document to be translated into all official languages with the least possible delay.

In Madrid the language staff accounted for the largest portion of all costs of the executive secretariat. Yet consensus will never be reached for dropping any one of the six official languages. Costs might rather be reduced by circulating all ephemeral documents in only one working language, the one in which they were originally drafted, leaving it in case of need to the delegations' language experts themselves to translate them. Such an arrangement would mean that secretariat translators would be required only in the last phase of the meeting in order to prepare the various language versions of the texts previously agreed by consensus.

Recommendation 15:

Journals of closed sessions should be produced only if there are decisions, formal reservations or interpretative statements to be registered. The verbatim texts of the opening and closing statements during the open sessions should be published only in the language in which they are delivered.

In Madrid 336 Journals amounting to 803 pages issued in six languages were published and distributed on a wide scale. A small number contain records of consensus on particular decisions or reservations and inter-pretative statements included at the request of one or more delegations. The rest are of no interest because all they contain is lists of which delegations contributed to the session, without the text of what was said. To carry out empty routines of this sort is totally superfluous.

The verbatim record of statements at the Madrid opening sitting filled 350 pages and of this record 782 copies were distributed, 100 in German, 270 in English, 73 in Spanish, 166 in French, 60 in Italian and 113 in Russian. The closing statements had a similar circulation. Publishing only a single text containing each statement in its original language would mean a significant saving of costs. The states themselves could then make what translations they liked in their own home capitals.

Recommendation 16:

All Plenaries should be open to the public but all meetings of both formal and informal working bodies should remain closed.

Opening all the Plenaries to the public would represent a recognition of the CSCE's character as a forum and would also strengthen its rule-supervisory function. As the fact of the matter is that each delegation at present supplies the press with texts of its own interventions in the Plenary it would seem more efficient simply to allow the press to be present at the sessions.

*) This contribution is based on the concluding chapter of Jan Sizoo & Rudolf Th. Jurrjens, *CSCE Decision-Making: The Madrid Experience,* Martinus Nijhoff Publishers, The Hague 1984.

10

Finland's Activity in the CSCE

Klaus Krokfors

Introduction

The process of enhancing European security and cooperation on fora designed for that purpose started with unofficial talks at the end of the 1960s. The tenth anniversary commemoration of signing of the Helsinki Final Act took place in the summer of 1985.

Finland did not choose to be a mere bystander in the course of events on the continent but has, from the beginning, attempted to influence them through active participation.

This report studies this major project of Finland's foreign policy, i.e. Finland's role in the Conference on Security and Cooperation in Europe (CSCE).[1]

Finland's role is observed from three different perspectives. First, Finland's **role:** the special tasks Finland has had in the negotiation mechanism. Finland's foreign policy can be seen as a tool, as instrumental conduct.

Second, Finland's **goals** in substantive questions: which issues Finland has addressed and what initiatives it has made.

Substantive issues have often been intertwined with instrumental conduct, and they have influenced the conference's general progress. On the other hand, the instrumental role of Finland's foreign policy may be a goal and a value as such, in attempts to prove the usefulness of a policy of neutrality. This is the case particularly in the CSCE, where Finland's instrumental role has become emphasized.

Third, Finland's **reference groups,** or its co-operation partners.

Commencement of Multilateral Negotiations

The international atmosphere improved clearly at the end of the 1960s and at the beginning of the 1970s, despite the events in Czechoslovakia, when several agreements normalizing East-West relations were signed. In this, the *Ostpolitik* of the Federal Republic of Germany played a key role. Economic co-operation, too, was undergoing changes.

In 1971, a significant factor of uncertainty in international relations was removed as the winners of the Second World War, France, Great Britain, the United States and the Soviet Union, reached an agreement on the status of West Berlin. The agreement to commence the Mutual Force Reduction Talks in Vienna in the autumn of 1972 enabled the United States to agree to a simultaneous conference on European security and co-operation.

Finland took advantage of international détente and proposed, on 5 May 1969, to all European nations, the United States, and Canada, that a carefully prepared conference on European security be arranged. The idea was not a new one. However, the timing of the proposal was favourable as both the Warsaw Pact and NATO members, in principle, had a positive approach to such a conference.[2] Since the 1950s, Socialist countries had proposed such negotiations. An irregular East-West dialogue on the subject had started in 1966.

In March 1969, the Warsaw Pact made a new proposal on the preparations for the conference. Finland received the proposal on 8 March 1969 and took a serious interest in it after a meeting of NATO's foreign ministers' which was held three days later. The meeting decided to study concrete issues which were negotiable. Later in April, a Nordic foreign ministers' meeting drafted rough outlines for a successful conference and gave its support to a Finnish initiative which was to be published later. The timing was to be favorable for positive results and all countries which had an influence on European security were to be accepted as participants.

Finland's initiative stressed that no prerequisites should be set for the conference. The purpose of this was to postpone such issues as the European *status quo* so that the negotiations could start in a positive atmosphere. Finland's initiative also stated that all participants should have the right to express their own ideas and proposals concerning European issues. Finland's note also determined the question pertaining to the US participation thus removing one obstacle to the upcoming conference.

In the proposal, Finland also cited the objectives set by the Nordic foreign ministers' meeting. No suggestions were made concerning an agenda. Despite earlier initiatives by other countries, Finland has always emphasized the independent character of its initiative.

Enckell's Round

After the submission of the proposal, the discussion on the conference gained momentum. It was important for Finland that it be informed about progress achieved in various contacts and consultations because Finland was a host candidate for the conference it had proposed. To continue its active role, the government of Finland ordered, in April 1970, that Finland's permament representative to the OECD, Ralph Enckell, assume the duties of roving Ambassador.

In the course of his 50 trips, Enckell surveyed the positions of various countries.

Following Enckell's negotiating tour, Finland submitted a new memorandum to all the countries concerned on 24 November 1970. The memorandum proposed that consultations be held in Helsinki with the Finnish Ministry for Foreign Affairs, either bilaterally or multilaterally as agreed, and noted that participation in such consultations would not require participation in the actual conference nor would it mean recognition of the European *status quo.*

The next year, NATO's foreign ministers' meeting gave its approval to the idea and decided to start bilateral talks in Helsinki. Technical preparations for the multilateral talks started in Helsinki in September 1971, in a positive international atmosphere. The US—Soviet relations had improved, particularly after the decisions on the status of West Berlin and the MFR talks. Significant restraints were removed the next year when the West Berlin Agreement and the Eastern Treaties were ratified. The final restraints were removed the year after.

Ambassador Enckell concluded his extensive round of negotiations in April 1972. In May 1972, Finland submitted a memorandum to European and North American countries, which stated that the duration of the upcoming preliminary consultations would be four weeks. All countries responsible for European security, including the United States and Canada, were defined as participants to the consultations.

In July, Finland inquired several countries if 22 November was a suitable date for starting the negotiations. By 9 November, Finland had received confirmation from all the countries, excluding Albania, that they would participate in the consultations. Two days later Finland extended the official invitations.

The Peak of Activity

Finland implemented an active and peace-oriented policy of neutrality displayed through the CSCE initiative. However, the conference initiative was not a completely new form of activity, but a continuation to Finland's earlier activities, of which good examples were the proposals on the Nordic nuclear-weapon-free zone and on the Finnish-Norwegian border peace treaty.

Since the 1960s, Finland had displayed its activity at the UN, in particular. Finland had emphasized her neutrality by developing relations with the two Germanys in a balanced way. The fact that Helsinki was chosen in 1969 to be the site for the Strategic Arms Limitation Talks indicated that a neutral Finland was an acceptable forum for negotiations. Consequently, other significant negotiations could be held here.

Finland's foreign policy activity peaked at the end of the 1960s and the beginning of the 1970s.

Through its proposals, Finland attempted to create long-term processes for enhancing European security. Besides general objectives, Finland had objectives based on its national interests. Strengthening common European security would guarantee and improve the status of such small countries as Finland and reduce speculation on that. Through an active international role, Finland hoped to gain recognition for its national foreign policy and its neutral status, in particular.

Neutrality was a prerequisite for initiatives which sought to produce concrete measures. On the other hand, Finland wanted recognition for its neutrality. Finland did not seek to get exclusive rights to the active pursuit of the conference. Any neutral state could work actively to serve the cause of peace and security.

It was natural that Finland should cooperate with other neutral countries — Austria, Sweden and Switzerland — in the CSCE. Under the new circumstances, neutral countries had an obvious opportunity to contribute by maintaining contacts, by seeking new methods and by acting as mediators.

The Dipoli Consultations and the Helsinki Foreign Ministers' Meeting

An ambassadorial level meeting in Dipoli, Espoo drafted procedural and agenda recommendations for the CSCE which were approved by the Foreign Ministers' meeting held in Helsinki. At the opening day of the Dipoli consultations on 22 November 1972, President Kekkonen defined Finland's role in Europe in the following way:

"Pursuing a policy of peace-oriented neutrality and of good relations with our neighbors, the people of Finland found its place in Europe and in the world years ago. Finland's neutrality built through consistent work has become a positive and permanent part of the European system of balance."

The Host's Difficulties

Finland was the first country to be tested as the host whereby it had to set standards for the future, too. Hosting the conference was not completely without problems. A few days before the Dipoli consultations started, the hosts were criticized for the seating arrangements. Consequently, they were changed to follow the French alphabetic list of names instead of the English so that the two Germanys could be seated next to each other. Since the French word for Germany begins with an A, problems were avoided. This was significant because Finland avoided taking sides in the Great Power conflict which still was unsolved. Finland's neutrality alone dictated the decision to change the seating arrangements.

Although Rumania proposed that a rotation system be applied in chairing the meetings to ensure each participant equal rights, Richard Tötterman, Director General of the Finnish Ministry for Foreign Affairs, was appointed chairman as had been agreed in advance. He chaired the Dipoli consultations through their duration. In addition, Finland had a strong representation in the assistance staff and in the secretariat. Ambassador Jaakko Iloniemi served as special adviser to the chairman.

In its statement in the plenary session of the CSCE's I phase, Finland noted that it might be suitable to charge neutral countries with the responsibility to study confidence-building measures. As a concrete proposal, Finland expressed a wish that President Kekkonen's initiative on the Nordic nuclear-weapon-free zone and on other corresponding zones be taken under investigation on a new basis.

Finland emphasized the comprehensive nature of the process throughout the preliminary phases of the CSCE: security and co-operation are inseparable. President Kekkonen's words at the inaugural session of the Foreign Ministers' meeting (3 July 1973) became widely known and frequently quoted:

"The meeting is not only a conference on security — it is also a conference on co-operation. A step has been taken in the right direction of development, which was coined in the 1960s in a Finnish aphorism with words: 'Security is not gained by erecting fences, security is gained by opening gates.'"

The Emergence of Reference Groups

The important procedural regulations which were put together in the Blue Book of the Dipoli consultations stated that every participant was to be an equal negotiating partner and that all decisions were to be made on a consensus principle. Despite differences of opinion between Rumania and the rest of the Eastern bloc and the occasional disagreements between the United States and the EC, the negotiations were, in practice, conducted between the East and the West. Consequently, a group of neutral and non-aligned countries remained outside the blocs.

The Nordic countries' group which in the UN, for instance, has traditionally formed a reference group for Finland was not, as such, applicable in the CSCE process, which addressed security issues in addition to questions concerning cooperation. Nordic NATO members naturally had different concepts of security from those of neutral Finland and Sweden. In this situation, the cohesion between countries outside the blocs on important security issues increased. Some non-aligned countries such as Yugoslavia, Cyprus and particularly Malta were also concerned about Mediterranean security which the others were not especially interested in including in the negotiations.

Finland's contacts with the other neutral countries originated from Ambassador Enckell's negotiating tour. Neutral countries' foreign ministers held official talks in Helsinki in January 1973.

Finland's Activities in Geneva

Finland's Role and Special Tasks

The Geneva meeting from September 1973 until the summer of 1975 were conducted in committees which corresponded to the "baskets" of the CSCE agenda. These committees were further divided into sub-committees by subjects. This was not an established system. Unofficial working groups were set up when deemed necessary. There were approximately 20 committees and subcommittees. Combining the documents from paragraphs, sentences, words and punctuation was a time-consuming task.

The coordination committee consisting of the heads of the delegations was the highest organizatory body for the negotiations. The committee's purpose was to strengthen the meeting's unity, coordinate the various activities and approve the final results.[3] However, all decisions were made by the committees among the negotiators.

Finland wanted to have political influence and participated actively in drafting the meeting's schedule. In the spring of 1974, the role of the neutral countries in formulating the agenda was established. Neutral as well as non-aligned countries' activities were influenced by their concern that a deadlock in the negotiations might result in a failure of the conference. In order to guarantee continuity, Finland proposed, in June 1974, that a follow-up committee be set up. This proposal was accepted.

The 1974 Summer Package

In the summer of 1974, Finland made an attempt to solve two difficult questions through the so-called package deal. The meeting was stalemated and could not reach an agreement on the preamble for the text of the third committee which handled so-called humanitarian issues. Nor could the meeting reach an agreement on the texts of the first basket principle concerning sovereign equality (I principle) and the principle of obligations under international law (X principle). The East emphasized each nation's right to its own laws while the West stressed international obligations.[4]

This was mainly a question of whether Socialist countries' established codes of conduct were to be recognized as legitimate or whether the West would get an impetus to criticize East's human rights policies by demanding increased individual contacts and a freer flow of information.

Finland discussed these problems with the other neutral and non-aligned countries but no agreement on the details was reached immediately. These talks were mainly based on a draft made by Finland. The draft was based on the text of the Helsinki Recommendations but the solution pertaining to the problems was reached in the package negotiations.

Finland made a proposal which was revised and presented a a joint neutral countries' proposal. A sentence concerning the participating states' rights to "choose and develop" their systems and to "determine (their) laws" was added to the principle of sovereignty. The principle of obligations under international law was amended to state that the countries, in executing their sovereign rights "conform with their legal obligations under international law". In other words, the principle of sovereignty does not annul international obligations, for instance those included in the CSCE. They are equally significant. These two clauses were linked with the preamble of the third basket and, consequently, with its contents.

The first, unofficial version of the package was submitted on 21 June

1974. The revised version was completed on 7 July. Finland, Switzerland and Austria, under the chairmanship of Ambassador Jaakko Iloniemi, conducted negotiations with the other participants and drafted the package version with necessary translations. On 11 July the package was presented as the joint proposal of the neutral and non-aligned countries.

After several delays and further negotiations the package was accepted in its revised form on 26 July 1974, at the last working day before the meeting's summer recess. The package, which was the neutral and non-aligned countries' first major venture, was prepared outside the official organization but the outcome was politically binding. This achievement gave significant encouragement to the stalemated meeting.

Finland as a Coordinator

The rotation principle was not applied on unofficial negotiations. In such negotiations, the chairman was not just a technical supervisor but also the engine who, through his own activity, contributed to the outcome. Finland had several special tasks which was an indication of the confidence Finland's conduct aroused in the CSCE.

Finland wanted to contribute to the political balance required by the document text. She was charged with an effort to accelerate the meeting's work by acting as a coordinator for the unofficial working group which drafted the preamble for the declaration of principles. Finland's representative also headed unofficial talks which put together the preamble for the section of industrial co-operation and projects of common interest. In science and technology, Finland coordinated unofficial talks which finally reached an agreement on regulations concerning business contacts.

The third basket issues which caused disputes were dealt with by a system in which each neutral country headed the negotiations on one issue. Finland was in charge of culture and thus escaped the most difficult East-West disagreements.

Finland advocated the follow-up process, which it found vitally important, in a follow-up working group in order to ensure the signing of the Final Act in Helsinki in 1975. The follow-up issue was one which remained unsolved until the last moment. After other problems were solved at the final stage of the Geneva negotiations, Finland participated in the negotiations on the demands by Malta. Finland was the only neutral and non-aligned country in those negotiations. Neutral countries have had special tasks in the CSCE's later phases, as well.

Participation in Substantive Proposals

In February 1974, Finland, Sweden, Switzerland, Austria, Yugoslavia and Cyprus made a joint proposal on confidence-building measures (CBM). These countries also proposed that other military issues be included. The proposal went through several revisions in March 1974. The six neutral and non-aligned countries' proposal on military aspects of security included CBMs, general negotiation principles and disarmament.

In the negotiations on military issues, Finland also presented her position on the Nordic nuclear-weapon-free zone and general security. Finland did not submit a written proposal on the NNWFZ. The issue did not create much discussion and regional projects of this kind were not included in the Final Act. Finland brought up the idea just to show its activity and also to gain recognition to the proposal as a legitimate initiative. From Finland's viewpoint, the main result was that the NNWFZ could later be reintroduced as a part of arms control and disarmament.

In the field of trade, neutral countries introduced Finland's comprehensive proposal on business contacts. The issue progressed in the talks headed by Finland and the section on business contacts was completed.

The deadlock in the field of industrial cooperation and major projects was broken by a proposal made by Finland. Finland's written proposal for the preamble was accepted after slight amendments in October 1974. Finland made an oral amendment to the proposal on research programmes and support activities and the contents of the proposal were accepted after Norway put it forward. The proposal on the harmonization of norms and standards which Finland submitted jointly with Switzerland and Austria was accepted without difficulty.

In the field of environmental protection, Finland submitted a written list of cooperation targets which was included, in detail, in the document text. Finland had made a proposal on an environmental subcommittee already at the Dipoli consultations.

In addition to the package deal, Finland made no other attempts to influence the contents of the third basket text. Finland did, however, propose that journalists' greater opportunities for travel be extended to other journalists besides accredited correspondents.

Finland proposed that the relationship between political and technical follow-up of the CSCE be solved through two committees: in addition to a technical follow-up committee, an administrative body for political multilateral negotiations. Finland suggested that a permanent committee be set up to organize the implementation of the decisions and to hold meetings of high officials. The suggestion aimed at covering both the implementation of the common decisions and the continuation of the consultations.

Finland had committed its prestige to the CSCE and, therefore, was particularly interested in securing the follow-up. The decision was finally made and it combined elements from various proposals but no permanent committee or other body for the follow-up was established.

The Nature of Finland's Activities and Reference Groups

Finland cooperated mostly with other neutral countries. On the second basket issues, Finland cooperated particularly closely with Sweden. The division of work among the neutral countries in the cooperation on humanitarian issues turned out to be successful. A similar division of work along each country's interests and resources was applied in the later stages of the CSCE process, as well.

The cooperation with non-aligned countries, which started in Helsinki through cautious surveys, intensified. Yugoslavia and the neutral countries started their cooperation as early as during the Dipoli consultations. In February 1974, Finland increased its contacts and dialogue with non-aligned countries.

As nobody took the floor at the meeting of the coordination committee held on June 6,1974, the neutral and non-aligned countries decided that Cyprus, whose representative was chairing the committee, was to invite all the delegation heads to an unofficial meeting. Thus, the neutral and non-aligned countries contributed to creating a new procedure.

The Emergence of the N+N Group

Contacts between the neutral and non-aligned countries started in the field of military issues. The cooperation became so close that the term Neutral and Non-aligned countries (N+N or NNA) became an established name for the group.

In 1975, contacts increased further as the heads of the N+N delegations started having meetings every other week. It was understandable, however, that this group was more heterogenous than the blocs and it cooperated only on certain issues, such as procedural questions and attempts to mediate in drafting the texts.

The Helsinki Summit - Summer 1975

The Helsinki Summit, at the end of July and at the beginning of August 1975, was short in duration. Nevertheless, it was the most significant stage in the history of the CSCE. At the same time, it was the highlight of Finland's post-war foreign policy.

The summit concluded the actual CSCE process and also put an end to Finland's role as the host. The fact that the Final Act was signed at the highest possible level has often been seen as the most valuable recognition for Finland's foreign policy. The group of signatories was impressive: 35 heads of states or governments including the US and Soviet leaders.

President Kekkonen said in Finland's official statement on 31 July 1975 that the Final Act tells of the desire of countries differing from one another as to their history, social objectives and political systems to overcome the separating factors and lay the main emphasis on uniting aspects, the need for security felt by each, the desire of each to promote common well-being at the governmental, national as well as individual levels.

President Kekkonen spoke for the increased emphasis on military issues and disarmament in the future:

"We believe that the contribution made even by the present Conference to the promotion of détente has brought us nearer to the day when the idea of far-reaching international disarmament is not only a remote prospect but an integral part of our cooperation. This belief is not just a wishful dream of a small country not belonging to any bloc. It is based on the consciousness that, rather than any system relying on the use of force, the cooperation initiated by us is the best guarantee of security."

Finland in the Belgrade Follow-up Conference

Finland's Role and Special Tasks

The preparatory meeting for the Belgrade follow-up meeting which started in June 1977 faced agenda problems because the United States, under the leadership of President Jimmy Carter, was executing an active human rights policy, supported by other Western countries, which was strongly targeted against the Eastern bloc. The dispute reduced optimism about a successful meeting. Détente was becoming past history.

In Belgrade, Finland tried to emphasize its role as the "godfather" of the CSCE and passed on to Yugoslavia the responsibility for promoting détente. To make this clear, Finland wanted to have a visible role in meeting. Consequently, Finland was the only foreign delegation allowed to make a statement at the opening session of the preparatory meeting.

The N+N countries distributed an unofficial procedural and agenda proposal which was officially presented on 15 July. It was a compromise which covered the Socialist countries' proposal to combine the review of the implementation of the Helsinki Final Act with the discussion on the future developments of the CSCE, and the West's demand that the achievements and new proposals be separated from each other and the review be given enough time.

Military Issues

Finland did not prepare any proposals of its own to the actual follow-up conference. However, Finland was prepared to cooperate on military issues, arms limitations and disarmament. After the CSCE had started a discussion on politico-military issues and experiences that had been gathered about their implementation, Finland, together with the other N+N countries, gave her support to the further development of CBMs and the establishment of a special joint body to deal with such issues. An attempt was made to complement political détente with military détente.

The Attempt by the N+N Countries

On 7 December 1977, the N+N countries made a proposal for the general political section of the concluding document. Two days later, the seven countries demanded that human rights be respected and deplored the unfavorable status in disarmament talks. Finland had disagreements with the other N+N countries after it had expressed, in a more moderate way, its dissatisfaction over the implementation of the Helsinki Final Act.

In order to accelerate the slow process, the N+N countries submitted on 1 February 1978, an unofficial concluding document draft. The 14-page draft included both individual N+N countries' substantive proposals and other countries' proposals on which compromises were seen possible. The N+N countries suggested that even more informal working procedures be adopted in the meeting. This was accepted.

After the rejection of their proposal, the N+N counties tried again to produce a substantive concluding document by submitting an unofficial four-page draft. The division of work resembled the system adopted in the Geneva meeting as Finland concentrated on the second basket, on the follow-up and culture which was a third basket issue.

The concluding document which the East and the West finally accepted, simply stated that the Belgrade conference had been held and that a new follow-up conference would be arranged in Madrid. In addition, it included a decision on certain expert meetings.

Participation in Substantive Issues

At the end of October 1977, the N+N countries' unofficial military expert group submitted the N+N group's CBM proposal. At the beginning of November, Finland introduced the N+N group's disarmament proposal which was received favourably. The N+N countries advocated, along with the Western bloc, that the clause in the Final Act dealing with notification on troop transfers be elaborated upon but the Eastern bloc rejected the idea. The N+N countries introduced a new procedure whereby notification on naval movements be made obligatory. There were obvious similarities between the proposals made by the N+N countries and by four members of NATO, which was the case in Geneva, too.

Although the Belgrade meeting failed to reach an agreement on a new document concerning military issues, old commitments remained in effect. Furthermore, the Madrid meeting offered an opportunity to discuss new ones.

In November 1977, the Nordic countries expressed their views about the need to develop the future role of the ECE in the implementation of the CSCE Final Act. Finland joined the statement by Sweden, Austria, Norway and the Eastern bloc which suggested that a clause be included in the concluding document about an environmental conference under the ECE's auspices. Together with other neutral countries, Finland proposed that bilateral economic co-operation be developed on the basis of multilateral recommendations by the CSCE.

After the Belgrade conference, there was domestic criticism of Finland's activities in the N+N group which had been unsuccessful in its mediation to produce a substantial concluding document. Critics said that the N+N countries had been too pro-Western which reduced the successfulness of Finland's initiatives.

Three Reference Groups

Finland's membership in three different reference groups showed that Finland had not committed itself to any third bloc outside the East and the West. Finland participated in proposals by joining the reference group which, in each case, seemed the most appropriate.

Finland did not make one single official proposal in Belgrade in its own name. Together with other neutral countries, Finland participated in the second basket issues. Finland also cooperated with the Nordic countries, which is Finland's oldest reference group. Finland worked together with the N+N countries in proposals concerning the agenda and the concluding document, as well as the follow-up. Finland's position moderated the concluding document in which other N+N countries and the West wanted to include qualitative assessments about the implementation of the Final Act.

Finland expected more of the Belgrade conference than was accomplished, to secure the continuation of the process. In its final statement, Finland expressed its dissatisfaction with the outcome, particularly in the field of disarmament and in second basket issues. Nevertheless, Finland was still optimistic about the future of the CSCE process.

Finland at the Madrid Follow-up Meeting
Finland's Role and Special Tasks

The negotiations in the preparatory meeting of the Madrid follow-up meeting which started in September 1980 were stalemated in the same way as the Belgrade preparatory consultations three years earlier. There were disagreements about the character and content of the follow-up meeting's working procedures.

The Soviet Union and other Socialist countries did not accept the procedural document achieved through a compromise at the Belgrade meeting as the basis for the Madrid preparatory meeting. According to the Eastern bloc "The Yellow Book" symbolized the failure of the Belgrade follow-up meeting.

The decision to start the Madrid follow-up meeting on 11 November 1980, was made in Belgrade in 1978, but the preparatory meeting was still in progress on 10 November. The clocks in the conference hall were stopped in order to gain more time. During the night, the neutral countries distributed a compromise proposition for the agenda and working procedures. The preparatory meeting concluded its work and any unsolved issues were left for the actual meeting.

Finland's address at the inaugural session of the actual Madrid follow-up meeting emphasized that peaceful settlement of disputes, implementation of human rights and cooperation are long-term processes. Thus, Finland indicated that it was prepared for difficult negotiations.

To break the 1981 deadlock, the Finnish delegation presented an unofficial draft for the concluding document on 31 March 1981, prepared with the N+N countries. The draft, which did not completely correspond to Finland's original objectives, included Finland's proposals for the follow-up. One of the key points in the proposal was a draft decision on the conditions for a European disarmament conference, which Finland, among others, promoted strongly. The Western bloc considered the proposal useful among other proposals, while the Eastern bloc saw it as a sufficient text basis.

The official meeting assumed increasingly unofficial forms.[5] The N+N countries which coordinated the shadow organization ("the contact groups") remained chairmen. Finland chaired a group which was charged with the drafting of the principles. Occasionally, these groups took even more unofficial forms ("coffee groups", "sherry groups") but the N+N countries maintained a key role in them.

Toward a Comprehensive Proposal

At the beginning of November 1981, the neutral countries started an informal dialogue to solve the remaining issues. Finland started independent negotiations but informed other countries of its attemps to solve the remaining humanitarian issues and the dispute over the confidence-building measures in the same package.

After Finland had made a package proposal to solve the most difficult issues between the East and the West, the other N+N countries did not submit alternate drafts, for example, for a moderated concluding document or for a recess proposal because the main parties wanted to continue the negotiations on the basis of the Finnish proposal. At the beginning of December, the Finnish proposal was complemented to form a package proposal of the neutral countries.

On 16 December 1981, the N+N countries presented, after the neutral countries' foreign ministers' meeting and unofficial negotiations, a comprehensive, 33-page proposal (RM.39) for the concluding document, which was based on Finland's working paper. Both parties recognized that it was well defined and that it observed the achieved accomplishments.

The proposal outlined a mandate for the Conference on Disarmament in Europe, CDE, which was the most significant expansion to the Helsinki Final Act.

After martial law was declared in Poland (13 December), the Great Powers left for Christmas recess without studying the proposal which the N+N countries considered acceptable in the form in which it was proposed.

At the end of February 1982, the N+N countries had unofficial consultations with all the participating countries initiated by Finland. These negotiations lasted one week. In March, Switzerland proposed, representing the N+N countries, a long recess which would go on until November because the discussion on the Polish situation had paralyzed the Madrid meeting.

After the Recess

After the long recess the atmosphere in Madrid was rather good despite the situation in Poland but the N+N countries realized that their role as mediators was limited in the negotiations on the concluding document's principles and section of information.

In December 1982, Finland commented on the human rights issues in a proposal stating that the draft was not necessarily in the form desired by Finland but in a form acceptable to all. In Finland's opinion, the trade union rights demanded by the West had no chance of being accepted.

In February 1983, Finland initiated small working groups which were coordinated by the neutral countries. Finland again chaired the group which negotiated on the principles. Coordination became more difficult because nobody knew how much bargaining the East and the West would be willing to do.

On 15 March 1983, the N+N countries presented a revised draft for the concluding document. The West's demands on the termination of radio jamming and deportation of journalists were omitted but a clause on trade union rights was added. The deadlines included in the proposal strived for a conclusion without long negotiations.

In the Soviet Union's view, the proposal was better than the previous one. The CDE's mandate satisfied the Soviet Union, the pro-Western human rights demands did not. The United States considered the proposal incomplete and ineffective. It suggested further negotiations but, at the end of April in 1983, the West announced that the version was an acceptable basis for the final negotiations.

On 18 April 1983, President Mauno Koivisto made an appeal for the successful conclusion of the meeting. The appeal was signed by the heads of five other N+N countries. Switzerland did not sign the appeal.

At the beginning of June, the N+N countries found new propoals useless. Nevertheless, the host country, Spain, introduced a package solution based on the proposal by the N+N countries, which addressed some of the issues considered important by the West. After the Soviet acceptance of the West's key condition concerning the mandate and date of the Bern meeting on human contacts, the main issues of the meeting were solved.

Finland expressed its satisfaction with the accomplished understanding, at the comprehensive concluding document, and, above all, at the Stockholm disarmament conference at the final session of the Madrid follow-up meeting.

Finland's Participation in Substantive Proposals

Finland co-operated with the other neutral countries in drafting several substantive proposals in order to achieve constructive dialogue, to enhance confidence and to reach an agreement on new methods of co-operation at the Madrid meeting. The proposals showed a clear interest in military issues. The N+N countries (with the exception of Malta) made a joint CBM proposal. Sweden and Yugoslavia made their own proposals on the Conference on Disarmament in Europe. Finland introduced an initiative on a European disarmament programme.

In addition to the above, Switzerland, Finland, Sweden, and Yugoslavia made a proposal on an expert meeting on the peaceful settlement of disputes to be held in 1982. Montreux (1978) had not succeeded in developing the actual settlement procedure although it had accepted the principle.

In their comprehensive proposal, the N+N countries proposed concrete measures to develop CBMs. These included increased attention to certain military manoeuvers, such as naval excercises and, in particular, amphibious troop manoeuvers, exchange of observers, information on military budgets and recognition of other measures serving in the implementation of the objectives of the Helsinki Final Act.

Finland's proposal for a European disarmament programme was submitted in December of 1980, and distributed in writing to the participants. Originally, an unofficial proposal had been submitted at the UN General Assembly's first committee in 1979. After that, Ambassador Esko Rajakoski had made an extensive tour of the foreign ministries of the CSCE countries. Finland's proposal aimed at defining and coordinating fora and proposals on arms reductions, arms control and other military issues. Finland emphasized the complementary, not competitive, character of the proposal. When the Madrid meeting started genuine work on a decision on a European disarmamant conference, the Finnish proposal was laid aside and it was not discussed in Madrid.

The N+N countries' proposal to develop CBMs in Madrid was a precautionary measure for a situation where no decision could be reached on a separate forum. The detailed proposal was based on a proposal made at the Belgrade conference which also advocated limitations on military activities.

On Finland's initiative, the Nordic countries again proposed that the ECE's role be strengthened. They also proposed that the position of small and medium-sized enterprises be improved in trade with the Western countries. To ensure a successful, high level meeting on environmental protection, the Nordic countries proposed that the mandate on this be given to the extention of the ECE's work. Together with Sweden, Finland made a proposal on the improvement of the conditions of migrant workers but was not very optimistic about the success of the proposal.

In the field of culture, Finland and Hungary made a proposal to increase the study of rare languages. Iceland joined the proposal later. In the field of education, the Nordic countries made a proposal, in which Finland was particularly interested, that post-graduate education for young researchers be arranged. Before the first Christmas recess, Finland proposed that a CSCE committee be established to improve the follow-up of the process. This proposal suggested that diplomats should meet between follow-up conferences.

The Nature of Finland's Activities and Its Reference Groups

Altogether 87 official proposals were made at the Madrid conference. Finland was involved in nine of them, alone or jointly with others. Finland co-operated with various combinations of the N+N countries in preparing a proposal on four different fields. In addition, important proposals were made unofficially. One of them was the above-mentioned disarmament proposal.

Finland's joint proposals with the various combinations of the N+N countries covered a considerable part of the official proposals in which Finland participated. However, Finland did not join the proposals concerning the third basket. Finland's emphasis on the continuation of the CSCE process became underlined through its solo proposal on the follow-up.

Traditional Nordic cooperation was particularly visible in Madrid as Finland cooperated with the Nordic countries three times, and only once with the N+N countries, on issues included in the second basket.

A good indication of the fact that Finland did not consider the established reference groups as the only alternative was Finland's cooperation with Hungary on a proposal to increase the study of rare languages. After Iceland joined the proposal, it became the first and only proposal in which the East-West line of recommendators was broken.

The first official N+N countries' foreign ministers' meeting in October 1982 showed how institutionalized the N+N countries' cooperation had become. The concluding document of the Madrid meeting is a manifestation of the success of this cooperation. 80 percent of the document is based on the proposal for the concluding document made by the N+N countries in December 1981.

The N+N countries' cooperation in Madrid was not without problems. The group had disagreements about the extent of the concluding document, in particular, about the long recess and about the efforts in the late spring of 1983.

Finland and the CDE

The preparatory meeting for the Stockholm Conference on Confidence- and Security-Building Measures and Disarmament in Europe opened in Helsinki soon after the conclusion of the Madrid follow-up conference in October 1983. Finland negotiated with the other participating countries already before the preparatory meeting.

Helsinki Preparations

On of the most difficult problems of the Helsinki preparatory meeting was the linkage between the CDE and the 1986 Vienna follow-up meeting. The problem was solved when a clause was added in the concluding document of the preparatory meeting, stating that the CDE will continue its work, unless otherwise decided by Vienna or by other consequent follow-up meeting.

In the beginning of November 1983, the host country, Finland, together with Sweden submitted to the preparatory meeting a proposal for a document. The other N+N countries had received the proposal earlier. A revised version of the proposal was presented by five N+N countries for a concluding document. It was accepted as the basis for the concluding document, and the meeting came to a successful conclusion as scheduled.

An Important Forum

The CDE, which started in Stockholm on 17 January 1984, is the first CSCE forum exclusively on military security. The CDE is also the first forum for negotiations on Europe's military security which includes all the countries responsible for the security of Europe — excluding Albania. For the N+N countries the CDE has given the first opportunity to conduct multilateral negotiations with allied countries on general European military issues.

The N+N countries started the conference by engaging in intensive work on the level of military experts and a drafting committee. On 9 March 1984, Sweden introduced the N+N countries' proposal on confidence- and security-building measures (CSBM). Finland had made several amendments to the proposal, including concrete measures such as the procedures of advance notice and monitoring, various limitations and the principle of non-use of force.

Finland emphasized the significance of informal contacts. In Finland's opinion, the main parties' basic proposals provided enough material to start the actual work phase. The first unofficial meeting of all the delegations was held at the end of June 1984, after long discussions. Finland summoned the meeting and coordinated the contact group. The objective was to form two working groups. In order to solve procedural issues Finland amended the stalemated proposal made by Sweden. After weeks of negotiations chaired by Finland, the N+N countries submitted a proposal to set up two working committees. Finland's proposal ensured equal treatment of all proposals in the two working groups.

On 3 December 1984, the CDE officially decided to establish two working groups. Group A was to handle political questions including the non-use of force, as well as proposals to increase the exchange of information. Group B was to study "traditional" CSBMs, such as advance notification of military manoeuvers and the exchange of observers. The decision was introduced to the plenary session by the Finnish delegation, after which the new groups could start their actual work on the proposals.

Despite persistent efforts by the N+N countries, there was no real progress in the negotiations during the first three quarters of 1985. However, in October 1985 the CDE decided to introduce informal meetings and chose five topics for a final document. Finland figured prominently in the making of this procedural compromise which opened the way for a transition to the drafting stage. The first major challenge of the CDE is to achieve results by the Vienna follow-up meeting.

Finland at the Ottawa Human Rights Meeting
Raising to Profile

At the expert meeting on human rights and fundamental freedoms in Ottawa, Canada, in May—June 1985, Finland strongly emphasized the right of the CSCE countries to voice their concern over human rights violations in other CSCE countries. Finland stated that concern over human rights does not mean improper interference in another country's internal affairs. Finland's representative who was allowed to make the first statement did, however, point out that loud criticism of or protests against another country are not always helpful or desirable.

Finland's statement included a list of the meeting's seven main issues. The list demanded that human rights issues and their relation to other problems, their potential order of priority, acceptable ways of inter- ference in another country's human rights problems and the influence of such interference on relations between countries and on European security, among other things, be defined. Finland noted in its statement that, in addition to its substance, the meeting was important for the continued implementation of the CSCE Final Act.

The agenda for the human rights meeting and the procedures were accepted after an unofficial working group reached a consensus on them. This consensus was largely based on the unofficial working paper prepared by the N+N countries in the preparatory meeting.

The Proposals

Dozens of official proposals were made at the actual meeting. Finland made a proposal on cooperation in human rights issues. Together with the other Nordic countries Finland also proposed that capital punish- ment be eliminated gradually. The N+N countries proposed that Finland be appointed chairman of the unofficial contact group which had already started its work. Finland divided the proposals in groups and drafted summaries of their conclusions and recommendations. Finland also prepared an unofficial draft for the preamble of the meeting report.

However, the experts' meeting could not agree on the conclusions and recommendations obligated by its mandate. Nevertheless, the Finnish representative noted at the final session that the meeting succeeded in conducting a genuine dialogue. According to Finland, the various and numerous proposals proved that an effort had been made which must be continued in the future, too.

The Tenth Anniversary Meeting

In his statement at the inaugural session of the tenth anniversary cele- bration of the signing of the CSCE Final Act in Helsinki on 30 July, 1985, the host country's Foreign Minister, Paavo Väyrynen, expressed Finland's satisfaction with the fact that the commemoration was arranged on a high political level. This facilitated important bilateral and other discussions outside the meeting agenda. During the preparations for the meeting Finland was in contact with all the participating countries through a tour by Ambassador Richard Tötterman.

In his welcoming remarks, President Mauno Koivisto said that there is no need to avoid criticism when the CSCE participants are gathered. According to Koivisto, the best outcome of this approach is achieved when it is combined with a willingness to listen to the others. The Presi- dent noted, in talking about human right issues, that security is not only a matter of states. Individuals living in the participating countries must feel security, which is based on the respect for human rights and fundamental freedoms.

In talking about Finland's role in the CSCE, Koivisto stated that Finland promotes European security by honouring her commitments and by maintaining good relations with all countries, particularly with the CSCE participants. Finland wants to be open to all directions and to show others the confidence which it hopes to get from them. Finland believes that other countries, too, benefit from its policy of neutrality.

When delivering Finland's statement on 1 August 1985, Foreign Minister Väyrynen said that, in view of the credibility of the CSCE, it is essential that the agreed commitments be honoured not only in words but also in deeds. Väyrynen saw environmental protection as a present-day challenge.

Due to human rights disagreements the CSCE tenth anniversary meeting failed to produce a final communique, for which Finland had prepared a draft. Most importantly, the United States rejected the proposal, because it didn't criticize human right failures strongly enough. The Soviet Union had accepted the short Finnish draft before the meeting. No consensus on a joint communique was reached. Nevertheless, Finland's foreign policy leaders did not see the failure as a prestige defeat. Instead of a final communique, Foreign Minister Väyrynen, who chaired the meeting, presented a unilateral final statement at the final session.

The meeting ended on 1 August 1985, a little over a year prior to the Vienna follow-up meeting. Finland believed that the precondition for the follow-up meeting in view of the third basket could still improve, because in addition to the CDE, the participating countries were to meet before the Vienna follow-up conference at least in conjunction with the "Cultural Forum" in Budapest and at the meeting on human contacts in Bern in 1986.

Notes

1. One of the main reference sources used in this report is the annual *Ulkopoliittisia lausuntoja ja asiakirjoja* ("Foreign Policy Statements and Documents") published by the Finnish Ministry for Foreign Affairs. The Finnish Institute of International Affairs' press files on the CSCE were also very helpful. The file contains CSCE-related material from major Finnish dailies. The 'eyewitness' main sources for the Helsinki and Geneva meetings are Luigi Vittorio Ferraris (ed.), *Report on a Negotiation, Helsinki-Geneva-Helsinki 1972–1975*, Alphen aan der Rijn: Sijfhoffs Noordhoff, 1979, and John J. Maresca, *To Helsinki. The Conference on Security and Cooperation in Europe, 1973–1975*. Duke University Press 1985. The main source for the Madrid follow-up meeting is Jan Sizoo & Rudolf Jurrjens, *CSCE Decision-Making: The Madrid Experience*, Martinus Nijkoff, The Hague 1984.

Other useful reference materials were the CSCE documents and several major Finnish studies and assessments which discuss Finland's role in the various stages of the CSCE process.

2. On the timing of the proposals see Jaakko Iloniemi "Finland and the Conference on European Security and Cooperation," in: Keijo Korhonen (ed.), *Urho Kekkonen. A Statesman for Peace*, Otava, Helsinki 1975.

3. On the coordination committee, the CSCE's organization and the CSCE's progress, see Ferraris, *op.cit.* and Maresca, *op.cit.*

Kaarle Nordenstreng analyzes the origins of the package deal and its significance in his article "Détente and the Exchange of Information between East and West," in the *Yearbook of Finnish Foreign Policy 1975*, The Finnish Institute of International Affairs, Helsinki 1976. See also Osmo Apunen's article "The Principles of Relations between the States of Europe," in the same publication.

5. The official and unofficial organization of the Madrid conference, see Sizoo & Jurrjens, *op. cit.*

11
Documentation

***Speech of welcome by Dr. Mauno Koivisto, President of the
Republic of Finland, at the Tenth Anniversary Meeting of
the CSCE, Helsinki 30 July 1985***

On behalf of the Government of Finland, I have the honour to welcome
you to Helsinki where you have come to duly commemorate the Tenth
Anniversary of the Signature of the Final Act of the Conference on
Security and Co-operation in Europe. It was signed ten years ago in this
very hall. Now is the time to reflect on its meaning today.

At the follow-up Meeting in Madrid in 1983 it was agreed to commemorate the tenth anniversary in Helsinki in 1985. Your presence here at the
high level of ministers responsible for foreign relations is a demonstration of firm commitment both to the Final Act and to the later agreements which have followed its signature. It proves that the governments
of the participating States intend to continue to give full effect to all the
results of the CSCE and of subsequent meetings held to ensure the
follow-up to the Final Act.

In the course of the coming days you will have the opportunity to
express the views of your government on the occasion of the Anniversary. You will certainly pay attention not only to the Final Act itself but
also to the whole series of unilateral, bilateral and multilateral activities
undertaken by the participating States, which has become known as the
CSCE process.

At the same time this is an opportunity to look forward. The Final Act
and the other CSCE documents are not simply monuments to past
efforts. They are a living programme for the present and a promise for the
future.

We all know, however, that the CSCE process does not run automatically like a well-oiled machine. The pace of progress depends on capabilities and resources. It depends above all on the political will of the
governments concerned. Many expectations have not been met. Disappointment has been expressed, also in Finland over the lack of results
or over slow progress in certain areas of the CSCE process. At the same
time, we know that it could hardly have been otherwise. There is no easy
road to the aims set forth in the Final Act. The performance of all the
participating States must therefore be open to critical scrutiny.

There is no reason to shy away from a critical approach when the CSCE States are meeting. This approach works best when it is combined with a willingness to consult with other participating States. In such a way we can seek advice, assistance and encouragement from each other. In such a way we can make our common commitments more precise and effective, and also, if possible, more ambitious.

The Final Act is a rich document. It means many things to all of the participating States. On this occasion I wish to call attention to some aspects of it which have seemed particularly pertinent to us in Finland.

First of all, the Final Act has established a broad concept of security. A strong basis is found in the the principles guiding relations between the participating States, which are part of the Final Act. These principles reflect the idea of security which permeates the Final Act as a whole.

In the Final Act, the CSCE States have emphasized that co-operation and contacts across international borders are a natural part of the security that we all need. They have also recognized that the building of confidence between States requires careful attention and elaborate rules. We realize that such confidence-building may be a helpful first step to military disengagement and disarmament.

Furthermore, it was recognized in the Final Act that security is not only a matter for the States. Security requires more than the protection of borders and social structures. The Final Act underlines that there must be security also in the lives of the individual inhabitants of the participating States, based on respect for human rights and fundamental freedoms. The security and confidence that human beings feel in their relations to others are an important part of the security of States.

Confidence, contacts and co-operation as essential elements of the broad concept of security are important to all of us. They are all the more important to the smaller participating States and to those that are outside the military alliances. The Final Act shows how even the smallest States and their inhabitants can make their contributions to the security of all. It is this understanding of the meaning of security which my distinguished predecessor, President Urho Kekkonen, crystallized in a short sentence twelve years ago, on the occasion of the first stage of the CSCE. He said that "security is not gained by erecting fences, security is gained by opening gates".

In this country, we try to live up to this ideal. We contribute to the security of Europe first of all by honouring our commitments, and by cultivating good relations with all other States, particularly the ones which are represented now in this hall.

For Finland, it has been a natural principle in a divided world to deal with all sides, to be open in all directions, to show others the confidence that we hope others will show us. This is our policy of neutrality. We believe that this policy is useful not only to ourselves but also to others.

The Final Act recognizes that the participating States have the right to be or not to be a party to treaties of alliance and the right to neutrality, as rights inherent in sovereignty. We have found many partners on the road of neutrality. Finland has been able to engage in practical co-operation throughout the CSCE process with other neutral and non-aligned participating States, trying to help this whole community to find acceptable solutions to problems facing us all.

In accordance with a decision taken in Madrid, Finland has assumed the task of preparing of organizing this Anniversary Meeting. The substance of the Meeting is now in your hands. Once more, I bid you welcome to our capital, hoping that your brief stay will be rewarding.

Statement by Paavo Väyrynen, Minister for Foreign Affairs of Finland, at the Tenth Anniversary Meeting of the CSCE, Helsinki, 1 August 1985

The Final Act of the Conference on Security and Cooperation in Europe opens with a pledge by the participating States to promote better relations among themselves and to ensure conditions in which their people can live in true and lasting peace from any threat to or attempt against their security.

For Finland it is vital that international security is sought through co-operation instead of confrontation. International security is not strengthened through the accumulation of arms but through effective agreements in the field of disarmament and arms control, effective means for the peaceful settlement of disputes, and effective impediments to the threat or use of force in international relations.

There is more to security than freedom from war. Ensuring conditions in which our people can indeed live free from any threat to their security requires action and co-operation across a broad spectrum of other concerns important to people in all our countries. The CSCE, with its many different aspects, manifests this broad concept of security.

We have assembled here to commemorate the signature, in this very hall, of the Final Act of the CSCE by the highest political leaders of our States.

Finland's assessment of the CSCE reflects her unwavering support for and active involvement in the CSCE process from its very beginning. Finland's destinies are linked with those of Europe as a whole. For Finland, the CSCE is a unique forum to pursue her policy of neutrality. While advancing her national interests she contributes to common efforts to find peaceful solutions to European problems, to promote closer co-operation between States irrespective of their political, economic and social systems, and to widen contacts between peoples.

The Helsinki Final Act is the cornerstone of the CSCE process. In it, the participating States have agreed to respect and put into practice ten fundamental principles in their mutual relations. Since 1975, these principles have become a common standard by which the participating States can, and do, measure each other's behaviour.

The Final Act is also a mandate for the future: it is an expression of political will, at the highest level, to seek progress in areas of common agreement, ranging from security to economic co-operation, culture, and human rights. The Final Act commits its signatory States indefinitely and with equal force with regard to each of its provisions.

It is of fundamental importance for the credibility of our joint endeavour that CSCE commitments are put into effect not only in word but in
deed. Regrettably the implementation of all provisions of the Final Act
has not been satisfactory. The reasons for this state of affairs are
evaluated differently by different States. Assessment of deficiencies of
implementation of CSCE commitments are both legitimate and necessary. It is equally important that such assessments are conducted with a
view to the enduring objectives of the CSCE.

For Finland, the significance of the Final Act transcends its specific
provisions. The Final Act outlines a vision for the future of Europe. It is a
vision in which co-operation has superseded confrontation, in which
confidence in the intentions of others has replaced suspicion and mistrust, in which exchanges and interaction between States and their
citizens have become a way of life, and in which the individual lives in
security fully enjoying his rights as a human being.

Implementation of agreed commitments and continuation of the multilateral diplomatic process are our means to bridge the gap between
vision and reality. They assure the possibility of progress. It is incumbent
upon us, as participating States, to make the best use of that possibility,
unilaterally, bilaterally and multilaterally.

The possibilities for further progress are examined in expert-level
meeting before the third follow-up meeting commencing in Vienna next
year. Finland seeks progress in each of them, on their own terms. It is the
task of the Vienna meeting on the basis of the results of the expert
meetings to see to it that the CSCE process retains its vitality as a whole.

In the field of military security, the real innovation of the Final Act is the
concept of confidence-building measures. The confidence-building
measures agreed upon in Helsinki are modest in scope and in their
degree of commitment. Yet, the experience of their implementation since
1975 is encouraging. They are a beginning, a promise. The Stockholm
Conference is mandated to make good on that promise.

In our view, the work of the Stockholm Conference has proceeded
well but slowly. However, the Conference is now approaching the point
where clarifications of positions and discussions alone will have outlined
their usefulness. The first priority of the Conference should be to get on
with actual negotiations. Tangible progress on concrete confidence- and
security-building measures in Stockholm would make it possible for the
Vienna follow-up meeting to supplement the mandate of the Conference
to cover disarmament as well. Despite all arms control efforts so far,
Europe remains the continent of the deadliest concentration of weapons,
both nuclear and conventional. The potential of the CSCE should be
effectively utilized in the field of arms control and disarmament.

Trade and economic relations are of major importance for the long-
term development of CSCE co-operation. The Final Act has already
given important political impulses to this co-operation. It is our
conviction that all CSCE countries benefit from the expansion of trade
and economic relations among themselves as their economies complement each other.

The work of the UN Economic Commission for Europe is particularly valuable for the realization of our common aims in the field of trade and economic relations. The ECE's role as the main international body responsible for implementing CSCE decisions in the economic field should be further strengthened.

Finland, whose economic well-being is closely connected with foreign trade, works for the maintenance of an open multilateral trading system and the abolition of obstacles to free trade. Trade between all CSCE States should be liberalized in the spirit of true reciprocity. Economic development will continue to provide new challenges for regional co-operation to which the CSCE will need to respond. One urgent challenge concerns co-operation to save our environment.

The CSCE process has already inspired two important conventions in this field, one relating to long-range transboundary air pollution and the other to the protection of the marine environment of the Baltic Sea.

Finland's commitment to the CSCE is not based on sanguine trust in easy progress or disregard for difficulties. Already at the signing of the Final Act ten years ago, President Kekkonen struck a note of caution by reminding his fellow leaders that "despite the straightness of our path, we are not yet safe from reverses".

For many years now, the international situation has been marred by deep mutual distrust in East-West relations. In this general climate of suspicion, the CSCE has also suffered. Difficulties in a number of CSCE meetings demonstrate that the CSCE process is neither a harmonious progression toward the goals of the Final Act nor immune to outside developments.

Yet, the reverses have not precipitated a reversal of course. Our common endeavour has survived, indeed developed. The Tenth Anniversary Meeting confirms the high political significance of the Helsinki Final Act.

Closing remarks by Paavo Väyrynen, Minister for Foreign Affairs of Finland, at the Tenth Anniversary Meeting of the CSCE, Helsinki, 1 August 1985

The Tenth Anniversary Meeting is now drawing to a close. Before concluding this Meeting, I wish to say a few words as the representative of the host country.

For the past three days we have been gathered here in Helsinki to commemorate the signature, exactly ten years ago in this very hall, of the Final Act of the Conference on Security and Co-operation in Europe. We have heard statements by the high representatives of the thirty-five participating States assessing the CSCE from the particular viewpoint of each participating State. These statements have dealt with the problems as well as the prospects concerning security and co-operation in Europe.

In my view the holding of the Tenth Anniversary, the statements we have heard in this hall, and the many contacts among the participating States during the Meeting show that the participating States continue to attach prime importance to the Helsinki Final Act and to the CSCE process as a whole. This Meeting has demonstrated the continued commitment of the participating States to implementing the provisions of the Helsinki Final Act and to continuing the CSCE process. This Meeting has shown that although progress has been made, much remains to be done to strengthen security, to foster co-operation and to solve humanitarian problems so that the commitments we all have assumed become the reality in the lives of our citizens.

I wish to thank all my distinguished colleagues for their valuable contribution to this Meeting.

On behalf of the people and Government of Finland, I wish to express our gratitude for the many generous remarks that you have directed to Finland as host of this Meeting.

I would also like to take this opportunity to thank the secretariat for its contribution to the smooth and orderly conduct of our proceedings.

And now I declare closed the Tenth Anniversary Meeting of the signature of Final Act of the Conference on Security and Co-operation in Europe.

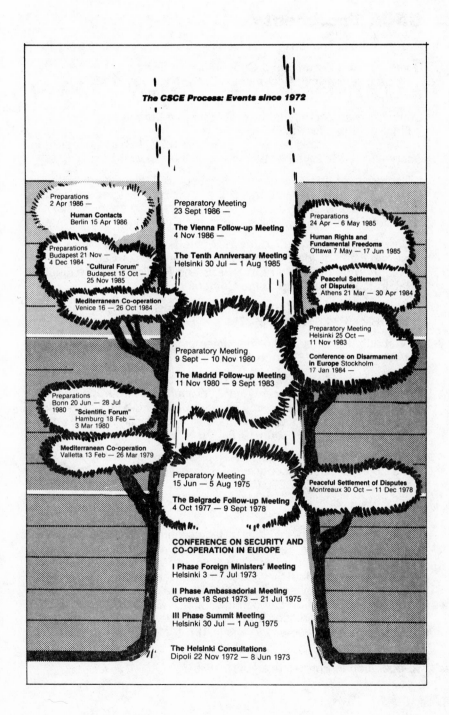

The CSCE Process: Events since 1972

Preparations
2 Apr 1986 —

Human Contacts
Berlin 15 Apr 1986

Preparations
Budapest 21 Nov —
4 Dec 1984 **"Cultural Forum"**
Budapest 15 Oct —
25 Nov 1985

Mediterranean Co-operation
Venice 16 — 26 Oct 1984

Preparations
Bonn 20 Jun — 28 Jul
1980 **"Scientific Forum"**
Hamburg 18 Feb —
3 Mar 1980

Mediterranean Co-operation
Valletta 13 Feb — 26 Mar 1979

Preparatory Meeting
23 Sept 1986 —

The Vienna Follow-up Meeting
4 Nov 1986 —

The Tenth Anniversary Meeting
Helsinki 30 Jul — 1 Aug 1985

Preparatory Meeting
9 Sept — 10 Nov 1980

The Madrid Follow-up Meeting
11 Nov 1980 — 9 Sept 1983

Preparatory Meeting
15 Jun — 5 Aug 1975

The Belgrade Follow-up Meeting
4 Oct 1977 — 9 Sept 1978

Preparations
24 Apr — 6 May 1985

**Human Rights and
Fundamental Freedoms**
Ottawa 7 May — 17 Jun 1985

**Peaceful Settlement
of Disputes**
Athens 21 Mar — 30 Apr 1984

Preparatory Meeting
Helsinki 25 Oct —
11 Nov 1983

**Conference on Disarmament
in Europe** Stockholm
17 Jan 1984 —

Peaceful Settlement of Disputes
Montreaux 30 Oct — 11 Dec 1978

**CONFERENCE ON SECURITY AND
CO-OPERATION IN EUROPE**

I Phase Foreign Ministers' Meeting
Helsinki 3 — 7 Jul 1973

II Phase Ambassadorial Meeting
Geneva 18 Sept 1973 — 21 Jul 1975

III Phase Summit Meeting
Helsinki 30 Jul — 1 Aug 1975

The Helsinki Consultations
Dipoli 22 Nov 1972 — 8 Jun 1973

CSCE Documents

Final Recommendations of the Helsinki Consultations. (Helsinki 1973)

Conference on Security and Cooperation in Europe.
  Stage I: — Helsinki. Documents (CSCE I/1, Helsinki 1973)
— Verbatim Records July 3—7, 1973 (CSCE/I/PV.1, Helsinki 1973)

Conference on Security and Co-operation in Europe.
  Final Act (Helsinki 1975)
— Stage III — Helsinki 30 July — 1 August 1975. Verbatim Records and
Documents (CSCE/III/PV.1)

Decisions of the Preparatory Meeting to Organize the Belgrade
Meeting 1977 of Representatives of the Participating States of the Confe-
rence on Security and Co-operation in Europe, held on the Basis of the
Final Act Relating to the Follow-up to the Conference (Beograd 1977)

Concluding Document of the Belgrade Meeting 1977 of Representatives on the Participating States of the Conference on Security and Cooperation in Europe, held on the Basis and Provisions of the Final Act
Relating to the Follow-up to the Conference.

— Verbatim Records of the Opening Statements 4—10 October 1977
(CSCE/BM/VR. 1, Beograd 1977)

— Verbatim Records of Closing Statements 8—9 March 1978 (CSCE/
BM/VR. 1, Belgrade, 8 March 1978)

Report of the Meeting of Experts Representing the Participating States
of the Conference on Security and Co-operation in Europe and Their
National Scientific Institutions, Foreseen by the Final Act of the CSCE
and the Concluding Document of the Belgrade Meeting 1977 to prepare
the "Scientific Forum" (Bonn 1978)

Report of the Meeting of Experts Representing the Participating States
of the Conference on Security and Co-operation in Europe, Foreseen by
the Final Act of the CSCE in Order to Pursue the Examination and Ela-
boration of a Generally Acceptable Method for Peaceful Settlement of
Disputes Aimed at Complementing Existing Methods. (Montreux 1978)

Report of the Meeting of Experts Representing the Participating States
of the Conference on Security and Co-operation in Europe. Foreseen
by the Concluding Document of the Belgrade Meeting 1977 to Consider,
within the Framework of the Mediterranean Chapter of the Final Act, the
Possibilities and Means of Promoting Concrete Initiatives for Mutually
Beneficial Co-operation Concerning Various Economic, Scientific and
Cultural Fields, in Addition to Other Initiatives Relating to the above
Subjects already under way. (Valletta 1979)

Report of the "Scientific Forum" of the Conference on Security and
Co-operation in Europe. (Hamburg 1980)

Decisions on the Organization of the Madrid Meeting 1980 of Representatives of the Participating States of the Conference on Security and Co-operation in Europe, held on the Basis of the Provisions of the Final Act relating to the Follow-up to the Conference. (Madrid 1980.)

Concluding Document of the Madrid Meeting of Representatives of the Participating States of the Conference on Security and Co-operation in Europe, held on the Basis of the Provisions of the Final Act relating to the Follow-up to the Conference. (Madrid 1983)
— Verbatim Records of the Opening Statements 11—18 November 1980 (CSCE/RM/VR.8)
— Closing Statements 7—9 September 1983 (CSCE/RM/VR.1)

Decisions of the Helsinki Preparatory Meeting on the Agenda, Timetable and other Organizational Modalities for the First Stage of the Conference on Confidence- and Security-Building Measures and Disarmament in Europe. (Helsinki 1983)

Report of the Meeting of Experts Representing the Participating States of the Conference on Security and Co-operation in Europe, foreseen by the Final Act of the CSCE and the Concluding Document of the Madrid Meeting, in Order to Pursue, on the Basis of the Final Act, the Examination of a Generally Acceptable Method for the Peaceful Settlement of Disputes aimed at Complementing Existing Methods. (Athens, 30 April 1984)

CSCE. Venice Seminar on Economic, Scientific and Cultural Cooperation in the Mediterranean within the Framework of the Results of the Valletta Meeting of Experts, (Venezia, 26 October 1984)

Report of the Meeting of Expert Representing the Participating States of Conference on Security and Co-operation in Europe, Foreseen by the Concluding Document of the Madrid Meeting, to Prepare the "Cultural Forum". (Budapest, 4 December 1984)

Conference on Security and Co-operation in Europe. Tenth Anniversary Meeting. Verbatim Record, 30 July — 1 August 1985. (Helsinki 1985)

The Contributors

Esko Antola, Senior Research Fellow, Academy of Finland, University of Turku; 1985—86 Visiting Fellow at Yale University, New Haven, Conn.

Hans-Henrik Holm, Associate Professor, Institute of Political Science, University of Aarhus

Juha Holma, Junior Research Fellow, Academy of Finland, University of Tampere

Pierangelo Isernia, Director of the Forum Humanum Project on "The Factor of Peace in the World Community", Club of Rome, Rome

Rudolf Th. Jurrjens, Professor, Institute of International Relations, Free University of Amsterdam

Leo Mates, Professor, Institute of International Politics and Economics, Belgrade

Philippe Moreau Defarges, Senior Research Fellow, Institut Français des Relations Internationales, Paris

Adam Daniel Rotfeld, Head of Department for European Security, Polish Institute of International Affairs, Warsaw

Lars B. Wallin, Senior Research Associate, Swedish National Defence Research Institute, Stockholm

Klaus Krokfors, Research Assistant, Finnish Institute of International Affairs, Helsinki

Kari Möttölä, Director, Finnish Institute of International Affairs, Helsinki